Administering central-local relations, 1871-1919

Administering central–local relations, 1871-1919

The Local Government Board in its fiscal and cultural context

Christine Bellamy

Manchester University Press ⊞

distributed exclusively in the USA and Canada by St Martin's Press, New York

Copyright © Christine Bellamy 1988

Published by Manchester University Press
Oxford Road, Manchester M13 9PL

Distributed exclusively in the USA and Canada
by St. Martin's Press, Inc.,
Room 400, 175 Fifth Avenue, New York, NY 10010, USA

British Library cataloguing in publication data
Bellamy, Christine
    Administering central-local relations, 1871-1919 : the Local
    Government Board in its fiscal and cultural context.
    1. Great Britain. *Local Government Board*—History
    I. Title
    352.041   JS3145

Library of Congress cataloging in publication data
Bellamy, Christine
    Administering central-local relations, 1871-1919.
    Bibliography: p. 276.
    Includes index.
    1. Local finance—Great Britain—History. 2. Central-local government
relations—Great Britain—History.
3. Great Britain. Local government Board—History
I. Title
HJ9422.B45   1988   336'.014'42   87-31368

ISBN 0-7190-1757-2 *hardback*

Typeset in Cheltenham ITC
by Koinonia Limited, Manchester
Printed and bound in Great Britain by
Anchor Brendon Ltd, Tiptree, Essex

Contents

List of charts

Acknowledgements

The research reported in this book was stimulated by a consultancy awarded under the SSRC Initiative on Central–Local Government Relations, and was subsequently financed by an SSRC small project grant. I am most grateful for the encouragement and practical assistance given by the Chairman and the Convenor of the Initiative, Professors George Jones and Mike Goldsmith. George Jones commented on an early plan of this book, and Mike Goldsmith read and provided most helpful advice on the typescript. I also profited from the contact with urban historians facilitated by the SSRC seminars organised in conjunction with the Initiative, and have been most appreciative of the interest subsequently shown in this work by John Garrard and Professor Peter Hennock. I hope that they approve of the outcome.

The work was undertaken while I was also engaged in a busy programme of teaching, administration and curriculum development. One consequence is that it has taken a long time to complete; another is that I have been obliged to trespass on the forbearance of my colleagues. I am grateful for the tolerance of my Head of Department, John Stancer, and for the supportive atmosphere engendered by the Politics staff for research work. The School of Human Sciences, Trent Polytechnic, also made a small grant from its research fund to enable the final stages of the research to be completed.

A project such as this necessarily depends on the co-operation of many librarians and archivists. I am particularly grateful to Fred Usher and Chris Maiden, at Trent Polytechnic, for their positive and helpful assistance at a time of increasing pressure of work, and to Robin Phillips, Peter Hayward and Helen Kirby at Nottingham University, where most of the research on the published official and historical sources was undertaken. I would also like to acknowledge the help of the staffs of the Public Records Office, Kew; the Manuscripts Department, British Library; the Department of Western Manuscripts, Bodleian Library, Oxford; the Social Sciences

Department, Birmingham Public Library; the House of Lords Records Office, the Wiltshire Public Office, Ministry of Agriculture Library, and Newcastle University Library.

Extensive use was made of photographic copies in PRO CAB 41 of original letters preserved in the Royal Archives, made available by the gracious permission of Her Majesty the Queen, and of papers under Crown Copyright in the Public Records Office. I am obliged to the PRO, to the Trustees of the Beaverbrook Foundation and the Clerk of the Records of the House of Lords, the Marquess of Salisbury, Lord Monk Bretton and Sir William Gladstone for permission to quote from papers in their possession or custody, and to the Association of County Councils for access to their records.

I owe a particular debt to those friends who have shared my fascination for politics and whose insights and ideas have inevitably influenced my own, especially my former colleague, Maureen Whitebrook, who also offered much practical support in both a professional and private capacity, and Keith Humphrey. Keith Humphrey commented on an earlier draft, and Roger Iles checked the chapters on local government finance. The errors of fact or interpretation which no doubt remain, are, of course, my own.

Finally, I am profoundly indebted to my family for the practical help and moral support that makes possible the combining of academic work with family life, especially my mother Edith Turner, who, sadly, did not live to see the publication of this book, and my mother-in-law, Nancy Bellamy. Celia Steward and Karen Marchant provided invaluable assistance in school holidays, without which the research would never have been completed. Alice Bellamy helped to organise and wordprocess the bibliography; and Robert Bellamy designed and drew the charts and figures, checked the proofs and undertook many of the clerical chores associated with the later stages of authorship. In a real sense, this work has been a family effort.

C.B.

Chapter One:
Introduction

This is a study of the national politics and administration of the developing relationship between central government and local government in England and Wales in the period from 1871 to the First World War. The choice of dates has been determined by the lifespan of the Local Government Board, the first comprehensive client department for the local government system that emerged in British central government. This period also spans the years when a comprehensive set of local authorities was established in England and Wales to provide the local field administration of the expanding state and when the central executive accepted a more active responsibility to assert the national interest in respect of a wide range of locally administered matters, particularly those relating to social welfare and the physical environment.

In this period, then, there occurred the institutionalisation of relations between the central and local administrative systems in the UK. By 'institutionalisation' I refer to the organisation of political behaviour into definable, persistent, routinised patterns, possessing normative prescription and political authority, which acquire a permanent place in the governmental arrangements of a state. In this sense, this is a study in constitution-making. It explores the historical foundations of a chronically unsettled aspect of our governmental system, one which, moreover, has been surrounded by much loosely conceived rhetoric.

One of the major problems in studying the history of central-local government relations, is that it is difficult to penetrate the rhetoric of twentieth century controversies to reach the contemporary meaning of nineteenth century evidence. Much recent academic work in administrative history has proceeded by a dialectical process, presenting a series of partial insights which have needed to be reconsidered and reintegrated. This is a field, indeed, where academic dispute and political polemic have come to be mixed in more than usual degree. Most academic comment on the Local Government Board, for example, has taken up uncritically the views of John Simon, the Webbs and other early twentieth century advocates of a statist model of central-local government relations, which was a counterthesis to the more influential pluralistic late nineteenth century model, without adequately noticing its dialectical context, because it happens to fit the social democratic ideology of twentieth century academic social policy.[1]

We are told by Stanyer[2] and by Rhodes[3] that the mid twentieth century interpretation of central-local government relations was dominated by a 'conventional wisdom', developed by academics but endorsed by the classic official reports on English local government in the 1960s.[4] This held that there has been an historical trend in the U.K. from a 'partnership' to an 'agency' model of central-local government relations. Here, the words 'partnership' and 'agency' are used rather crudely as indicators of 'centralisation' and 'decentralisation':

> In the agent model, local authorities implement national policies under the supervision of central departments. Local authorities have little or no discretion. In the partnership model, local authorities and central departments are co-equals under Parliament. Local authorities have considerable discretion in designing and implementing their own policies.[5]

The 'conventional wisdom' asserted that the trend from partnership to agency has occurred for two reasons. First, central government exercises increasingly tight control over capital expenditure whilst, at the same time, local authorities have become increasingly dependent upon central grant. Second, central departments have acquired more administrative controls over local authorities. That is, there is an assumption that the centre naturally seeks to expand its influence over localities. This is not an assumption which is borne out by this study. At least until the First World War, much more political and intellectual effort was dedicated to defining and patrolling the boundaries of the central-local divide, limiting the incursions of localities into national politics, and, especially, restricting their demands on the national Exchequer and the London money markets. This shows, indeed, the force of Bulpitt's central thesis, that 'the official mind at the centre developed an operational code for territorial politics which emphasised the desirability of autonomy for the Centre in matters of high politics, and indirect rule of the periphery by local elite collaborators'.[6] The study presented here, however, points to major problems in the development of collaborative relations between the centre and the members and officers of the local authorities. For the centre perceived there to be not only a disparity of social status, but, also (and consequently) a disjunction of cognitive and normative structures, powerfully inhibiting the development of 'partnership'.

Rhodes goes on to point out that the 'conventional wisdom' was questioned in the late 1960s and 1970s by an opposing critique[7] – the 'conventional critique' – which, by inviting the study of local authorities as discrete local political systems, emphasised the importance of factors in the politics of different localities, which induced significant variations in the levels and nature of local services. That is, this counter-thesis has accepted the conceptual framework of the agent/partnership dichotomy, but has taken issue with its over simplified presentation of historical trends.

Rhodes goes on to argue that central-local relations should be approached not through concepts of control and hierarchy, but through an analysis of the mutual power dependency of tiers of government. In this model of central-local relations, the key concepts are reciprocity, power and exchange. It invites consideration of complex and multifaceted relationships in which both tiers appear not as monocratic, unified governments but as pluralistic organisations with shifting political resources for power bargaining. Building on the apparent paradox of central-local relations in Britain in the 1970s, that the centre possessed a multitude of detailed controls over local authorities yet demonstrably lacked the power of strategic direction,[8] Rhodes postulates a system in the UK characterised by 'the rationality of ambiguous confusion'. Central controls are seen here as bids in processes of political exchange, which are ad hoc, pragmatic and negotiable. They produce irritation and confusion, but are nevertheless a rational response by central government to the logic of its power dependence on local authorities and to their financial, political, ideological, legal and other power resources (which are by no means the monopoly of the centre). Although Rhodes describes a political system displaying a significant degree of order and formal continuity – he speaks of a 'game' with 'rules' – the policy system is disorderly. In contradiction to both the agency/partnership thesis and its counter thesis, government displays at both national and local level little scope for the rational, confident, uncompromised resolution of issues.

The present study may offer some useful clues to the historical origins of the contemporary 'rulebook' of the game of central-local relations, and points to some persistent features of the domestic policy system. Its perspective on the pre-First World War central-local system is closer to Rhodes' model than to one where either the language of 'partnership' or 'agency' is appropriate. It suggests also that we should be wary of the assumption made in many debates in the 1980s about the constitutional status of local government in England, that a study of history would validate a doctrine and authentic practice of local government as the political organ of the local 'community'.[9]

Nevertheless, the language of 'partnership' and 'agency' points to an important thrust in Victorian and Edwardian ideas and practice, one to which, rightly, importance has been attached by administrative historians. It probably originates from the Webbs: here is a passage from the 1909 Minority Report of the Royal Commission on the Poor Laws (which is taken from an extended critique of the Local Government Board's management of local authorities):

> To attempt by preremptory orders, meticulous in their detail, having the force of law, to concert the thousands of representatives of the ratepayers, in all this work of administration, into mere mechanical agents of a Central Government Department is, in our opinion, at once to court failure and to destroy local government.[10]

The context of this remark is a passage urging the limits of detailed coercive powers to obtain local compliance to national policy. The Report envisages, rather, an organic unity, based not on the imposition of a multitude of individual controls (regardless of local circumstance) but on that consistency of principle which tolerates local flexibility. In this vision, 'control' stems not from regulation but from the sharing by local elites in the cognitive and normative framework of national policy, and much of the Minority Report is a discussion about how this may be promoted.

If we stand back from the familiar language of central-local relations, and consider the ordinary, every-day meaning of 'partnership', it conjures up images not of detachment and autonomy but rather of common purpose and 'working together'. 'Partnership', doubtless, involves the mutual recognition of functional separation, but it also involves sufficient congruence of values and understanding to ensure a certain compatibility of aim and method. In central-local relations, it implies local authorities which enjoy discretion, but discretion which is ultimately controlled by a shared, national administrative ethos. 'Agents' in contrast may act on behalf of principals in specific respects, but it is not supposed that they share their aspirations: the word is silent as to any organic connection between agent and principal.

This interpretation of agency and partnership clearly cuts right across what, in the 'conventional wisdom' appears as a parallel dichotomy, the centralisation/decentralisation dichotomy. It turns our mind from questions which address the extent and success of hierarchical domination to those concerned with the integration of tiers of the state. In scorning an 'agency' relationship, Beatrice Webb was nevertheless seeking a more profound degree of integration in public life, to be organised around nationally articulated principles: the Minority Report is written from a deep frustration with the disorderliness of social policy. And her battles were with the central administrative agents who possessed a growing volume of controls but who apparently lacked the will and the capacity to exercise strategic leadership over the local authorities. This is the paradox which this study explores.

Beatrice Webb was merely the latest representative of a tradition[11] in nineteenth-century English public life which embraces Bentham, James Mill, Chadwick, G.C. Lewis and John Austin and (with some qualification) J. S. Mill. Without engaging in the tedious and over-protracted debate about the 'individualistic' or 'collectivist' nature of 'Benthamism', we can assert that the common and significant thrust of this work was a vision of the state as a purposive instrument of social change and improvement. Of itself, the notion of 'instrumentality' is neutral about the principles upon which society should be organised. What connects these writers is less an agreement about the balance between collective and private duty and action, than an understanding of the significance of the modern state in the determination of social and economic organisation. They looked to a state which is capable of concerted and rational effort in the public welfare, informed by organised knowledge and general principle, and mobilised by enlightened opinion rather than special interest.

In constitutional terms, Benthamism was a reaction to the model of 'mixed government'. This model was popularly associated with Blackstone[12] and described a system of checks and balances articulated through the institutional separation of powers, reflecting divisions between the sectional economic and possessive interests on which the state rested. The significance of this model for the present discussion was that Mixed Government was highly sympathetic to the role of traditional elite interests, the aristocracy, the gentry, the Church, and the corporations. Contemporary theories of representation, notably the theory of 'virtual representation', discounted popular influence in favour of a balance of interests in Commons and Lords. In the work of William Paley[13] and Jean de Lolme[14], the understanding that political 'influence' and deference arose from the economic and social dependence of the lower classes on their landed and industrial masters was used to justify the claim that independent economic or political interest – that is the possession of personal, unfettered property, office or social position – was the necessary qualification for political rights. This had two important consequences for nineteenth century politics. First, it was used until the 1880s to limit the political power of those classes who were deemed by virtue of their economic and social position – as labourers, traders, tenants, for example – to be incapable of articulating an independent, authentic political voice. And, second it bestowed on the possession of certain economic, social and official privileges a political significance which successfully countered concepts of national or (in local terms) community interest. That is, the Mixed Government model and concepts of interest and political relations inherent in it, discouraged the emergence of a notion of a transcendental state in the UK.

Benthamite ideas reflect a deep antagonism to the corruption, particularism, and inefficiency which was legitimised by the Mixed Government model. For Bentham and James Mill, the public interest was indivisible: the efficiency of government, its accountability and its responsiveness, required clarity of responsibility and unity of action rather than the separation of control and the balance of power. In place of constitutional doctrines which defended traditional rights and the diffusion of political power, they promoted the notion of an autonomous, inclusive integrated state acting through general, universal legislation. The positive state is legitimised by the rational consent of individuals rather than by the negotiated, compromised, exclusive consensus of possessive interests.

The centralising tendencies of such ideas emerge strongly in Chadwick's 1834 Report on the old poor law.[15] Local government is equated with particularism and ignorance; national organisation with the application of general principle and knowledge; local control with corruption and favouritism; national control with consistency and justice. Given the abuses of poor law administration uncovered by the Commissioners, 'any discretionary power left to local officers must be a source of suspicion'.[16] We find consequently in the work of Nassau Senior[17] and John Austin[18], who took the 'centralisation' side in the arguments about the New Poor Law and public health in the 1830s and 1840s, a deep suspicion of local office holding based on traditional or inherited status and a desire to promote a national bureaucracy staffed by disciplined functionaries.

Chadwick recognised, however, that it was politically inexpedient to contemplate a national poor law organisation: local administration was cheaper; increasing national taxes to pay for a national system was politically impossible; and the introduction of the workhouse test would be smoothed if the interests of ratepayers could be harnessed to the new principles. But he also realised that general legislation would be useless without the means of enforcing its local implementation. The Report presents, therefore, a plan for a new central authority for the superintendence of a standardised system of local poor relief, composed of Commissioners and Assistant Commissioners who would personally supervise the local authorities and who would have powers to make detailed regulations for the conduct of the poor law within the guiding spirit of its general principles. Their authority would be derived from their expertise and their political independence. At the same time, the influence of public opinion upon local authorities would be enhanced by a fuller, clearer system of financial accounting, and local officers would be detached from local influence by being appointed under regulations laid down by the central authority.

It can be seen that this blueprint for a national poor law system reflects deep hostility to local government: it is contemptuous of the administrators of the old poor law; it entirely discounts local knowledge; and its arguments for local administration are practical and financial rather than ethical or traditional. But it recognises the centre's power dependency on local government stemming from the incapacity of the centre to fund and manage a national system, and from the need to mobilise local political authority behind the new dogmas. What is particularly important for our argument is that Chadwick discusses more than mechanical, legal and financial controls on local authorities and begins to address how a nationally integrative cognitive system to support the new laws can be developed and disseminated. His report exploits the direct financial interest of ratepayers in economical administration, but it is also founded on the hope that a wider, more disinterested 'public opinion' is available to be mobilised by an administrative system built on technical authority and political independence.

A similar distrust of local government is displayed by J. S. Mill in his *Essay on Representative Government* in which, in the chapter on local representative institutions, he discusses strategies for extending the influence of an enlightened central bureaucracy to support and supplement the exercise of formal, legal powers. What comes clearly across in this chapter is Mill's contempt of local representatives and officials, for whose failures of imagination and intelligence he finds a structural cause; their detachment from the generalised experience and knowledge shared by those at the centre. The central-local relationship is, therefore, for Mill and, indeed for most members of the mid Victorian progressive liberal elite, inherently tutelary.

But Mill sees that central government is dependent on local authorities for the administration of some functions of more than local interest. He distinguishes three kinds of functions which are administered through local institutions: firstly, functions which are 'general' and 'universal', the essence of which is uniform, consistent and efficient administration: secondly, functions in which the national government has a proper interest but where there should be flexibility to take account of local circumstances: and, thirdly, functions which are 'purely local – which concern[s] only a single locality' and in which 'the nation at large is interested... in no other way, than that in which it is interested in the private well-being of all its individual citizens'.[19]

The criteria underpinning the distinction between 'national' and 'local' services are interest and benefit; the distinction is one between the particular and general interest and how directly the function in question addresses the essential purposes of the state. Mill gives as examples of his first category policing, prisons and the administration of justice, because they involve 'security of person and property, and equal justice between individuals [which are] the first needs of society and the primary ends of government'.[20] But he recognises that functions of general application may need local or field administration. It is useful 'even necessary', Mill goes on, 'from the scarcity in the localities of officers representing the general government', that these duties should be under local execution but 'whatever are the best arrangements for securing these primary objects should be made universally obligatory, and, to secure their enforcement, should be placed under central superintendence'.[21] Mill's third category includes paving, lighting, street cleansing, house drainage, and here the issue of central control does not arise, because they are 'in ordinary circumstances... of little consequence to any but [the] inhabitants'.[22] It is worth noting here that, like many others who commented on this issue throughout the nineteenth century, Mill places in this third category many aspects of town improvement, which formed the legislative basis of public health and housing administration, and in which local property rights were most obviously involved. It is when these spill over into matters which directly affect the health of the country that Mill has most problems: the poor law and 'sanitary regulation' form the second category and here the issue is the balance of local discretion and central supervision.

The principle is, says Mill, that localities should be legally allowed to mismanage their own affairs, but the law should intervene to prevent the violation of the interests of others and to protect the principles of justice. But even where Parliament does not choose to intervene, a central administrative authority has the right of influence.

> ... as an adviser and critic, an enforcer of the laws, and a denouncer to Parliament or the local constituencies, of conduct which it deems condemnable, the functions of the executive are of the greatest possible value.[23]

What Mill apparently envisages is a form of 'partnership', in which the local authorities are to be given a sphere of independent action and discretion but will be taught to share a national ethos. It is a partnership in which the centre is very much the dominant partner.

In practice, the late nineteenth state was far from realising the clarity of purpose and the control of the legislative and administrative process by coherent, general principles of public action to which the Benthamites aspired. The concept of an instrumental state which is promoted in this literature, and the expanding activity of the state in social, environmental and economic life, which has been so often ascribed to its influence, should not blind us to the problematical nature of government in the late nineteenth century. This study reflects some of the difficulties arising from the turbulence of party politics, from the overload of the bureaucracy and of Parliamentary business arising from the expansion of public administration, and the problems presented by its fiscal demands. The present day political scientist studying the contemporary sources cannot help but notice the fitful legislative process, its compromised outcomes and patchy implementation.

Likewise, the accretion of formal powers over local authorities by central administrative agencies – the expansion of powers and functions under new general legislation and the transfer to the bureaucracy of controls hitherto exercised by the judiciary or Parliament – was real and it was considerable. But, largely because of problems of political management, it was strategically incomplete. The lacunae both signal and reflect the persistence of earlier political forms and of the intransigence of fiscal conflicts, which very severely constrained the centre's management of local authorities. The growing volume, complexity and detail of powers was formidable: indeed, it contributed to a profound sense of overload at the centre. But in the poor law and in environmental control and public health, the Local Government Board continued to lack certain key powers. Instead it was entangled in a mass of detailed procedural checks in which strategic direction was unavailable. In particular, the Board failed to develop technical authority in the policy areas falling within its responsibility and to assert a formative role in general service development.

This is a syndrome familiar to students of the latter years of the Local Government Board, who have been scornful of the mentality of those officials who rose to the top of its hierarchy to whose influence has been attributed much of the 'frustration of social policy' before the First World War. Certainly, departments have 'minds' and officials influence, and the Local Government Board is a good example of the fact that this is not an exclusively twentieth century phenomenon. What I argue in this study, though, is that the style of the Board in the 1890s and 1900s was determined by more than the personalities, inclinations and abilities of those officials who happened to occupy its top posts: what they were reflecting was a departmental ethos which arose from structural and cultural factors in the situation of the Board and especially from its legal, fiscal and normative context.[24] There are two fundamental and interconnected factors which inhibited the vigorous assertion and implementation of national policy, and discouraged attempts by the centre to build a partnership with local authorities. The first is the prolonged and unresolved fiscal tension which accompanied the expansion of the domestic functions of the state. This was created by the disproportionate burden placed on the rates, and from pressures from taxpayers and orthodox 'sound money' doctrines, for retrenchment in imperial finance. The failure of central government to share fully in the burdens of local authorities brought local finance and the politics of central-local relations into 'high politics', severely exacerbating the problems of their management, and inhibited the development of grants, subsidies and public loans as positive instruments of central influence. The second is the persistence of ideas and constitutional conventions more suited to an understanding of local government under a constitutional model of 'mixed government'. This understanding of local government I propose to label 'local possessive pluralism'.

The connection between these two factors is the way in which the 'localness' of interests was assumptively defined in nineteenth century politics. For most purposes, 'local' interests articulated in national politics are those of classes of localities; boroughs against counties, urban against rural, industrial places against farming places. What distinguishes these classes – and determined the nineteenth century structure of local government – is the perception that they rest on different property relations and on different kinds of rate base. Their distinctive interests were represented in parliamentary politics by the national organisations of economic and fiscal interests, the most coherent and powerful of which were the national organisations of rural and farming ratepayers rather than of urban or industrial interests.

The notion of local authorities as managers of collective consumption, representing constituencies composed of persons interested in general service delivery rather than as ratepayers and property holders, is one which was only weakly articulated until the 1900s. The perception of local government which continued to have most influence on the nature of central controls was 'local possessive pluralism'. Local possessive pluralism essentially contradicts the notion of a unitary or transcendental 'community', but rather assumes that there is within a locality a structure of interests defined by relations to its real or immoveable property – its houses, parks, rivers, farms, woods, mines, factories, markets and so on. These relations reflect its economic and social structures and determine the nature of its politics. Within these relations, the local authority was not perceived to occupy a neutral place. Particularly at the district and town level, local authorities were assumed by virtue of their franchise, their pattern of political recruitment and their duties, to represent a constituency predominantly composed of ratepayers, that is occupiers, rather than of landlords. Moreover, members of local authorities possessed a direct interest in local property and financial relations as trustees for the corporate property of the authority and for the ratefund. The significance of local possessive pluralism for the growing administrative state was that the general and private law of local government continued to bind local authorities into a system of privileges and duties traditionally ascribed to private property, at the cost of their ability to promote a general or community interest.

The security of local possessive rights was guaranteed by three sets of checks and balances: the first was the composition of the local authority itself: until 1894 separate representation was reserved for landowning interests as a check on the dominant occupiers.[25] The second were the reporting and accounting procedures to which local authorities were subject. In this category, I include not only local electoral processes but also the process of audit and the requirements for financial returns imposed by the centre. The third was the containment of the local authority within a procedural framework which subjected the acquisition and use of certain legal powers to external arbitration with competing interests.

It was a principle recognised by the statutes relating to mid nineteenth century local authorities that the authority to exercise three types of power was not granted except on condition that the holders of certain interests had given positive consent, or had special rights of appeal. These were: the taking of new powers by private bill or under adoptive clauses of public acts (where it was usual to require the referral of an application for consent to a meeting of ratepayers and owners or to a public inquiry where their views could be sought): direct interference with or appropriation of local property, for example the taking of land, the removal of nuisances, the closure of slums (where it was usual to provide for reference to the county magistrates or a jury): and the disturbance of corporate property and local fiscal burdens by the alteration of boundaries (where it was traditional to require parliamentary confirmation). A few Acts also granted certain interest holders the right to apply to an external authority in default of the local authority, a right that was postulated on the premise that the exercise of nuisance and sanitary functions was essentially a duty to local occupiers and owners.

The influence of these conventions on the development of central-local relations in the second half of the century was very great. It was natural that the central authority was drawn into policing these safeguards, as an agency independent of local competitive interests. That is, possessive local pluralism opened the local government system to central regulation and control, but it was control undertaken by the state less in pursuit of positive public policy than the protection of individual and corporate rights. Moreover, possessive interests formed a political and psychological barrier against the creation of directive and coercive central powers where these involved the disturbance of local property and political rights. We can see this particularly in relation to public health, but its effects were felt even in the New Poor Law which at first glance appears to have created very intrusive and thorough powers over local authorities. The Poor Law Board lacked, however, two powers of strategic importance to the full implementation of less eligibility: it had no power to compel the building of efficient workhouse accommodation and it had no very effective powers over the boundaries of Unions. That is, it had no positive control over the capital structure of the poor law authorities.

The preoccupation with possessive rights and fiscal politics also determined the nature of information flowing to the centre about domestic services. The Local Government Board maintained several inspectorates, the district audit and a relatively large statistical capacity within its headquarters administration. However, we will see that this machinery was more than fully taken up with ensuring effective local stewardship so that the generation of information for central policy development was discounted. That is, the duty of the centre was interpreted to be the certification of the accuracy of financial and statistical returns, and the checking of forms for local compliance with statutory and departmental regulations, rather than service review.

Without denying the extent and significance of administrative growth in this period, this study points to the persistence of political values and administrative practices which owe more to liberalism and pluralism than to collectivism or statism. It may also go some way to providing historical explanations for some rather longer term features of the British administrative system. The Local

Government Board has been much maligned, but its internal organisation and its approach to the management of central-local relations demonstrate common characteristics of late nineteenth century and twentieth century government. In particular, the subordination of the technical expert to the generalist administrator – the sidelining of rational, scientific modes of thought in government first by the gentlemanly cadre of the unreformed civil service and then by the liberal meritocrat, which has been a special grievance expressed by historians of social policy (especially health policy) against the Local Government Board[26] – represents a more general preoccupation with internal diplomacy and conflict avoidance which cannot be explained merely by rehearsing the mechanical distribution of power within a specific policy community. Hence it is difficult not to fall back on propositions which call attention to the weakness of statist doctrines in the UK.[27] In this sense, this study endorses Bulpitt's view that

> ... the Centre lacked the support of any positive coherent doctrine of an independent community-oriented state... laissez-faire may have lost its former intellectual hegemony, but nothing more positive or coherent arose in its place.[28]

Nevertheless, by the early 1900s, both at local and at national level, the failure of the state to formulate and carry forward coherent responses to poverty and slum housing did lead to the assertion of statist concepts of government, and calls for more integration between tiers founded on a rationalistic model of central-local relations. Although its protagonists proposed the extension of formal *controls* over local authorities, the essence of this model was the assertion of positive *leadership,* founded on technical and professional authority, dedicated to the achievement of objective, impersonal standards of service. That is, if we characterise the dominant model of central-local relations in the late nineteenth century as 'diplomatic-political', the counter model was a 'technical-bureaucratic' model.

The growing awareness of the social problems of Edwardian England therefore led to more strident calls for the powers of the centre over local authorities to be strengthened and for more effort to be made to incorporate local authorities into national policy.

The fundamental issue which they raised was the nature of the centre's authority over localities, but the controversy increasingly focused on narrower questions of machinery and powers. The Local Government Board took on the role as symbol, and therefore as scapegoat, of a style of central-local relations which took the blame for the frustration of policy. What was a far more pervasive problem was put down to a failure of will on the part of politicians and administrators attached to a particular government department, to be remedied by an administrative reorganisation. The issue which appeared on the national political agenda was the call for a Ministry of Health.

The Local Government Board is, therefore, more than a convenient handle on which to hang a study of central-local relations at this time: it was in the eyes of contemporaries the reification of a dominant model of central-local relations. Certainly the Board played a large role in the development and management of the local government system: it dealt with structure, rating, grants, elections, boundaries and audit. And it also sponsored the widest range of domestic services ever encompassed by a single, unitary department, including the poor law, public health, housing, town planning, vaccination, food and drugs administration, alkali inspection, highways, traffic management and old age pensions. A central purpose then of this book is to explore the nature of the Local Government Board as a central authority and the assumptions on which it was organised for the conduct of central-local relations.

NOTES TO CHAPTER ONE

1 The two major contemporary sources for the reputation of the Local Government Board are John Simon, *English Sanitary Institutions*, 1890, reprinted Johnson Reprint Co. Ltd, 1970, and Sidney and Beatrice Webb, 'English poor law policy', *English Local Government*, X, Frank Cass, 1963 and 'The last hundred years', *English Poor Law History*, II, Longman's, 1927-9; and Beatrice Webb, *Our Partnership*, 1948, (ed.) B. Drake and M. Cole, London School of Economics and Cambridge University Press, 1975.
Views of other contemporaries are to be found in Randolph S. Churchill, *Winston S. Churchill*, II, Heinemann, 1967; Lucy Masterman, *C. F. G. Masterman; a Biography*, Nicholson and Watson, 1935; R. C. K. Ensor, *England, 1870-1914*, Oxford, Clarendon Press, 1936; Christopher (Viscount) Addi-

son, *Politics From Within,* Herbert Jenkins, 1924 and *Four and a Half Years,* Hutchinson, 1934.

The reputation of the Local Government Board has been freely cited and reinforced by academics, for example: Sir Ivor Jennings in H. J. Laski *et al., A Century of Municipal Progress, 1835-1935,* Allen & Unwin, 1935; K. B. Smellie, *A Hundred Years of British Government,* Allen & Unwin, 4th ed., 1948; J. L. and Barbara Hammond, *James Stansfeld; a Victorian Champion of Sex Equality,* Longmans 1932; Kenneth D. Brown, 'John Burns at the Local Government Board', *Journal of Social Policy,* VI, 1977, pp. 157-170; Kenneth D. Brown, *John Burns,* Royal Historical Society, 1977; R. Davidson and R. Lowe, 'Bureaucracy and innovation in British welfare policy, 1870-1945', in W. J. Mommsen (ed.), *The Emergence of the Welfare State in Britain and Germany,* Croom Helm, 1981; Douglas E. Ashford, *The Emergence of the Welfare States,* Oxford, Blackwells, 1986.

There are accounts of the Local Government Board, at first or second hand, from men who worked in it, in: Susan Liveing, *A Nineteenth Century Teacher: John Henry Bridges,* Kegan Paul, 1926; Herbert Preston Thomas, *The Work and Play of a Government Inspector,* Blackwells, 1909; Horace Butler, *Confident Morning,* Faber & Faber, 1949; Sir Arthur Newsholme, *The Last Thirty Years in Public Health: Recollections and Reflections on my Official and Post-Official Life,* Allen & Unwin, 1936; and W. A. Ross, 'The Local Government Board and after', *Public Administration,* XXXIV, 1956, pp. 17-25.

2 Jeffrey Stanyer, *Understanding Local Government,* Fontana, 1976, p. 211.

3 R. A. W. Rhodes, 'Some myths in central-local relations', *Town Planning Review,* LI, 1980, p. 270.

4 There are full references in Rhodes, *ibid.* The more important representatives of this tradition are D. N. Chester, *Central and Local Government,* Macmillan, 1955; W. A. Robson, *Local Government in Crisis,* Allen and Unwin, 1966; and P. G. Richards, *The Reformed Local Government System,* Allen & Unwin, 1973.

5 Rhodes, 'Some myths in central-local relations', p. 270.

6 J. P. Bulpitt, *Territory and Power in the U.K.,* Manchester University Press, 1983, p. 3.

7 Again, there is a full bibliography in Rhodes, but see, John Dearlove, *The Politics of Policy in Local Government,* Cambridge University Press, 1973; D. E. Regan, *Local Government and Education,* Allen & Unwin, 1977 and John Gyford, *Local Politics in Britain,* Croom Helm, 2nd ed. 1984.

8 Rhodes' work was developed for the SSRC initiative in central-local government relations. See, R. A. W. Rhodes, *Control and Power in Central-Local Government Relations,* Farnborough, Gower, 1981. There is a critique of his approach in the light of the work undertaken as a result of the initiative in R. A. W. Rhodes, 'Power-dependence theories of central-local govern-

18 Introduction

ment relations: a critical assessment'. in M. J. Goldsmith (ed.) *New Research in Central-Local Relations,* Aldershot, Gower, 1985.

9 The view that local government represents an authentic tradition of the organic local community in England, is seminally developed in the work of Joshua Toulmin Smith, an antiquarian and lawyer, whose polemics were published in the 1840s and 1850s against the statutory regulation of water supply, especially in London. His position was that Parliamentary Sovereignty was a symptom of Norman oppression, and that the natural constitution of England was a confederation of local communities in which sovereignty resided. This is clearly nonsense. Nevertheless, his rhetoric lives on; e.g. W. H. Greenleaf has argued that 'his works constitute a particularly good instance of a certain kind of libertarian thought about public administration', and illustrate an important aspect of the British political tradition. W. J. Greenleaf, 'Toulmin Smith and the British Political Tradition', *Public Administration,* LIII, 1975, pp. 25-44. There is a much more balanced discussion of the notion of community in Dilys M. Hill, *Democratic Theory and Local Government,* Allen and Unwin, 1974.

10 *Report of the Royal Commission on the Poor Laws and the Relief of Distress,* 1909, (Cd. 4499) xxxvii 1 'Minority Report', p. 357.

11 Sir William Blackstone, *Commentaries on the Laws of England,* Oxford, Clarendon Press, 1765-69. The important distinction between the Mixed Government model and the Separation of Powers model, and their relative influence in the U. K. is covered in my thesis, Christine Bellamy, *Some Aspects of Constitutionalism in England in the Nineteenth Century,* unpublished PhD thesis, University of Nottingham, 1974. See also, M. J. C. Vile, *Constitutionalism and the Separation of Powers,* Oxford University Press, 1967, chapter 3.

12 On this 'tradition', Shirley Letwin, *The Pursuit of Certainty,* Cambridge University Press, 1965.

13 William Paley, *The Principles of Moral and Political Philosophy,* 2nd ed. London, 1786.

14 Jean de Lolme, *The Constitution of England,* G, Kearsley, London, 1775.

15 *Report from Her Majesty's Commissioners for Inquiring into the Administration and Practical Operation of the Poor Laws,* 1834 (44) XXVII, 1.

16 *Ibid.* p. 162.

17 Nassau Senior, 'Poor Law Reform', *Edinburgh Review,* LXXIV, 1841, pp. 1-44.

18 John Austin 'Centralisation', *Edinburgh Review,* LXXXV, 1847, 231-32.

19 J. S. Mill, *Essay on Representative Government,* Oxford University Press, 1912, p. 373.

20 *Ibid.* p. 374.

21 *Ibid.*

22 *Ibid.* p. 373.

23 *Ibid.* p. 379.

24 Some easement of the general censure of the Local Government Board
has been made, on these grounds, by Roy M. MacLeod, *Treasury Control
and Social Administration,* Bell, 1968, and Jose Harris, *Unemployment and
Politics: a Study in English Social Policy, 1886-1914,* Oxford. Clarendon
Press, 1972, pp. 267-9. Harris has also contributed a short but extremely
useful note on 'Social policy and the problem of local taxation', *Ibid.* Appendix A.

25 The constitutive acts of nineteenth century local authorities provided for
the following:
The Poor Law Amendment Act, 1834: franchise – ratepayers and owners
of property, by plural voting according to wealth: qualification for Guardians – property qualification up to £40 fixed by the central authority, and
J.P.s *ex officio.*
The 1835 Municipal Corporations Act, 1835: franchise – ratepayers for two
years, resident within seven miles (i.e. burgesses); qualification for councillors and aldermen – property qualification varying with the size of the town.
Public Health Act, 1848: franchise – all owners of land and ratepayers, by
plural voting according to wealth; qualification – residence within seven
miles, plus real or personal property qualification up to £30 fixed by central
authority.
Local Government Act, 1888: franchise – ratepayers, and £10 occupiers
qualified for Parliamentary elections; qualification – residence and property qualification to be fixed up to £10.
Parish Councils Act, 1894: franchise – all parish electors for county council
and all parliamentary electors; qualification – parish electors resident
within three miles for twelve months.
B. Keith-Lucas, *The English Local Government Franchise: a Short History,*
Oxford, Blackwells, 1952.

26 Roy M. MacLeod, 'The frustration of state medicine 1880-1899', *Medical
History,* XI, 1967, pp. 15-40; Jeanne L. Brand, 'John Simon and the Local
Government Board bureaucrats, 1871-1876', *Bulletin of Medical History,*
XXXVII, 1963, pp. 184-194; Jeanne L. Brand, *Doctors and the State: the British
Medical Profession and Government Action in Public Health, 1870-1912,*
Baltimore, John Hopkins Press, 1965; R. J. Lambert, *Sir John Simon, 1816-
1904, and English Social Administration,* Macgibbon & Kee, 1963; A. S.
MacNalty, 'The history of state medicine in England', *Journal of the Royal
Institute of Public Health,* II, 1948, pp. 9-46.

27 I am grateful to Maureen Whitebrook for clarifying my views about theories
of the state in Britain. C. A. Bellamy and M. F. Whitebrook, 'The state and
the theory of the state in Britain', *Canadian Journal of Political Science,*
XIV, 1981, pp. 727-743; Kenneth Dyson, *The State Tradition in Western
Europe,* Oxford, Martin Robertson, 1980, chapters 1 and 7.

28 Bulpitt, *Territory and Power,* p. 124.

Part One
The national politics
of local finance

Chapter Two
Expenditure and grants

The relationship between the central bureaucracy and local government in the second half of the nineteenth century and early twentieth century cannot be understood except in the context of the national politics of local government and taxation. The growth of the local state disrupted the distribution of fiscal burdens, producing a chronic grievance amongst those who claimed to bear the economic burden of ratepaying. The conflicts arising from this simple fact, are dominated by the categories of possessive pluralism: that is, the politics of local taxation assumed and reinforced, to the almost total exclusion of other considerations, the perception that local government belonged specially to the interests associated with real property, on which rates were levied. This is important for central-local relations in two respects. It inhibited the emergence of fiscal doctrine able to address the problems of redistributing finance to local authorities in such a way as to ensure the universal capacity to meet national minimum standards, and it delayed the development of grants as a mechanism of central influence on local government. For the national politics of local finance were largely an extension of the struggles between local possessive interests, carried on their terms. That is, the conflicts focussed on the relationship between fiscal duties imposed on, and the benefits from public expenditures accruing to, different categories of property in urban possessive structures and rural possessive structures. And this argument was applied by extension to central-local financial relations: since the development of local government was largely a response to nationally defined interests, the national taxpayer, it was argued, rather than the local ratepayers, should bear the cost.

What is especially important is the capture in the early part of our period of the political right to speak for ratepayer interests by a national pressure group – the Local Taxation Committee – dominated by farming and landowning interests. These interests achieved a particularly salient presence in Parliament until 1885, disrupting the orderly management of national politics and financial affairs, and compelling the centre to seek a settlement. After 1888, these interests were able to exploit their special position in Conservative and Unionist politics, producing a persistent bias in the financial relations of local and central government in favour of the rural areas. In the years before the First World War, moreover, the Liberal Government found itself faced with national associations of local authorities dominated by Conservative and Unionists, justly resentful of the chronic failure of governments to build an adequate financial base for the expanding local services of the state.

The centre's capacity to respond to and manage ratepayer demands was limited by its own financial problems and, until 1909, by orthodox financial and administrative doctrines. Gladstonian financial orthodoxy held that local authorities should be disciplined by the establishment of a direct connection between local expenditure and rates, and resisted the use of subventions as an instrument of central policy. The Treasury consistently opposed financial arrangements involving detailed monitoring of local government by central departments, because of the establishments implications for the civil service. And national politicians regarded with great suspicion any proposal which gave local lobbies an interest in the yield and nature of imperial taxes.

It is possible, therefore, to identify a bi-partisan central-government strategy aimed at protecting the Exchequer from local demands, founded on an increasingly untenable distinction between the local (and private) and general (and public) activities of the state. Pressure from ratepayer lobbies meant that this strategy could not be consistently sustained; nevertheless, an important feature of local finance in this period is the relative success of the centre in limiting its financial contributions to local government. The growth of local administration was largely financed by other means (Figure 1). And where the grant system was expanded, it was more often a response to local pressure than to central bureaucratic pressure for greater control of local

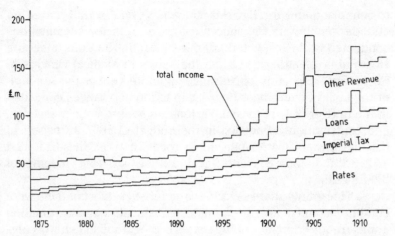

Fig. 1 Local Authority Income, 1875-1913, from rates, imperial taxes, loans
and other revenue
Note: The peaks of 1904-5 and 1909-10 are due to the capital expenditure
on the formation of the Metropolitan Water Board and the Port of London
Authority, respectively.
Sources: Local Taxation Returns and Annual Reports of Local Government
Board

administration. The culmination of this strategy was the substitution of assigned revenues for conditional specific grants in 1888.

Although the growth in local expenditure was led by changes in
national legislation, there was, until Goschen's reforms of 1888, no
systematic aid to local authorities based on an explicit distributional principle. Rather, there were a number of specific grants,
conceded *ad hoc* as the price of securing particular legislative or
administrative change. They were: grants towards the salaries of
poor law medical officers and teachers, conceded by Peel in 1846[1]
as compensation to agricultural districts for the abolition of the
corn laws; the grant paid under the 1856 Police Act[2] by which police
forces certified by HM Inspector of Constabulary to be efficient
received a quarter of the cost of pay and clothing; gratuities paid
on the certificate of the Medical Inspector of the central authority
to public vaccinators under the 1867 Vaccination Act,[3] as a financial
incentive to increase the number of successful vaccinations; grants

to schools, under the Revised Education Code of 1861, based on attendances and on the success of children in the examinations conducted by the Inspectors of Education; contributions under the 1872 Public Health Act[4] of half the salary of Medical Officers of Health and Inspectors of Nuisance appointed under the sanction of the Local Government Board; capitation allowances conceded in the Budget of 1874 for pauper lunatics sent to county asylums; and contributions conceded in the Budget of 1882 in respect of half the cost of maintaining main roads. In 1888 these totalled £4,268,222 compared with local authorities' rate income of £22,194,836.

These grants share several characteristics: most of them were conditional and many (for example, the education and vaccination grants) required significant increases in the establishments of central departments to provide for the routine inspection and heavy burden of administration they implied. And the total grant paid was determined by the level of expenditure or activity undertaken at the local level. Several of these grants were, therefore, also the subject of chronic dispute between the central authority and the Treasury, especially the lunatic, vaccination and education grants.

The pauper lunatic grant was conceded under pressure from the Lunacy Commissioners for the removal of lunatics from general workhouses into specialist asylums. In its first full year, 1875-6, it was set at £330,000; by 1887-8 it had risen to around £450,000.[5] The Treasury formed the view that lunatics were being sent unnecessarily to asylums to obtain the grant, and that it was the duty of the Local Government Board to limit the practice: and it regularly challenged the Board's estimates.[6] Reminded that this was a grant voted by Parliament in pursuit of national policy, the Treasury usually backed off, but the ritualistic nature of its complaints does not obscure the Treasury's want of sympathy with the grant.

By contrast, the vaccination grant was small, but vaccination was a contentious issue in Parliament and the grant was a source of constant irritation to the Treasury. The annual vote was, in consequence, the subject of much official correspondence in Whitehall. The history of this grant was one of constant under-provision and supplementary votes, caused by the Treasury's persistent refusal to accept the Board's estimates. Eventually, in 1876,[7] the Treasury attempted to cut the estimate from £17,000 to £6000, and demanded a review of the grant on the grounds that the inspection of individual vaccinations could not economically be a central function, and that public health was a local function. The grant was saved by a strong protest to the President, George Sclater Booth, from the Secretary, John Lambert, and E.C. Seaton, the Board's Medical Officer, who were convinced that the vaccination scheme had operated uniformly only since gratuities were introduced, and that qualified, local MOHs were too few and far between for inspection to be devolved to local authorities.[8] The grant continued to grow year by year, often financed by savings on other heads, but the Treasury continued to be reluctant to show Parliament the true costs and to insist that it was understood to be 'merely provisional and temporary'.[9]

Education grants, of course, produced the greatest call on the Exchequer and the greatest administrative problems. By the mid 1880s, there were some 18,540 schools in receipt of grant, for each of which a grant had to be calculated, a cheque written, a payment accounted for. The system was riddled with opportunity for dispute, and the Education Department had evolved the most complicated rules to protect itself from challenge. Nevertheless, it was in constant trouble with the Public Accounts Committee.[10] In 1885, the Permanent Secretary to the Treasury. Ralph Lingen, pressed Hicks Beach, the Conservative Chancellor, for the devolution of the grant administration to school boards, and for the substitution of a capitation grant for the system of payment by results. This would free HMIs for a badly-needed policy development role in the Education Department.[11] The Government was, however, unwilling to load the already contentious issue of local government reform with educational controversies, and education finance remained untouched by the 1888 settlement.

The pre-1888 grants were also limited in range, and, as Figure 1 shows, represented a falling share of local income. Ratepayer grievances stemmed, therefore, from the correct belief that rates were bearing the burden of an expanding range of functions, many of which were not peculiarly local in the benefit which they created. That is, rates offended against a central canon of contemporary fiscal doctrine: that the burden of expenditure, especially new expenditure, should fall on those who benefited from it, and that expenditures of general benefit should be borne by 'equal sacrifice' of the different classes in society.[12]

By the 1860s, the grievances of ratepayers had become specially attached to agriculture. Peel's concessions of 1846 had created an assumption – endorsed by Disraeli in the 1850s for example[13] – that economic damage to agriculture would be compensated by further adjustments in local finance. Resentment was fuelled in the late 1860s by an upturn in rate-borne expenditure, (caused by an increase in the rate of pauperism, by heavier investment in poor law buildings and local improvements), by the disturnpikement of main roads, and by the prospect of a national Education Act.[14] However, the factor which, above all, brought rates into national politics was the formation of a pressure group capable of the national organisation of the agricultural interest.

The Central Chamber of Agriculture was formed in 1867 to build on the experience and success of the farming community's campaign in 1865-6 for action on the cattle plague, to promote and co-ordinate local chambers and to organise national farming opinion. By late 1868 it had 15,000 members organised in some 66 chambers, a permanent office in London and a full time, paid Secretary.[15] From the first, local taxation issues played a prominent part in its business. In May 1868, Sir Massey Lopes, a Conservative MP and Devon landowner 'inaugurated the Parliamentary intervention' of the Chamber by moving the first of a series of annual resolutions drawing attention to the injustice of levying local taxation exclusively on real property.[16] In 1869, the Chamber's interest in the rating issue achieved national recognition, when a deputation to Gladstone in February was promised that the Government 'would at all time during the progress of this matter' confer with the Central Chamber.[17]

In the spring of 1869, the Central Chamber agreed to sponsor an organisation 'to promote the adopting of concerted measures by Ratepayers of Towns and Ratepayers of Counties, and to raise a special fund for the diffusion of information upon the subject of local taxation'.[18] The Local Taxation Committee was established as a separate body, with its own committee (under the Chairmanship of Lopes), its own funds, its own office and its own full time

Secretary, in order to appeal to a wide body of ratepayers, urban as well as rural.[19] In its first year, the Committee circulated all local chambers of agriculture, all Quarter Sessions, all Boards of Guardians and (with the co-operation of the London ratepayers organisation, the Metropolitan Poor Rate League) all London vestries, calling for the transfer of national services to the Exchequer.[20] The campaign of the late 60s/early 70s is therefore notable for the political connection that was attempted between the agricultural interest and ratepaying organisations in the cities, especially London, Liverpool, Birmingham and Leeds to which its circulations were subsequently extended. By the end of 1871, the Committee was claiming credit for well attended meetings in London and other urban centres which resulted in some 270 petititions to Parliament,[21] and it was able to list in its membership some eighty-three MPs (almost entirely, however, Conservative county members).[22] In 1872, it claimed that twenty-three out of the thirty-nine London vestries subscribed to the Metropolitan League.[23]

In the late 1860s, the President of the Poor Law Board, J. G. Goschen, responded to the agitation by measures designed to reduce the rate of pauperism; by pressing Boards of Guardians for stricter local poor law administration,[24] by instituting special inquiries into poor relief in the agricultural counties,[25] and by inviting the co-operation of voluntary bodies in London in disciplining the poor through the organisation of charity.[26] But the Government conceded the inevitability of rating reform when Gladstone opposed Lopes's 1869 motion for a Commission of Inquiry, on the grounds that what was required was less an investigation than a policy.[27] In 1870, however, he agreed to a Select Committee, chaired by Goschen, to inquire into the division of rates between owners and occupiers. Goschen meanwhile commissioned from the statistician, Robert Giffen, a report[28] which sought to drive a wedge between urban and rural ratepayers, by showing that the political emphasis on the increase in rates obscured changes in the relative distribution of taxation and of the economic value on which it was raised. When taken together with imperial taxation, land was shown to be less heavily taxed than in any other European country, and the increase in rates on land to be more than matched by that in property values. In the towns, however, where rates had risen most steeply, occupiers of dwellinghouses had been hit both by rising rents and by rising rates. The inference was that rating was primarily a grievance of the urban occupier.

There followed in 1873 a controversy generated by R Dudley Baxter, the statistician and publicist of the Local Taxation Committee.[29] Baxter argued that not only was the rise in rates far greater than Giffen had shown, but also that the income generated by real property was taxed at a significantly higher rate than the income generated by personal wealth or by industry. Baxter was also able to show that Giffen's figures and methods were far from robust. He pointed out that Giffen had used, as his base year for the calculation of the rise in rates, a year in which rates had been untypically high; that he had failed to take account of revaluations; that he had used inappropriate tax schedules to calculate the fiscal contributions of railways and similar properties; and that his foreign comparisons were invalid because he had failed to notice the different proportions of real and personal property in the countries which he had surveyed. Giffen's report also contained a number of arithmetical mistakes which hardly enhanced its credibility.

One of the strengths of the Local Taxation Committee was that it was consistently able to draw on authoritative statistics to support its case: Baxter died suddenly in 1875, but his work was carried forward by P. G. Craigie, who had become the first Secretary to the Committee. But though the Committee proved technically very strong, Goschen's paper achieved its political objectives: Baxter's and Craigie's analysis allied the Committee to a perspective which was very much more sympathetic to the cause of agriculturalists and landowners than to housedwellers and urban ratepayers. The local taxation lobby was never again able to claim to unite urban and rural ratepayers. The Members who spoke for the Committee in the Commons – Lopes, the Conservative MPs Albert Pell of Leicestershire and Clare Sewell Read, a tenant farmer from Norfolk, and (after 1880) the Liberal MP for Herefordshire, Thomas Duckham – were clearly identified with the agricultural interest, and the vast majority of the Parliamentary subscribers to the Local Taxation Committee continued to be Conservative members sitting for agricultural counties.[30] Although Pell and Lopes occasionally remembered to point out the adverse effects of high agricultural rates on the price of food in towns, the main thrust of their campaign was directed against the damage inflicted by the expanding rate bill on the profitability and effectiveness of agriculture.

The Committee's short term objectives were to secure subventions towards the costs of locally administered services where control by central government had become so great that local authorities were, in effect, its agents – vaccination, lunatic asylums, major highways, education and the poor law were often cited. And they pressed for the transfer to the centre of 'national' functions – prisons, the administration of justice and, more contentiously, the police. Pell, who had come into public life through poor law administration and who was very active in the Poor Law Conference movement for a stricter poor law, also pressed strongly for a national capitation grant towards the maintenance of the indoor (as opposed to the outdoor) poor, as a financial inducement to Guardians to apply the workhouse test. Most urban and many Liberal MPs argued, in contrast, that the greatest rate rise was in towns, generated by improvements – drainage, street making and lighting, embankments, clearances, and so on – which increased land values to the economic benefit of landlords. Tenants paid twice, through higher rates and through increased rents. On this analysis, subventions merely transfered the costs of improvements from occupiers to income and indirect taxpayers (who were often the same people as ratepayers), unjustly increasing the burden on labour and working capital. Liberal leaders preferred, rather, to transfer part of the rate burden to landowners: Robert Lowe, who was Gladstone's Chancellor in the early 1870s, believed that this would weaken the ratepayer lobby by driving a wedge between landlords and tenants.[31] In 1866 the Select Committee on Metropolitan Local Government[32] had proposed that this transfer be effected by dividing the rates, that is compelling landlords to bear half the rates by deducting them from rents. The 1870 Select Committee endorsed this scheme.[33] But Gladstone's strategy throughout the 1870s and 1880s was that the local taxation card must be saved to effect a resolution of an even more contentious issue, and this was the reform of local government.

Goschen had become convinced that the issue of local taxation

was inextricably linked with problems of local government structure. Local government in England and Wales was the product of
the incremental, ad hoc development of general statute law and of
a mass of private local Acts: there were administrative counties
under the non-elected magistrates; municipal corporations (often
acting as improvement commissions); urban local boards; parishes
(sometimes acting through vestries and sometimes through committees for special functions); unions of parishes for the Poor Law;
and even special rating districts within parishes under the 1866
Sanitary Act.[34] The size of parishes varied enormously, union and
county boundaries bore no necessary relation to each other or to
those of municipal corporations, and parishes were frequently
divided between town and county or between counties.[35] Each
authority had its own (different) financial year, electoral arrangements, and issued a separate rate demand. Local Government,
wrote G. C. Brodrick in 1875, suffered from a 'striking and almost
obtrusive lack of unity'.[36] Aside from the obvious inefficiency of
such arrangements, it was argued with some force that the confusion rendered local authorities practically unaccountable for their
finance and the performance of their functions.[37] To many in central
government, especially those like Gladstone, Lowe, Goschen and
Northcote with strong views about the conduct of public finance,
the state of local government in the early 1870s was indefensible.

Tackling local government structure raised very contentious
issues, however. The very overlapping of areas meant that no
rational structure could be achieved without considerable disturbance of local financial arrangements, property, and poor law
settlements. The problem was compounded by rating valuations,
which were made separately for each parish by overseers working
to Union assessment committees. Any interference with parish or
union boundaries involved, therefore, not only the assimilation of
rates but also of rateable values. The Poor Law Board and the Local
Government Board assumed that, as with the formation of Unions
after 1834, a reorganisation of union boundaries would disturb
settlements, produce an inbalance of workhouse accommodation,
and provoke major local political conflict; and that adjusting county
boundaries to union boundaries was ruled out by the effect on
parliamentary boundaries.[38] The conventional wisdom of the Poor

Law and Local Government Boards was, therefore, that parishes (with rationalised boundaries) and petty session districts, rather than unions, should form the electoral units for representative county authorities. And this is what Goschen proposed.

In 1871, Goschen introduced two bills[39] which, taken together, amounted to a comprehensive reform of the whole question. He proposed the division and consolidation of rates, the abolition of various exemptions to widen the rate base, and the standardisation of assessment procedures as a first step towards valuation reform. He also proposed to implement the recommendations of the Royal Sanitary Commission of 1871 by establishing a comprehensive system of rural and urban sanitary authorities and consolidating the central authority under a new Local Government Board. The rationalisation of local government was to be completed by the reform of parish government, and by the establishment of indirectly elected county financial boards to which the administrative and rating functions of magistrates were to be transfered.

The Liberal Government absolutely refused to contemplate subventions in aid of rates. But on the strict condition that the local government clauses were passed, Goschen offered to assign to local authorities the house duty, worth some £1.2m annually, for the relief of the rates. The incidence of this tax was such, he argued, that it would relieve the ratepayers most in need of relief, that is the urban ratepayers. But he had offended too many interests to pass his bills: the agriculturalists wanted subventions not assigned revenues; the division of rates was dismissed as a diversion from the main issue, and his own backbenchers rejected the principle of indirect elections.[40] Only the clauses providing for the establishment of the Local Government Board were saved.

The political cost of failing to deliver on the local taxation issue became dramatically apparent to the Liberal Government in the 1872 Session. It is clear that unease about rates went beyond the Conservative membership of the Local Taxation Committee to the Liberal backbenches. Aware of unfulfilled pledges on the Royal Sanitary Commission's report, the Government introduced a Public Health Bill to establish local sanitary authorities. With one eye on this Bill and another on Gladstone's anticipated budget surplus (which turned out to be in excess of £2m), Lopes moved on 16

April that the House should accept no more legislation imposing burdens on ratefunds unless that legislation also provided for Exchequer contributions for national services.[41] Two hundred Liberals abstained and the Government suffered a spectacular defeat by a hundred votes.[42] Progress on the Public Health Bill was suspended while James Stansfeld, the President of the new Local Government Board, hurriedly negotiated with Lopes. Lopes was conciliated by the offer of a conditional grant towards the salaries of the local Medical Officers of Health (the only new expenditure envisaged in the bill) and by a special cheap rate for public works loans for sanitary purposes. A grudging Gladstone was placated with the assurance that the health officers' grant was 'a temporary arrangement, without prejudice on either side'.[43]

The Local Taxation Committee had shown that it possessed a veto on domestic legislation, so long as the local taxation issue remained unresolved. Parliament was, however, left in no doubt as to Gladstone's price for settlement: further progress was conditional upon Parliament accepting reforms which strengthened local government by widening representation and equalising the burdens between occupiers and owners, and which promoted the general economy and efficiency of administration.[44]

This statement settled the Liberals' long term strategy, but the Government was embarrassed for a short term response. Eventually, on Stansfeld's advice that the establishment of sanitary authorities had taken the urgency from the structure issue, an uncertain Cabinet agreed to a programme (urged by Lambert) of single issue measures to pave the way for local government reform, rather than another grand measure.[45] Accordingly, in 1873, a Select Committee was nominated to consider the rationalisation of parish boundaries.[46] However, a bill to tackle rating exemptions was defeated in the Lords (after being much compromised in the Commons by concessions to special interests), and a valuation bill was quietly dropped after an apathetic reception in Parliament.[47] In the autumn of 1873, the Cabinet discussed a measure for 'Local Government as compared with local taxation' and appointed a cabinet committee to discuss representative county government.[48] But in January 1874, the Government fell, and a budget surplus of over five million pounds, which Gladstone had earmarked to fulfil his long ambition of reducing or abolishing the income tax, was left for a new Conservative Government.[49]

In opposition, the Conservative leadership had exploited the issue by supporting the Local Taxation Committee, and, in March 1874, a Local Taxation Committee deputation to Disraeli was promised that relief would now be forthcoming.[50] In his first Budget in April,[51] the new Chancellor, Sir Stafford Northcote, announced additional grants worth £1.25m a year in aid of rates: poor law authorities were to receive four shillings a week for every pauper lunatic sent to a county asylum; the police grant was doubled, and some £170,000 a year was made available in lieu of rates on government property. He also announced that the Government was considering the finance of local criminal prosecutions and promised a major review of the income tax, which would address the issue at the heart of the question – the fiscal relationship of real and personal property. But Northcote was careful to spell out the assumptions under which these concessions were made, to head off future raids on the Exchequer. The grants, he declared, were an acknowledgement of long standing grievances which stood in the way of the Government's social policy, and they were offered only in respect of 'national' services.

In 1877 prisons were transfered to central management. But this was as much as Northcote was able to do. Anxieties in the years between 1875 and 1879, that tax revenues would prove insufficiently elastic to cope both with the demands of domestic policy and Disraeli's expansive foreign policy, ruled out fiscal reform.[52] In 1875, Northcote deferred his review of the income tax, because his surplus was too small to finance changes in taxation: in 1877 the budget went into deficit.

In 1876, George Sclater Booth, Stansfeld's successor at the Local Government Board, tried to persuade Northcote and the Cabinet to extend subventions to highways.[53] The future of disturnpiked main roads had been the subject of much agitation by the Local Taxation Committee on the grounds that main roads in rural areas were mainly used by urban and commercial traffic, and their complaints had been endorsed by House of Commons Select Committees on disturnpiked roads in 1874 and 1875.[54] The Local Government Board wished to promote the rationalisation of district

government by forming highway districts with the same boundaries
as the new sanitary districts. Sclater Booth therefore pressed the
Cabinet for the compulsory districting of local roads and the transfer of main roads to indirectly elected county road boards, to be
effected by offering a highways subvention. The Cabinet was
unsympathetic, partly from a feeling that ratepayers' grievances
had been dealt with in 1874, and partly on the grounds allegedly
expressed by Lord Derby that 'there is nothing so local as a road'.[55]
Sclater Booth and Northcote discussed the possibility of assigning
a share of the carriage tax towards the cost of roads, but this
proposal collapsed on the difficulty of finding a formula for relieving
the rural ratepayer by means of a tax that was largely generated
in London and other urban centres.[56] Sclater Booth therefore
retreated from compulsory districting, and the bill that was passed
in 1878 provided only permissive powers for highway districts.[57]

The Conservatives' approach to the issue of local taxation
turned out, in practice, to be much the same as that of the Liberals.
That is, they continued with a series of paving measures: a Rating
Act in 1874; an Act in 1876 to deal with the boundaries of divided
parishes by administrative action; Valuations Bills in 1876 and 1877
(which failed to pass); and the Highways Act of 1878.[58] And they
too paid the price in political embarrassment for their inability to
propose a full measure of local government reform.

For the Central Chamber of Agriculture had become committed to reformed county government, as a countervailing influence
on extravagant local authorities. In 1876, they approved a scheme
by Craigie for county boards, to be composed of one third nominees
of the magistrates (who were supposed to represent landowners)
and two thirds elected by the Guardians (to represent ratepayers).[59]
On March 9, 1878, Clare Sewell Read moved an amendment in the
Committee of Supply calling for county boards to take over the
administrative and rating functions of the magistrates.[60] For the
Liberals, Stansfeld felt unable in principle to vote against the reform
of county government. The Government issued a whip to oppose,
but faced, in a near-empty chamber, with Read's obvious cross-
party support from county members, Sclater Booth merely
announced that he recognised the inevitability of county government, and declined to divide the House. As the *Times* commented,

both parties were now committed to the reform of county government: 'Mr Read. . . checkmated the Government and the Opposition at the same time'.[61]

During the winter of 1877-8, the Conservative Government apparently decided that the least damaging way to handle the question of county government was to bring in a measure for indirectly-elected Boards that stopped short of the schemes for representative county councils circulating among MPs and ratepayer organisations.[62] A Bill was introduced early in the 1878 session, but debates on a concrete proposal revealed what Sewell Read's resolution had obscured, that there was no consensus on which a measure could be passed.[63] On Second Reading, Stansfeld announced that the Liberals' support was conditional on the Government accepting direct elections. The representatives of the Central Chamber backed the bill in principle, but Pell spoke for the Poor Law Conferences in favour of Unions as the electoral divisions for the new councils (rather than the petty sessional districts proposed in the bill). On the Tory wing of the Conservative Party, Churchill denounced it all as democratic, radical and dangerous. Nor could the Liberals hold a consistent line: Chamberlain announced that the Radicals could not support the Conservatives' narrow view of county government. The Irish began to obstruct, and Northcote eventually accepted an adjournment motion from Parnell. An amended bill was reintroduced in 1879 but was pursued with no great enthusiasm.[64]

There was never a likelihood that Gladstone's second administration would legislate on local government. Its programme was overloaded with contentious bills and subjected to constant harrassment from Irish obstruction. There was still in the 1880 Parliament a sizeable contingent of Liberal county members,[65] some of whom sympathised with the Local Taxation Committee on the rating issue, and there was little chance of finding a consensus on the future of county government between them, the Chamberlainite radicals and the Whigs. Gladstone chose to regard the local government issue less as a problem of its own than as a symptom of wider constitutional and fiscal questions, including those raised by Ireland, and toyed with schemes of devolution as a counter to parliamentary obstruction and with a major review of the incidence of taxation.[66] His priority in 1880-1 was the Irish Land Bill.[67] Gladstone's preference in 1881 was, therefore, for a full, official investigation of the subject, chaired by J. G. Dodson, the new LGB President, which would discuss

> local government in the three kingdoms, an assessment of the incidence of local taxation, a review of forms of assistance from central funds, would consider how to alleviate the time of Parliament and should lead to the reconstruction of local government, and the establishment of general rules governing the discretion of local authorities and obviating the direct intervention in local government of the central authority.[68]

As Dodson understood, the Government needed not an inquiry but a policy.[69] The Local Taxation Committee had again been active in Parliament, calling for a Select Committee on Local Taxation and pressing for relief for the maintenance of roads.[70] The rating issue was kept alive by a Lords Select Committee on Highways and by the Royal Commission on the agricultural depression.[71] On 10 November 1881, the Cabinet decided to give a high priority in the forthcoming session to local government and appointed a committee to develop a measure.[72] An interdepartmental committee composed of Cavendish, the Financial Secretary, Rosebery from the Home Office, Dodson and Hibbert, his Parliamentary Secretary, was established to consider the financial arrangements.[73]

The principles for the financial settlement which Dodson developed in the winter of 1881-2[74] anticipate much of the thinking underpinning Goschen's scheme in 1888, and the discussions in the committee anticipate some of the problems which were encountered in its implementation. Dodson was clear that the Government needed a permanent settlement that would finally close the Exchequer door on ratepayer demands, provide an incentive for economical local administration, and yet give the centre sufficient control to check neglect and jobbery. He was also adamant that a scheme would only be acceptable if the Government conciliated the local taxation lobby by increasing Exchequer contributions. He proposed that expenditure-led subventions should be replaced by a stereotyped block payment, to give local authorities a direct financial interest in economy, but he also sought a device to attach assigned revenues to specific 'national' expenditures: he was not interested in giving general support to the ratefund. The plan was, therefore, for new grants for roads and for the indoor poor, which would be commuted with existing subventions into a fixed grant to be paid to the new counties, who would in turn be required to administer the existing specific grants to the minor authorities.

In principle there was a consensus for these views, but there was considerable disagreement about how to fund the Exchequer contribution. Dodson was unhappy about assigning localisable revenues direct to the counties in which they were collected, for the reason that the usual candidates – licences, house duty, carriage tax – were not necessarily raised where expenditure was greatest. Cavendish was especially worried about the potential loss of grant to the metropolis, where police expenditure was particularly high.[75] The committee concluded that a reformed carriage tax would match the distribution of the costs of main roads. It also discussed a proposal to assign the product of a penny or twopence income tax, but there were misgivings about giving localities a direct interest in national taxation, and the Treasury was fearful that it would expose anomalies in assessments for rates and income tax.

There was also difficulty about the distribution of the county grant. Worried about the prospect of piloting a measure through Parliament, Dodson believed that the only acceptable scheme would be one that disturbed existing allocations as little as possible: that is he wanted grants to be stereotyped on the basis of the commuted grants. Cavendish argued that this rewarded past extravagance, that it would stereotype all sorts of anomalies into the grant system and would be too insensitive to population changes: such a system would eventually give rise to much resentment. He therefore proposed a grant allocated according to population. Cavendish's view prevailed: it was decided that the counties should receive an exchequer grant equal to their commuted grants, plus the carriage tax to offset the highways and poor law grants which they would be required to make to minor authorities, plus a share of the income tax distributed by population.[76] However, Gladstone's government never introduced a county government measure, and so this scheme was never publicly revealed.

On 21 February 1882 a resolution moved in the House of Com-

mons for the Local Taxation Committee calling for immediate relief
to ratepayers was lost by only five votes,[77] and on 24 February a
motion on highways subventions, which was generally expected
to pass, forced Gladstone to concede that if, as seemed likely, a
local government bill was delayed by parliamentary congestion,
the government would provide a subvention for highways.[78]
Gladstone was accordingly obliged to propose in the 1882 Budget
a temporary grant for disturnpiked roads, to be financed by an
increase in the carriage tax.[79] In the event he was unable to carry
the carriage tax increase, and, in August, Dodson was forced to
take a supplementary vote for £250,000.[80] The grant was paid as a
fixed proportion of the costs incurred by highway authorities on
roads declared by the county magistrates to be a 'main' road.
Gladstone had therefore conceded the kind of grant to which he
most objected, a grant committing the Exchequer to open-ended
payments towards local expenditure. And in the absence of local
government reform, this 'temporary' expedient lasted till 1888.

The discussions within the Government in 1882-3, which
resulted in the decision to give priority to London Government
and franchise reform, have been throughly analysed elsewhere.[81]
Lambert's advice to Gladstone was that there were significant technical problems in organising county registers in advance of reforming the county franchise, and that the Liberal Party should first
secure the rural working class vote by measures of social reform.[82]
Dilke, who replaced Dodson in December 1882 at the Local Government Board, believed that a Liberal county government bill could
not be passed through the 1880 Parliament but that the Government
needed the appearance of action,[84] and began in April 1883 to work
on a measure. Indeed the Government continued under too much
Parliamentary pressure to admit that it could not legislate on local
government. On 17 April 1883,[84] a motion in the name of Pell for
the immediate relief of local taxation was successfully met by a
Government-sponsored amendment calling for the local taxation
issue to be dealt with only in conjunction with local government
reform. But thirty-one Liberal MPs who had supported the Government signed a memorial calling for the Government to redeem its
pledges on local taxation, and this was delivered to Gladstone,
amid embarrassing publicity.[85]

By the autumn of 1883, however, the chances of reform had further receded: the Chamberlain-dominated National Liberal Federation pressed for priority for franchise reform,[86] and a Cabinet Committee established to consider local government was divided on key issues between the 'too complete' scheme drawn up by Dilke, which was supported only by Chamberlain and Childers, and a measure enjoying majority support, drafted by Fitzmaurice, his Parliamentary Secretary (which Dilke thought 'good but very timid').[87] The main question came to be whether a bill should be completed and announced, even though a serious attempt to pass it could not be made.[88] The Queen's Speech for 1884 promised franchise reform and municipal government for London.[89]

The Government continued to be harrassed sporadically on the local taxation issue: on 28 March, the House refused to support the Government against a motion, put down by Pell, for immediate relief of local charges.[90] And the failure to make any progress on this issue was the ostensible justification for the opposition amendment to the Budget of 1885 which led, on 8 June 1885, to the fall of Gladstone's Government.[91] For Childers, the Chancellor, proposed to meet a massive deficit of some fourteen million pounds, arising partly from the Afghan War, by bringing the death duty on real estate, which had hitherto been treated more gently than personalty, into line with the duty on personal wealth. Dilke for the Government declined to agree with Conservative frontbenchers that the lenient treatment of land was a *quid pro quo* for the rate burden. Nevertheless, thereafter, death duties became inextricably linked with the rating issue.

The timing and terms of the great local government bill of 1888 have usually been considered through the politics of the Conservative-Unionist coalition which emerged in 1885-6.[92] But the Act also reflects changes in the national politics of central-local relations, towards an apparently more pluralist structure. In the first place, the Local Taxation Committee was weakened by the retirement in 1885 of several of their most prominent spokesmen in the House, including Pell and Lopes, and by declining support amongst MPs.[93] Redistribution and changes in patterns of political recruitment were reducing the number of Tories with connections in traditional local status systems, and there were more carpetbagging careerists, often with professional or commercial back-grounds.[94] Of particular importance for the politics of 1888 was the Conservative electoral domination of London,[95] which created an organised group of metropolitan MPs, who were prepared to be aggressive in defending their electoral interests.[96]

By 1888, moreover, economic and fiscal doctrine was becom-ing more sensitive to the problems of urban development. The 1885 Report of the Royal Commission on the Housing of the Working Classes had drawn attention to the effects of rising capital values on the supply of building land and on ground rents.[97] Although Salisbury had dissented from the main report on rating, he had publicly acknowledged that the narrowness of the local tax base was a powerful barrier to the expansion of municipal action.[98] In 1886, the economist, Thorold Rogers, successfully moved in the Commons for the rating of urban ground rents:[99] the consequence was the nomination of the Select Committee on Town Holdings, which provided an important forum for a number of schemes designed to transfer to landowners a significant share of urban taxation; including the division of rates; the rating of site values; the taxation of reversionary interests in leasehold property; a municipal death duty on real property; and the taxation of better-ments.[100] These schemes reflect the growing salience of land reform as a political issue. But we can also see in the conflicting evidence to the Committee the general shift in Liberal fiscal doctrine, to the view which was to come to fruition in the Budget of 1909, that the community should take to use for public benefit the unearned increment in the value of real property created by public urban improvements and economic change.

The extent to which the Conservative and Unionist coalition was awakened to urban interests can be seen in the movement between the financial proposals developed for the local govern-ment bill in 1885 and Goschen's proposals in 1888. The first bill was clearly a Tory bill, designed to meet the agriculturalists' demands. Since the late 1870s, when it had become apparent that representative county government was inevitable, both the Local Taxation Committee and the Conservative Party had become con-verted to the principle of dividing the rate, to make apparent what they held to be the economic reality, that landlords shared the rate burden because increased rates reduced rents and depressed the income from land. The direct payment of rates would also give the county gentleman a claim to *ex officio* seats on the new county councils. In the autumn of 1885, the Chancellor, Michael Hicks Beach, who was in charge of the financial arrangements of the bill and who had been long associated with the Central Chamber, proposed that the county councils should include nominees of the magistrates, and that the rate be divided between owner and occupier.[101]

Hicks Beach was also anxious to satisfy a central demand of the local taxation lobby, to incorporate personalty into the tax base of local government. He therefore commissioned a paper on a local income tax to be levied on business profits. But he was advised that it was technically impossible without a politically unacceptable extension of bureaucratic machinery, that a profits tax would be non-localisable, and that it would divorce voting and ratepaying. His financial recommendations were, therefore, to assign the house duty and excise licenses (which totalled around a million pounds more than the existing subventions), and to assign public house licences to local authorities on the assumption that licensing would be transfered to the counties. Hicks Beach also proposed the partial derating of agricultural land, on the grounds that rate borne expenditure was largely a function of population and buildings. In January 1886 A. J. Balfour (the LGB President, who was not a member of Cabinet) submitted his Bill, but it left many significant issues wide open and failed to secure Cabinet agreement.[102]

When the Conservatives returned to office in July, the exigencies of Conservative politics brought Randolph Churchill (now a leading proponent of Tory Democracy in the Government and potentially the key to successful coalition building with Chamberlain and the Unionists) to the leadership of the House and to the Exchequer. Salisbury offered the Local Government Board to 'Squire' Henry Chaplin, 'the natural leader of the Tories in the House of Commons',[103] but, angered by not being offered a Cabinet seat, Chaplin turned it down.[104] But Salisbury now considered that 'local government has quite as much to do with town as with the country, perhaps more',[105] and eventually offered the post to C. T. Ritchie, a London member who had a reputation as a 'roughish diamond', able but brusque and belligerent.[106] He was given a 'good country member', Walter Long, as his Parliamentary Secretary, to reassure the Tory gentlemen.[107]

The bill which Ritchie drafted with the full collaboration of Churchill, omitted – with Long's full support[108] – both the division of rates and the representation of JPs, and proposed county and district councils, wholly elected by ratepayers, for all local functions including the management of the poor. It provoked a major crisis within the coalition. Both Hartington, the Unionist leader, and Hicks Beach, who had become Irish Secretary, were deeply uneasy about the poor law provisions, especially seen as a precedent for the reform of Irish Local Government. In the end, a compromise suggested by Hartington – that both the division of rates and the transfer of the poor law to local government be dropped, and that co-option of JPs be permitted – was reluctantly agreed.[109]

Churchill's view was that the country gentlemen would accept any bill if the financial terms were good enough. 'The pill will be gilded', he promised Salisbury.[110] Churchill proposed to commute grants and to make an additional £2.5m available to relieve the ratepayers by the transfer to the county councils of local licences, house duty, carriage tax and public house licenses. There would also be the assignation of a new horse tax, and an Exchequer contribution of £800,000 allocated by the rate of indoor pauperism.[111] But as part of his package, Churchill also proposed to rationalise and assimilate the death duties on real estate to those on personalty, and to introduce an element of graduation. Salisbury calculated that country gentlemen would pay an additional ninepence in the pound taxation, 'which is gilding of a negative kind'. He received the less than satisfactory assurance that changes in the succession duty would take '12 years to work up'.[112] Churchill's financial proposals renewed the political crisis within the Cabinet, and contributed directly to his resignation in January 1887. However, the main lines of the financial settlement with the ratepayers were now clear. The financial deal which Goschen, the new Chancellor, offered in his 1888 Budget[113] shows, in its bias to the towns, continuity with the analysis in his 1870 report, but it was not dissimilar in its distributive effects from Churchill's scheme, though he postponed, on technical grounds, the reconstruction of the death duties.

Goschen's major claim for the 1888 Budget was that it at last effected the separation of central and local finance. For he proposed the interception of the revenues to be assigned to local authorities into a special Local Taxation Account: henceforth, they would cease to be voted by Parliament and to figure in the public accounts. Each county would maintain an Exchequer Contribution Account to receive payments from the Local Taxation Account, from which grants to minor authorities, including the indoor pauper grant, would be disbursed.

Goschen proposed to assign to the Local Taxation Account the local licenses (including a reformed carriage tax) and half of the annual yield from the probate tax. Probate was offered as the contribution from 'realised personalty' to local expenditure, and to give the local authorities a share in the growing national wealth. Its allocation was to be redistributive. 'Nothing would be more unjust', Goschen asserted, than to distribute the tax on the basis of the old grants.[114] He therefore proposed to share out the probate grant according to the incidence of indoor pauperism, which indicated 'where the shoe pinches most'. This would also advantage London where the existence of the Metropolitan Poor Fund had produced a particularly high ratio between the indoor and outdoor poor.[115] He also proposed to transfer liquor licensing to the county councils. Goschen announced that he had rejected a local income tax, because it would fall on the very taxpayers most burdened by residential rates, and on enterprise and labour. The whole package was worth an additional £2.9m.

This package did not, however, pass through Parliament without radical modification. By April it was clear that reforms in the carriage and horse taxes would be nullified by the range of commercial interests claiming exemptions.[116] Ritchie was also obliged to withdraw the liquor licensing clauses, as a result of pressure from the temperance lobbies.[117] The county councils were given the revenues, but the right to set the price of licenses was not transferred: the Government thus undermined Goschen's central proposition, that assigned revenues were localisable taxes rather than imperial grants. And Stansfeld raised the obvious constitutional objection to the interception of revenues to the Local Taxation Account: '. . . they had not only not given to the localities any power over these taxes, if they were to be called taxes, but they were taking away all power from themselves'.[118] The Government were also forced to amend the allocation of the probate grant, and to adopt the very principle which Goschen had stated to be the most indefensible.

Goschen's problem was that, in his own word, every part of his scheme was 'anomalous' (in the sense that it was not distributionally neutral).[119] Although under any principle of allocation, the bulk of the grant would go to London and the more densely populated areas, Goschen had tried to manipulate the exact balance between between London, the large provincial cities, the smaller boroughs and the counties, so that their interests were balanced. He assumed, as previous Chancellors had assumed, that the carriage tax, licenses and the use of indoor pauperism to allocate the probate money would all benefit the towns and industrial counties, and refused to reinforce this skew by the transfer of the house tax – despite pressure in Parliament from the temperance lobby and from borough members in his own party to substitute it for the liquor licences.

The metropolitan area did better under the indoor poor criterion than if population or rateable value had been used. But the small and medium sized boroughs would have gained more if the probate grant were allocated by population. The borough members also argued that the distribution was too favourable to the rural counties, where populations were falling. The Government's own estimates of the income of counties and boroughs from centrally collected taxes and from the commuted grants[120] show that – doubtless due to the historically low rate poundages, expenditures and, therefore, grants in many shire counties – the percentage increases under Goschen's proposals would have been highest in rural counties, and lowest in the populous counties and cities, including London. Many borough and London members were able to quote the grant in terms of rate poundage relief to show similar effects.[121] But the use of indoor pauperism meant that some forty-three counties gained less than if Goschen had simply allocated the probate duty according to commuted grants: only thirteen counties gained more, none significantly. Indeed, several county members argued that the county councils would be net losers by the time they had paid grants, particularly highway grants and indoor poor grants, to the minor authorities.

Probably the clearest winner would have been London, and the relative losers, the small boroughs and rural counties. But by involving the poor law, Goschen provided a lever for his opponents to prise open his scheme. He was accused of using financial incentives to 'drive paupers into the workhouse' and radical opponents of the poor law (including some London Liberals) combined with Tory county gentlemen and borough members of all parties against the use of grant as an instrument of central poor law policy.[122] London Conservative members fought a rearguard action in defence of the principles of 1834 and on the grounds of the special needs of London, but after a stormy ride in the House on 9 July,[123] the Government was forced to drop its proposals for the indoor poor and to reconsider the probate grant; and resorted to the stereotyping of historic grants.

It is often assumed that only a Conservative Government could have introduced representative county government in 1888, because only a Conservative Government could have taken on the country gentlemen. What the outcome of 1888 also reflects, however, is that the very decline in the numerical strength of the country wing in the Conservative Party created a political need for its conciliation by the leadership. The growing influence of 'villa conservatism' paradoxically made Salisbury the more anxious not to alienate his country gentlemen and rural voters.[124] It is this sensitivity to the internal politics of the party, as much as pressure from an external pressure group, which kept the rating issue to the fore of Conservative politics after 1888.

Rating also continued to be an issue simply because the 1888 settlement failed in all Goschen's major objectives: it satisfied neither local or central government. It failed to prevent renewed demands for grants, and it failed to separate the politics and management of local and imperial finance. It failed to relieve the burdens of agriculturalists hit by the Great Depression, and it failed to meet the growing revenue needs of the urban centres, especially London.

Goschen's immediate problem, especially in the light of an anticipated two million pound deficit in the 1889-90 Budget, was the shortfall in the funds accruing to the Local Taxation Account due to the withdrawal of the 1888 Customs and Excise Bill. The county authorities had 'lost' some £800,0000 a year: the Government held that local authorities had been promised an assigned tax, not a quantity of cash.[125] But as the new county councils began to pay grants to the minor authorities, this was not a helpful argument in quelling their resentment.[126] It was the more awkward for Goschen, moreover, because of the agitation, led by Chaplin and 'some our friends connected with the landed interest', against proposals in the 1889 Budget to begin the reconstruction of the death duties.[127] These changes were necessary to pay for military expenditure, and Goschen tried to justify them as a *quid pro quo* for 1888. In 1890, he was therefore obliged to try again to transfer revenues to the Local Taxation Account, without obviously conceding a general grant-in-aid.[128] He proposed a surtax of sixpence on a gallon of spirits and threepence on beer – yielding about £1.3m a year – to be distributed to local authorities with the probate money. The money was intended to strengthen police superannuation funds (which were in many places in a scandalous condition) and for the purchase of public house licenses to promote temperance.

As in 1888, the 1890 Customs and Excise Bill ran into trouble with the temperance lobby, who objected to the principle of compensating publicans. At the end of June, the Government announced that it was withdrawing the licensing clauses, but, since the price increases had already been listed, it could not withdraw the surtax. The county councils would therefore keep the 'whiskey money', with a strong recommendation that it be used for technical education.[129] Technical education was not however, a mandatory duty of county councils: 'whiskey money' became, in effect, a grant in general aid of county rates.

In the early 1890s, the Conservative leadership faced mounting pressure from agricultural and landed interests in the party (for whom Chaplin, who had much influence in the National Union, was the acknowledged spokesman) to adopt protectionism as a response to the great agricultural depression. By 1893-4, Chaplin had acquired an important platform on the Royal Commission on Agriculture, and together with Middleton, the Conservative National Agent, was warning Salisbury and Balfour of the electoral dangers, especially in the Eastern Counties, if they failed to make special acknowledgement of the farmers' problems.[130] Moreover, the fiscal claims of real property were brought forcibly back to the political agenda by Harcourt's reform of the death duties in 1894.[131] It seems that Salisbury decided upon partial agricultural derating to head off protectionism and bimetallism.[132]

When the Conservatives were returned in 1895, Henry Chaplin was given the Local Government Board, and immediately began work on a scheme. Early in 1896, he abruptly forced through the Agricultural Commission (by a majority of one) an interim report[133] – validated by statistics showing the incidence of taxation on real and personal property worked up by Alfred Milner, Chairman of the Board of Inland Revenue[134] – calling for differential rating of agricultural land. The representative of the Local Government Board on the Royal Commission was Cornelius Dalton, the Assistant Secretary for the statistics and audit division. Dalton's recommendations[13]to Chaplin assumed that the political problem was to make a bill acceptable to non-agricultural ratepayers: the deficiency in rural rates must therefore be met by a government grant. The grant should be stereotyped, partly because of the administrative problems of recalculating the deficiency each year, and partly to discourage local authorities from deliberately increasing the rate to maximise their grant. Dalton believed that the county councils would not accept the task of processing the volume of payments required by the bill, and recommended that the grant be paid direct to each individual spending authority.

Dalton's scheme was strongly opposed by Treasury officials,[136] who objected both to the principle of subsidising an industry and to the heavy administrative work involved. They therefore pressed for a temporary subvention, rather than derating. Although they were overruled, Chaplin was obliged to concede that no grant would be paid to authorities with a deficiency of less than a penny rate and no grant was paid to overseers, parishes and burial boards, saving around £60,000. Nevertheless, the initial work imposed on the Local Government Board by the Agricultural Rates Act of 1896 was immense, and set back the routine statistical work for some months.[137] Thus, there was a large administrative disincentive to amend the grant as rates increased: the upshot was that the burden thereafter fell disportionately on non-agricultural ratepayers, giving grounds for great resentment, particularly in the suburban areas where both rates and land prices were rising, and where, over the years, boundary changes obscured the rationale of the sums paid to authorities.[138] However, the officials of the LGB, who generally continued to hold to the Gladstonian fiscal doctrines current in the Board's early years, supported the renewal of the grant in the early 1900s on the grounds that the benefit derived by agriculture from rate-borne expenditure was significantly less than that enjoyed by housedwellers and urban commercial interests.[139]

The problems for urban and suburban development arising from the rating system were well aired in the 1890s, but nevertheless failed to find a secure place on an active agenda. There were a number of reasons why this was so. The Conservative Government had secured political control of the Town Holdings Committee in 1887, and, after five years of taking evidence which demonstrated the need to widen the urban tax base, the Committee reported in 1892 against site value rating in favour of the division of rates.[140] The most systematic political case for the reform of urban rates was made by land reform groups in London and, towards the end of the 1890s, in other urban centres, notably Glasgow.[141] In the House, the special rating of urban land was pursued by radical, Liberal and, after 1900, by Labour MPs[142] and consequently acquired an identification as a highly partisan proposal. But, although urban site rating was the brand leader of urban rating reform, the Progressive LCC decided in 1889 to press for the division of rates,[143] the Chairman of its Finance Committee, the veteran and authoritative Lord Farrer, together with B. F. C. Costelloe, the Chairman of its Local Taxation Committee,[144] supported a municipal death duty, and, as we have seen, several different schemes were pressed on the Town Holdings Committee. There was, then, no very great consensus as to the fiscal instrument through which the taxation of urban land values should be pursued.

Moreover, the national organisation of the large urban authorities, the Association of Municipal Corporations, was too divided, both in party political terms and in the range of the borough interests which it represented, to be able to press the matter strongly. Although many of its member authorities were becoming acutely aware of the problem of land shortages, especially in relation to housing, the Law Committee of the AMC produced in 1895 a divided report on the subject;[145] and the Association took no further official action until 1904, when, following a joint conference of local authorities called by Glasgow Council, the Association's President, the maverick London Conservative MP, Sir Albert Rollit, led a deputation to Walter Long, the Conservative President of the Local Government Board.[146] However, it is clear that by no means all of Rollit's members supported him on this issue, and many colleagues in London Conservatism were actively hostile.[147]

The Conservative Government were therefore more hard pressed by the rural rating issue than by the urban rating issue, in party management terms. And the Liberals enjoyed office between 1886 and 1905 for only three years, dominated by Home Rule and parish council reform. Their less than comprehensive response to the issue of urban rates, was to commission an official report[148] on the incidence on different classes of property of local taxation, to update and revalidate Goschen's 1870 report on the special problems of urban rates, and to force through Parliament a bill for the equalisation of the metropolitan sanitary rate, largely for electoral reasons.[149]

Nevertheless, the Conservative Government felt sufficiently embarrassed by the obvious partiality of the Agricultural Rates Act to make two concessions to the bitter opposition they encountered in its passage; they agreed that it should be limited to five years, and they set up, under the Chairmanship of Lord Balfour, the Scottish Secretary, a Royal Commission to review the whole question of local taxation, both urban and rural. The papers prepared for the Royal Commission reveal considerable disillusionment with the principles of 1888, not only on the part of the local authorities but also within the central bureaucracy.

Many aspects of the arrangements made in 1888 were a source of irritation to local authorities. Assigned revenues were inconvenient for county authorities who had to find the grants to poor law authorities and districts, yet received no statement of their revenue until the Treasury calculated the final receipts from probate after the end of the financial year. They were particularly resentful when, as in 1894-5, the receipts fell and the grant was smaller than they had anticipated.[150] Furthermore, assigned revenues proved insufficiently elastic to keep pace with local spending: yet the grants which counties paid to minor authorities, continued to be expenditure led. Above all, the historic criterion adopted in 1888 was, by definition, incapable of adjusting the revenues to changes in population and rateable values, or responding to the special problems of particular areas. In particular, the share taken by London became a perennial source of grievance exploited by Liberal and Radical members in the House, especially when their party was in power.[151]

A memorandum prepared by the former Permanent Secretary to the Treasury, Lord Welby,[152] for the LCC in May 1898 pointed out that in the period from 1888, the services covered by the assigned revenues had risen from £140,000 to £240,000, so that the LCC had lost, in assigned revenues, some £100,000 worth of discretionary spending power. But the income the LCC received from assigned revenues had fallen, because the Government deducted the LCC grant for the metropolitan police before handing over the revenues and this grant had increased from £458,000 to £524,000. Welby argued that the LCC should at least press for the restitution of the old arrangements, but that a preferred solution would be the more complete separation of local and imperial finances by the transfer of 'national' services to central management and by the transfer of the power to levy 'local' taxes to local authorities.

Welby's position is very close to that urged on the Royal Commission by the Treasury's representatives, Sir George Murray and Sir E. W. Hamilton.[153] Their view was that assigned revenues were not only inconvenient for local authorities, but also for the Government. The partition of revenues had not proved politically sustainable, their interception into the Local Taxation Account meant that significant sums which the Treasury could have exploited lay fallow till disbursed to the local authorities, and the assignation of part shares of taxes confused national financial statements. But, above all, assigned revenues offended the constitutional doctrine that 'all revenue raised by the state should be paid into the Exchequer, and that all expenditure for which the State was responsible should be issued out of the Exchequer'. Hamilton and Murray therefore pressed for the re-establishment of clear public accountability for finance by the attachment of revenues either to Parliamentary votes or to local authority budgets: assigned revenues should be made truly local, that is, they should be levied and collected by local authorities.

Hamilton and Murray believed that the state should contribute only to those 'national' functions administered by local authorities which were 'onerous' to ratepayers because they were performed for the general good of society rather than for the special benefit of local property-holders: they disapproved of the 1896 grant because it was made in general aid of the rates, unattached to any specific service. In contrast, Dalton's view[154] was that the politics of local taxation were so fraught that the only sustainable course was to maintain existing arrangements: the abolition of the Local Taxation Account would open the Exchequer to the claims of every special interest, especially London. He proposed, therefore, that the grievance of ratepayers be acknowledged by concessions within existing arrangements, and suggested the transfer of the management of lunatics to the state and the assignation of the House Tax.

The Final Report of the Royal Commission, published in 1901, is closer to Dalton's strategy than to Hamilton and Murray's views. The Majority[155] argued that the problems of assigned revenues arose from the complex procedures adopted in 1888 rather than from difficulty in principle. They therefore recommended that the arrangements be simplified by the abolition of the county Exchequer Contribution Accounts, and by the payment of revenues direct to spending authorities. Indeed, they proposed to *add* to assigned revenues by transfering further licences, stamp duties on legal documents and the House Tax; the latter, they believed, would particularly help the more densely populated urban areas. What they did take, however, from Hamilton and Murray's analysis was the distinction between 'onerous' and 'local' services, and they recommended a list of 'onerous' clients for new capitation grants – lunatics in workhouses, poor law children, the sick poor, and the indoor poor – which would have redistributed grant to the more densely populated areas. They also proposed a new grant for main roads, an increase in the police grant, and more money towards the cost of the metropolitan poor. Most importantly, the Commission accepted the implication of Hamilton and Murray's distinction, that the state had an interest in the efficiency of the 'onerous' services to which it contributed, but there is almost no discussion about how this might be monitored or enforced. The Majority considered but refused to recommend the rating of urban land values.

To the embarrassment of the Conservative Government,[156] Lord Balfour not only signed (together with Hamilton, Murray and James Stuart, the Progressives' representative) a Minority Report[157] calling for the reform of the urban rating system, but also made separate recommendations,[158] endorsing a Report submitted by Hamilton and Murray[159] publicly condemning the agricultural rates grant and calling for a reformed grant system organised on new principles.

Hamilton and Murray proposed new block grants, for 'onerous' services only, to be distributed according to a formula which took account both of the level of expenditure necessary to maintain an efficient local service, and of varying local capacity to raise that expenditure. Under this formula, which in principle was the forerunner of the new Block Grant introduced in 1980, a local authority's grant for each grant-bearing service would be the difference between the yield of its standard rate poundage and a standard expenditure (based *per capita* on the number of units or clients demanding expenditure). They recommended that the standard rate poundage should be set at a level low enough to produce a grant for the majority of authorities.

The Hamilton and Murray Report shows clear continuities with past Treasury attitudes to grants. Its central purpose was to re-establish on a more authoritative conceptual foundation the distinction between the financial responsibilities of central and of local government, to limit the call on the Exchequer. And to achieve this, they applied the old principle, that expenditure should be borne by those who benefit. But they also began to reach towards an amended principle, namely that, in respect of 'national' functions, the same rate burden should be made to yield the same value of service, and that the grant system should be the agency through which this is promoted. But as we will see, it was not until the 1912 Departmental Report that the use of grant system as an explicitly redistributive instrument was officially advocated.

The Royal Commission had been appointed to reconcile the urban ratepayers to the 1896 Act. However, the contemporary estimate was that it would cost the Exchequer between two and three million pounds to implement the Majority's recommendations.[160] It was clear that even such a sum would not easily be forthcoming. The pressure on public expenditure by the Boer War was not significantly relieved when hostilities ceased, because of the costs of the pacification of South Africa and military expansion: indeed, the end of war enhanced the Government's embarrassment because it became less easy politically to justify high taxes.[161] A major embarrassment in 1901-2, and again in 1904-5, was the need to renew the Agricultural Rates Act, which meant that a debate in Parliament on the urban rates issue could not be avoided.[162] Moreover, the rural authorities also felt aggrieved: the fall in the value of land in the 1890s meant that the grant turned out to be around one and a quarter million pounds less than anticipated,[163] and, as a fixed grant which was never updated, represented a falling share of rising rates, especially in areas with declining populations and rateable values. And Balfour's Government continued to be sensitive to the growing political strength of the protectionists in the party, and vulnerable to the claim that the revenues generated by tariff reform could be used for domestic policy.[164] They were therefore obliged to find some movement on the local taxation issue, while protecting the imperial revenues from ratepayer claims. The chosen stategy – as so often before – was to promote a contentious paving measure as a precondition of a fiscal settlement, pushing the latter out of the short term political agenda.

In 1899, the Royal Commission had submitted an interim report calling for the urgent reform of rating valuation.[165] The argument was that non-standard valuations made it impossible to calculate the relative burden of rates in different areas: valuation reform was a necessary condition, therefore, of a financial settlement between ratepayers and taxpayers, and especially of the equalisation of the rate burden between localities. In December 1901, the Conservative Government decided that a bill should be immediately prepared, to counter pressure in the House on the rating issue during the 1902 session.[166]

The Royal Commission's report listed a long series of unsuccessful valuation bills, dating from the 1860s: while there had long been a consensus in principle for valuation reform, specific proposals had always collapsed on the question of machinery. For central government had always insisted on the intervention of a national agent – the Surveyor of Taxes – to standardise valuations from county to county, to protect the centre's interest in valuations for imperial taxation. Local property holders assumed that national valuation would lead to higher rates, but they also suspected that its purpose was to increase the yield from income tax and death duties. The 1899 Report, however, created further political complications, by recommending that valuation should be a county responsibility, guaranteeing the antagonism of the AMC and the minor local authority associations.

A Valuation Bill was introduced in 1904.[167] It embodied the recommendations of the Royal Commission and it predictably met strong opposition: a bill for valuation by district councils was subsequently prepared for 1905, but never introduced. However, Arthur Balfour and his brother, Gerald, who taken over the Local Government Board in March 1905, were able to assert that the introduction of the measure in 1904 had formally redeemed the government's pledges on local taxation.[168]

The new Liberal Government of 1905 inherited its own commitments to the reform of rating. During the Conservative years, backbench Liberals had continued to pursue the issue of urban rating reform. Bills for site value rating had been introduced in 1902 and 1903 by Dr Macnamara, the Liberal Member for Camberwell South, and a Land Values Bill, sponsored by C. P. Trevelyan, had a second reading in 1904.[169] The new President of the LGB, John Burns, formed the view, however, that the overlap of local boundaries and the question mark against the future of unions raised by the Royal Commission on the Poor Laws, made it unwise to consider rating reform based solely on local valuations, and argued in Cabinet (which in 1907 instructed him to prepare a bill) for priority for national valuation machinery for both imperial and local taxation.[170] In 1908, Asquith appointed Macnamara, who was generally considered to be intellectually better prepared than Burns to tackle the complexities of rating, to be Parliamentary Secretary to the Board.[171] However, the bill was never introduced, and the rough ride given to a Scottish measure in 1907 and 1908 signalled that any proposal for urban site rating would be vetoed by the Lords. In the end, national machinery for the assessment of site values became a necessary corollary of the 1909 Budget.

Meanwhile, during his years at the Exchequer, Asquith had begun the implementation of those parts of the Treasury's 1901 agenda that related to technical procedures. The Local Taxation Account was abolished in the 1907 Budget and, in 1908, the Government transfered the levying and collection of local licences to local government. This process, which was completed in 1909 and 1911 by Lloyd George,[172] deprived local authorities of the benefit of any elasticity in these revenues, but it largely detached local government from an interest in the yield and structure of national taxation. It also put full square on central government the responsibility for ensuring that grants to local authorities were adequate for national policy. This the Liberal Government patently failed to secure before 1914: indeed, the problems of financing local authorities for their role under the New Liberalism brought local finance into national questions of the most contentious kind, through the 1909 and 1914 Budgets.

Until 1909, it had been assumed that the taxation of land values was essentially an issue of local possessive politics, one intimately concerned with the distribution of local burdens and the relationship of the local authority to the market in land. But in the 1909 Budget,[173] Lloyd George proposed for purposes of imperial revenue to impose a twenty per cent incremental value duty on the sale of land, a duty of ten per cent on the reversion of leases, a tax on undeveloped land and a duty on the rental value of mineral rights. He also proposed the stereotyping to 1909 levels of Exchequer contributions to local authorities from the enhanced revenues from motor taxation and public house licences. The local authority associations immediately demanded compensation for their 'loss' of revenues, and the AMC demanded indemnity against loss of rateable income from any reduction of values in land and public houses resulting from the Budget.[174] The Conservative Opposition exploited their resistance in the House: Balfour could not approve the new taxation of real property, he said, but, if real property was taxed, the revenue belonged peculiarly to the localities: the new taxes were, therefore, doubly expropriatory; they deprived both landowners and local authorities of their rights.[175] On the other hand, the Government's case for nationalising land taxes was, simply, that a significant part of the incremental value arising from urban development was not localisable to the towns which generated it; that is it occurred in suburbs and near-lying rural areas.[176] Moreover, the transfer of centrally-collected land taxes to local authorities would merely have re-established the discredited assigned revenue system.

To meet the opposition, Lloyd George conceded that half of the land taxes would be diverted to local authorities, pending the full settlement of the local taxation question. To the AMC he claimed that that the Road Fund announced in 1909 would yield £600,000 a year to be spent on roads, to the relief of local authorities who would otherwise bear their burden, and promised 'to make some progress with the re-adjustment of the relations with local finance'[177] in the course of the next year. However, there was much dispute between the local authority associations about the principle by which the land tax money should be distributed: the AMC pressed for distribution by rateable value, and rather than stereotype some less acceptable criterion, agreed that the grant be postponed till 1910-11. In 1910-11, Lloyd George therefore announced an interim payment of £328,000 in lieu of the land taxes, and as compensation for a recent fall in the beer and spirit revenues.[178] In March 1911, the Government announced a Departmental Committee under the Chairmanship of the Comptroller and Auditor General, Sir John Kempe, to reconsider the principles of central-local financial relations. The Committee reported early in 1914.[179]

The Kempe Report recast the principles of central-local financial relations, in two major ways. Firstly, it marked the official end of the long search for a distinction between local and central responsibilities, which the Committee believed to have become pointless as a result of geographical mobility and the political nationalisation of a wide range of social issues. In particular, they noted the nationalisation of public health issues, particularly housing, which had hitherto been considered specially 'local'. Secondly, in consequence of a special request from Lloyd George in 1912,[180] the Report focussed on the distributional effects of grant. The Report applied to a wider range of local functions the principle elucidated by Hamilton and Murray in 1901 in respect of 'onerous' services, that it is the duty of government to ensure that every authority is capable of a minimum expenditure. The report also endorsed the arguments against assigned revenues, warning the government against assigning any of the 1909 revenues – or indeed establishing urban site taxation as a local tax – particularly on the grounds that the 1888 arrangements disadvantaged the most populous and needy areas, and that the centre would lose control over the way in which the money was spent. Rather, it recommended a series of block grants for specific services, calculated both to reflect the local need to spend and the local capacity to finance that expenditure. The formula proposed for the grants varied from service to service: Kempe recommended a series of capitation or unit-based grants (numbers of clients, miles of road, and so on), supplemented for some services by a deficiency grant to make up the rate product where it fell below a defined yield per unit. It also asserted the important principle, that to the extent the centre paid for local services, the centre should be also be assured of the efficiency of local administration, and there is some inconclusive discussion of mechanisms for identifying whether authorities are meeting national standards. The emphasis on finding a formula to distribute grant compared to the scrappy discussion of central controls shows that the Kempe Committee must be seen primarily as a response to the acute crisis in financing local government, not as an instrument for securing better central influence over the nature and standards of local administration.

The implications of Kempe are important, indeed revolutionary, in the context of the previous fifty years of fiscal history. Rather than attempting to free itself of financial and political responsibility for 'local' services, the centre was now claiming all domestic services to lie potentially within its sphere of interest. Moreover, Kempe would have radically redistributed Exchequer aid from the pattern set in 1888: the use of capitation and unit grants meant that, to an extent, its proposed arrangements would have reflected historic patterns of expenditure, but they were also chosen to reflect population changes, deficiencies in rateable value and the geographical incidence of social problems. And these criteria would have benefited London, the cities, large towns and the growing counties at the expense of those counties with static or falling populations. However, Kempe was never implemented; rather, it sank in the disaster of the 1914 Budget. And, as this study shows generally, the centre did not, before the First World War, develop mechanisms for defining minimum national standards and their enforcement over the broad set of local functions.

In the Budget statement of 1914,[181] Lloyd George accepted the principles defined by the Kempe Committee, and announced a comprehensive recasting of local grants, to be implemented in 1915 and to be based (with some modifications) on the Kempe Report. The whole package represented a potential increase of some twelve million pounds, for the grants were specifically stated to be in anticipation of new social responsibilities to be laid on the local authorities. He proposed to pay for it by a graduated income tax, by increasing super tax and by the liberation of funds from the sinking fund. But he made the grants conditional on the separate valuation of land and buildings, so that the relief to the rates would apply only to buildings and not to land. Gilbert has described how the Budget was destroyed by a revolt of Liberal backbenchers, revealing starkly the political limits of the New Liberalism:[182] the valuation and revenue conditions for the new block grants were never met.

The failure to achieve a practical resolution of the problems of central-local financial relations before the First World War, condemned central government to increasingly bitter confrontations with the national representatives of local government. The antagonism was doubtless exacerbated by the political influence in the County Councils Association of Conservatives and Unionists who were palpably unsympathetic to the New Liberalism. However, the unresolved financial questions allowed the CCA to make fellow feeling with the more progressive AMC, which seriously damaged the chances that local government would join full heartedly with the centre as a partner in social policy. Although both the AMC and the CCA had actively sought new functions in the 1890s and early 1900s – and been more than insistent on taking education over from the school boards – the almost complete absence of protest at the by-passing of elected local authorities in the administration of national insurance and unemployment policy, is particularly noticeable. The local authority associations protested about the establishment of the Roads Board in 1909[183] – and the Government was obliged to conciliate them by granting them membership – and there was some unhappiness about the non-representation of the corporations on the Poor Law Commission in 1905.[184] But there was certainly no pressure for the New Liberalism to become the special instrument of local self government. In turn, the negative reaction of local government confirmed many prejudices held by national reformers about its capacity and attitudes, and did nothing to discourage the tendency towards ad hoc machinery; if anything, it led, as we will see in the last chapter, to the search for more coercive techniques of control over localities. That is, we can see that the New Liberalism paradoxically hindered rather than encouraged a notion of partnership between centre and locality in social policy. The more conflictual relationship between central government and the national representatives of local government is particularly noticeable in the case of the CCA, which under Conservative Governments in the 1890s and early 1900s had exhibited a much closer community of values and style with officials in central government than the more assertive and independent-minded AMC.

The CCA emerged as a formal local authority association in 1890 from the Association of County Clerks, the organisation used by the LGB to consult the administrative counties during the formulation and passage of the 1888 Local Government Act.[185] Although, like the AMC, the CCA established a Parliamentary Committee of MPs to which it regularly referred legislative business and through which it mobilised parliamentary support, the CCA was, from its early days, clearly more oriented than the AMC to the pursuit of its interests through the central bureaucracy. Partly, this orientation reflects the issues which predominated in its early years, many of which concerned the administrative and financial arrangements set up under the 1888 Act: partly it reflects the fact that, having no powers to promote private Acts, the county councils were entirely dependent on government sponsorship of legislation to extend their power; and partly also, it reflects the closer administrative involvement of central departments with county than with municipal administration: the counties took the district audit and came to the bureaucracy for loan sanctions and adoptive powers. But the departmental orientation of the CCA is also a function of the fact that its leadership enjoyed strong insider connections with Whitehall, through experience of office, and greater empathy with its attitudes and values. Its first President was Sir John Hibbert,[186] of Lancashire, who had been heavily involved in the Poor Law Conference movement in the 1870s, was subsequently Parliamentary Secretary to the LGB under Stansfeld and Dodson, and was a frequent member of important inquiries into local government affairs until his death in 1906. The Vice President was Lord Thring,[187] who, as Parliamentary Counsel, was responsible for the 1888 Local Government Act and several other important local government measures. J. G. Dodson (now Lord Monk Bretton) was active in the association in its early years. By the turn of the century, the Chairman of the Parliamentary Committee was Sir John Dorington,[188] a prominent leader of the Conservative country wing, and Henry Hobhouse,[189] the Liberal Unionist MP, and formerly a Parliamentary Draftsmen, became the first Chairman of the important Education Committee.

We may deduce, too, from the opinions of its active membership, that the association's insider stance reflects the role of county councils within the central-local system to which many prominent county councillors aspired. It is clear that they saw the new county councils as a vehicle to reassert the declining political authority of local status systems based on landowning and county society, against the growing influence of interests based on urban economies and the democratisation of local government. We will see in the last chapter that a dominant theme in its affairs in its first two decades was the devolution of central bureaucratic powers over district councils to county councils, which aspired to become intermediate authorities between centre and locality. This was an aspiration, however, that brought the CCA into regular, direct clashes with the AMC and the minor local authority associations.

In contrast, the AMC was historically oriented to pressure in Parliament, and it was organised on the assumption that its primary interest lay with the legislative process. The catalyst for its formation was the passing of the Borough Funds Act of 1872, which limited the corporations' rights to apply for private powers, and it continued to take a close interest in the private bill procedure. Its member authorities were largely free of routine administrative connections with the Board – the corporations did not take the district audit and many went to Parliament for powers and borrowing sanctions – and a primary objective of the AMC was to protect and enhance its independence from Whitehall. Its style of leadership also differed from that of the CCA: the most important and powerful committee was the Law Committee, which was dominated by town clerks who had little independent relationship with – and lower status than – the officials of central government, but who possessed considerable expertise in the details of statute and private law. The AMC's political leadership in the 1890s and 1900s was largely monocratic: from 1890 to 1906 its President was Sir Albert Rollit,[190] an agressive, independent-minded urban conservative with strong collectivist aspirations and a weak sense of party loyalty in Parliament so far as municipal affairs were concerned. He was not a man, however, to empathise greatly with the bureaucratic style of the Local Government Board.

In the 1880s and 1890s, the pattern of relations between the LGB and the AMC was detached and formalistic. It was conducted through the periodic submission of resolutions, the mutual exchange of letters, and occasional large, rather ritualistic deputations. However, in the early 1900s there were signs of a closer, clientelistic relationship, one that was more consultative and informal. This was the result of informal agreement between Rollit and Walter Long, who now sat for an urban seat in Liverpool and who, despite a reputation for being a blunt and bombastic colleague in Government, operated typically through direct, warm personal relations. In 1901, he and Rollit agreed to repair relations which had been damaged by the nomination of the Joint Committee of Parliament on Municipal Trading,[191] an act widely interpreted to be hostile to the corporations. A deputation on 29th November

1901 presented Long with an extensive agenda for legislation in the interests of municipalities.[192] Long undertook action on the Borough Funds Bill and the deputation was followed by fruitful informal consultation betweeen Long and Rollit on valuation reform and other matters dear to the municipalities. Rollit concluded that this process was worth repeating, and that the AMC should again seek 'to see the Minister before he crystallises the views of his Department in a bill, and to represent to him those practical considerations which the Local Authorities are probably alone able to suggest'.[193] After the the mid 1900s, when both Long and Rollit left their offices, the relation reverted to the earlier style. In contrast to Long, John Burns's approach to the local government associations – as to all over whom he exercised official authority – was didactic and patronising, but not close. And the AMC's leadership was taken over by Sir Harmood-Banner, a new MP, with networks in the professional and commercial world rather than in Whitehall.[194]

The major formal problem in the relation of both associations with the Local Government Board was finance, and especially education finance. The issue of the finance of education dominated discussions of local taxation within the major local authority associations, for the transfer of the cost of education to the local education authorities in 1902 transferred the fastest growing nonremunerative expenditure to their rate funds (Figure 2): it was also an expenditure which represented a very significant proportion of the county councils' total expenditure, and one over which the local authorities experienced a high degree of central control. Moreover, the system of capitation grants, the rates of which were not generally increased before the First World War, had no inbuilt mechanism to respond to rising unit costs or to the burdens of capital development. Yet, after 1903, the Board of Education undertook the revision of the Education Codes and regulations, which imposed significantly higher standards of staffing, accommodation and equipment.[195] The implication of the grant system was that the costs of these improvements were to be borne by the new LEAs, yet they were clearly generated by changes in national policy. There was, moreover, no automatic way by which the grant system responded to the extension of the scope of the service: school

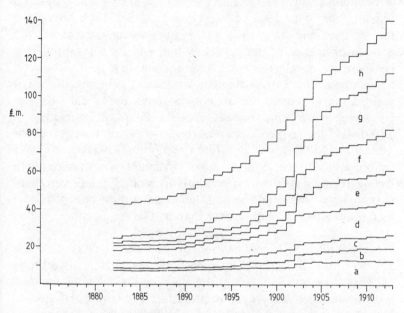

Fig. 2 Local Authority Expenditure other than from loans, 1883-1913, on poor
relief (a); lunacy and hospitals (b); police (c); highways and public
lighting (d); sewerage, water, refuse collection and public baths (e);
public utilities (f); education (g); and others (h) to make aggregate.
Sources: Local Taxation Returns and Annual Reports of the Local
Government Board

meals in 1906, medical inspection in 1907, the youth employment
service in 1911 and special facilities for epileptic and defective
children in 1913.[196] It is not surprising, then, that such extensions
of service became the subject of continual conflict between central
and local government. Both the AMC and the CCA established
special committees for education after 1902, and there was active
collaboration between the assocations, involving also, more
sporadically, other educational and ratepayer pressure groups,
religious organisations and the Central Chamber of Agriculture, on
this issue.[197]

Education was not, however, the only source of financial con-
tention between central and local government in these years. There

were similar representations on the cost of main roads, the financial implications of the 1905 Unemployed Workmen's Act, provisions for lunatics and imbeciles, and regular complaints about the general principles of the grants system and local taxation. This pressure was usually met by an open acknowledgement of the need to secure a financial settlement with local government, but it yielded very few financial concessions: the grant for the Unemployed Workmen's Act made in 1906 with a ceiling of £200,000;[198] the reintroduction of the necessitous areas grant for education in 1907, worth £200,000 a year;[199] and £100,000 for single-school areas in 1907,[200] all relatively insignificant compared with the aggregate growth of expenditure. In general, the Government continued to hold to its line that the question must be resolved by a comprehensive scheme rather than by piecemeal concessions.

It was not till 1912-14 that any real urgency can be detected in the government's response. The cause of this change in attitude appears to be two-fold. Firstly, the clamour, inside Parliament and out, became noticeably more insistent, largely because of the focussing of the fiscal issue in 1909 and delays in the settlement promised in consequence of the Budget.[201] But secondly, Lloyd George came to the active realisation that the further development of social policy through local administration was dependent upon dealing with the local taxation issue. In 1912-13, his mind was concentrated by a revolt of the county authorities, that is, a more-or-less point blank refusal by the county councils to undertake further new duties, especially the provision of accommodation for the treatment of tuberculosis which threatened to render that part of the National Insurance Act, 1911 a dead letter.[202] The Government was obliged to offer a grant to meet half of the county councils' expenditure, a commitment of some £500,000 a year.[203] In 1913, also, the Government proposed a grant of £100,000 as a half contribution to the loan charges of local education authorities and a grant of £50,000 towards the cost of school medical inspection, pending the introduction of a new block grant for education when Kempe reported.[204] The CCA found the medical inspection grant inadequate and advised its members to decline to accept it:[205] the bill was never passed and, as we have seen, Kempe was never implemented. At the outbreak of war the financial tension between central and local government remained unresolved.

We can see, then, that the reluctance of national politicians and bureaucrats to admit the claims of local authorities to a share of national taxes, even for the administration of services developed in pursuit of national policy, inhibited the development of grants as a mechanism used by the centre positively to promote national policy. The language of the argument, especially before 1900, served to legitimise a concept of local government as a service to possessive interests. By the end of the period, however, financial doctrine recognised the importance of grants to mitigate the problems for local service delivery arising from the unequal financial capacity of local authorities but, before the First World War, finance was seen by central politicians less as an entrée to the quality, level and nature of local administration, and more as a source of political conflict, bringing local interests into national political arenas and interfering with the management of national domestic policy. Likewise, the national associations of local government saw new services less as an opportunity for expanding their political status or administrative influence, and more as a burden on the ratepayers who continued largely to finance their activities. And, as we will now see, many of the same comments can be made of the financing of local capital development.

NOTES TO CHAPTER TWO

1 83 H.C. Deb. 3s. 27 January 1846 col. 238.
2 19 & 20 Vict. c. 69 s. 16.
3 30 & 31 Vict. c. 84 s. 5.
4 35 & 36 Vict. c. 79 s. 10.
5 Figures taken from yearly estimates of grant submitted to Treasury by Local Government Board in PRO MH 19/209-218, 1874-1888-9.
6 The original estimate for the grant is in LGB to Treasury, 41066/74 June 11 1874, PRO MH 19/209; subsequent correspondence is in 64149/75, October 1875, PRO MH19/210; 1889/79 9 January 1979, 5901/79 23 January 1879, 13590/79 14 February 1879, 90908/79 6 December 1879, 110857/79 18 December 1879, 95086/80 6 January 1880, 110857/80 15 December 1880, PRO MH 19/213; 114755/81 December 1881, 112587/82 28 November 1882, PRO MH 19/214; 111539/83 1 December 1883, 12250/84 27 December 1884,

PRO MH 19/215; 8639/87 20 January 1887, PRO MH 19/217.

7 Treasury to LGB, 4886/76 22 January 1876; Treasury to LGB, 14552/76 2 March 1876, PRO MH 19/211.

8 Seaton to President and Lambert, 9 August 1876, ibid; Lambert to President, 18 August 1876, ibid.

9 Treasury to LGB, 12377/77 14 February 1877, PRO MH 19/212.

10 A. S. Bishop, *The Rise of a Central Authority for English Education,* Cambridge University Press, 1971, p. 112ff; G. Sutherland, *Policy-making in Elementary Education, 1870-1895,* Oxford University Press, 1973, p. 70ff.

11 R. R. W. Lingen, 'Public education and local government', 16 January 1885, Hamilton Papers, PRO T 168/82. E. W. Hamilton *Diary 1880-1885* ed. D. W. R. Bahlman, Oxford, Clarendon Press, 1972, p. 782.

12 H. V. Emy, 'The impact of financial policy on English party politics before 1914', *The Historical Journal,* XV. 1972. pp. 103-131. For a contemporary review, R. Dudley Baxter, *The Taxation of the U.K.,* Macmillan and Co., 1869.

13 103 H. C. Deb. 3s. 8 March 1849 col. 424; 108 H. C. Deb. 3s. 1 February 1850 col. 218; 108 H. C. Deb. 3s. 19 February 1850 col. 1026.

14 *Report of the President of the Local Government Board to the Treasury on the Incidence of Taxation,* 1870 (470) LV 177; P. G. Craigie, 'The cost of local government', *Journal of the Statistical Society,* XL, 1877, pp. 262-288; P. G. Craigie, 'The English Poor Rate', *Journal of the Statistical Society,* CI, 1888, pp 450-93.

15 Central Chamber of Agriculture, *3rd Annual Report,* December 1868.

16 192 H. C. Deb. 3s. 12 May 1868 col. 136. Similar resolutions moved 199 H. C. Deb. 21 February 1870 col. 638 and 204 H. C. Deb. 28 February 1871 col. 1037. The comment is from A. H. H. Matthews, *History of the Central Chamber of Agriculture 1865-1915,* P. S. King, 1915, p. 76.

17 Central Chamber of Agriculture, *4th Annual Report,* November 1869.

18 *Ibid.*

19 Speech of Sewell Read to delegates from the municipal corporations, *The Times,* 31 May 1872 p. 10.

20 Central Chamber of Agriculture, *4th Annual Report,* 1869, 'Report of Local Taxation Committee'.

21 Local Taxation Committee, *Annual Report,* 1871.

22 Ibid. There are two Liberal MPs listed as subscribers, H. Matthews, MP for Dungarvon and Sir William Russell, MP for Dover. Of the Conservative members, 23 sat for boroughs, including a Member for Manchester and a Member for Liverpool.

23 Local Taxation Committee, *Annual Report,* 1872.

24 *Circular from Poor Law Board to Boards of Guardians on Outdoor Relief,* Circular 15, 1868-69, 9 December 1868; *Circular from Poor Law Board to Boards of Guardians on Outdoor and Indoor Relief,* Circular 1, 1870-1, 8 April 1870.

25 'Special Reports of Poor Law Inspectors', *Poor Law Board Annual Report 1870-1,* 1871 (C. 396) XXVII I, Appendix B.

26 *Minute of J. G. Goschen to Boards of Guardians in the Metropolis,* Poor Law Board Circular 4, 1869-70, 20 November 1869.

27 194 H. C. Deb. 3s. 23 February 1869 col. 268

28 *Report of President of Poor Law Board to Treasury,* 1870.

29 *The Times,* 10 October 1873 p. 10; 15 October p. 10; 12 November p. 5; 26 December p. 3; *Transactions of the Association for the Promotion of Social Science,* 1873 pp. 522-566: all collected as R Dudley Baxter, *Local Government and Taxation and Mr Goschen's Report,* R. J. Bush, 1874. Goschen's response; *The Times* 13 October 1873 p. 10.

30 By 1880, only 48 MPs subscribed to the Local Taxation Committee. Of these, two were Liberal Members. Local Taxation Committee, *Annual Report,* November 1880.

31 Lowe to Cabinet 8 November 1872, Hamilton Papers, PRO T 168/82; Lowe to Gladstone 27 October 1873, Gladstone Papers, Add Mss 44302.

32 *Second Report from the Select Committee to Inquire into the Local Government and Local Taxation of the Metropolis,* 1866 (452) XIII 317

33 *Report from the Select Committee to Inquire into the Division of the Rates between Owners and Occupiers,* 1870 (353) VIII 9.

34 29 & 30 Vict. c. 90 s. 5.

35 The confusion of areas of local authorities was the subject of a series of Parliamentary returns showing the overlapping boundaries of unions, parishes, boroughs and counties: 1862 (488) XLIV Pt II 1; 1867-8 (114) LIII 122; 1873 (102) V 5; 1878 (228) LXV 5. See also, V. D. Lipman, *Local Government Areas 1834-45,* Oxford, Blackwell, 1949, chapter II.

36 G. C. Brodrick, 'Local government in England', in J. W. Probyn (ed.). *Local Government and Taxation,* Cobden Club Essays, 1875, p. 6.

37 viz. examples given by W. Rathbone et al, *Local Administration,* Swan Sonnenchien, 1885 p. 70.

38 *Circular to Poor Law Inspectors,* 5 November 1869, Poor Law Board Circular 3, 1869-7; Inspectors' responses, 1870 (122) LVIII 261; Lambert to Cabinet 19 December 1871, Gladstone Papers, Add. Mss. 44609; *Report of Select Committee of the House of Commons on the Boundaries of Parishes, Unions and Counties,* 1873 (308) VIII 1, Evidence of Andrew Doyle and of John Lambert; Lambert to Gladstone, 6 January 1883, Gladstone Papers, Add. Mss. 44235.

39 1871 (106) V 317; 1871 (105) III 263.

40 Local Taxation Committee, *Annual Report,* 1871; 205 H. C. Deb 3s 3 April 1871 col. 1115.

41 210 H. C. Deb. 3s. 16 April 1872 col. 1331.

42 'The incident resembled more the sudden defeat of a strong ally on the very day of battle, the disappearance or the desertion of a whole wing,

than any common casualty of Parliamentary warfare', *The Times,* 18 April 1872 p. 11.

43 Stansfeld to Gladstone, n. d. 1872, Gladstone Papers, Add. Mss. 44640.

44 213 H. C. Deb 3s 1 August 1872 col. 245.

45 Lambert to Cabinet, 19 December 1871. Local taxation discussed in Cabinet on 14 October, 7 December and 10 December 1872, PRO CAB 41 4/45 4/53 4/55. Views of Cabinet Ministers, including Stansfeld, Hamilton Papers, PRO T 168/82 November 1872-January 1873.

46 *Report of the Select Committee on the Boundaries of Parishes,* etc, 1873.

47 Rating (Liabilities and Valuation) Bill, 1173 (146) IV 403.

48 PRO CAB 41 5/42, 28 November 1873.

49 PRO CAB 41 6/2 23, January 1874.

50 Local Taxation Committee,*Annual Report,* 1874. *The Times* 24 March 1874 p. 8.

51 218 H. C. Deb. 3s. 16 April 1874 col. 651.

52 Financial statements at 223 H. C. Deb. 3s. 15 April 1875 col. 1018; 228 H. C. Deb. 3s. 3 April 1876 col. 1100; 233 H. C. Deb. 3s. 29 March 1877 col. 989; 239 H. C. Deb. 3s. 4 April 1878 col. 536; 245 H. C. Deb. April 3rd 1979 col. 275.

53 Sclater Booth to Disraeli, 31 January 1876, Disraeli Papers, B/xxi/B/637; Draft Bills and Memorandum to Cabinet, 25 January 1876 PRO HLG 29/6; *Report of the Select Committee of the House of Lords on the Highways Acts,* 1881 (371) X. 1, evidence of Sclater Booth.

54 *Reports of the Select Committees of the House of Commons on the Continuance of the Turnpike Acts,* 1874 (205) XI 565 and 1875 (205) XIV 545.

55 *Select Committee on the Highways Acts,* Q. 290.

56 *Ibid.* Q. 300ff.

57 41 & 42 Vict. c. 77.

58 Rating Act, 1874 37 & 38 Vict. c. 54; Divided Parishes Act, 1876 39 & 40 Vict c. 61; Valuation Bills, 1876 (59) VII 527 and 1877 (63) VII 63.

59 Central Chamber of Agriculture, *Annual Report,* 1875 and 1876.

60 232 H. C. Deb. 3s. 9 March 1877 col. 1653.

61 *The Times* 10 March 1877 p. 10.

62 e.g. R. S. Wright *Two Memoranda on Local Government,* privately circulated, 1877, R. S. Wright and H. Hobhouse,*Local Government and Taxation* Maxwell and Son, 1884, p. v; Probyn *Local Government and Taxation.*

63 237 H. C. Deb. 3s. 28 January 1878 col. 583 and 14 February 1878 col. 1854.

64 County Boards Bill, 1879, 1878-9 (105) II 129.

65 Of 171 county seats in England, the Liberals took 53 in the 1880 election. Their total strength at the beginning of this Parliament was 352. F. W. S. Craig, *British Parliamentary Election Results 1832-1885,* Macmillan, 1977.

66 This had been a theme in the Midlothian campaign. e.g. his speech of 26 November 1879, *Midlothian Speeches,* Leicester University Press, 1971; also, Gladstone to Dodson, 10 January 1882, Monk Bretton Papers, Box 52.

67 Dodson to Gladstone, 4 November 1880, Gladstone Papers, Add. Mss. 44252; Dodson to Gladstone, 19 January 1881, Monk Bretton Papers, Box 50.

68 Gladstone to Dodson, 4 November 1881, Monk Bretton Papers, Box 53.

69 Dodson to Gladstone, 7 November 1881, Gladstone Papers, Add. Mss. 44252.

70 'A committee of farmers' friends from both sides of the House will be certain to make an inconvenient report. If you have any intention of dealing with grants in aid in any way, an intimation to that effect might perhaps keep them quiet'. Dodson to Gladstone, 18 January 1881, Gladstone Papers Add. Mss. 44252; 252 H. C. Deb. 3s. 17 February 1881 col. 1076; 259 H. C. Deb. 3s. 15 March col. 1056; 260 H. C. Deb. 3s. 28 March col. 42; ibid 7 April col. 886; 261 H. C. Deb. 3s. 23 May col 1084.

71 *Final Report of the Royal Commission on the Agricultural Depression,* 1882 (C. 3309) XIV, 1.

72 PRO CAB 41/15.

73 Notes of meetings (undated) in Monk Bretton Papers, Box 53.

74 J. G. Dodson, *County Councils,* PRO CAB 37 6/31 and *Grants in Aid* PRO CAB 6/33, both November 1881; *Grants in Aid,* February 1882, Monk Bretton Papers, Box 50.

75 Cavendish to inter-departmental committee, 16 February 1882, *ibid.*

76 J. G. Dodson, handwritten undated notes on financial arrangements, Monk Bretton Papers, Box 55.

77 264 H. C. Deb. 3s. 21 February 1882 col. 1285.

78 Ibid. 24 February col. 1542.

79 268 H. C. Deb. 3s. 24 April 1882 col. 1273.

80 273 H. C. Deb. 3s. 11 August 1882 col. 1575.

81 J. P. D. Dunbabin, 'The politics of the establishment of county councils', *The Historical Journal,* VI, pp. 353 - 379; A. Jones, *The Politics of Reform,* Cambridge University Press, 1972.

82 Lambert to Gladstone, 8 January 1883, Gladstone Papers, Add. Mss. 44235.

83 Dilke to Chamberlain, 3 February 1883, Dilke Papers, Add. Mss. 43886.

84 278 H. C. Deb. 3s. 17 April 1883 col. 437.

85 *The Times,* 26 April 1883, p. 9.

86 *The Times,* 18 October 1883, p. 6.

87 Dilke to Gladstone, 19 November 1883, Gladstone Papers, Add. Mss. 44149; Dilke *Diary,* 19 November 1883, Dilke Papers, Add. Mss. 43925.

88 Dilke to Gladstone, 11 January 1884, Gladstone Papers, Add. Mss. 44149; Sir E. W. Hamilton to Dilke, 27 January 1884, Dilke Papers, Add. Mss. 43885.

89 284 H. L. Deb. 3s. 5 February 1884 col. 8.

90 286 H. C. Deb. 3s. 28 March 1884 col. 1023.

91 298 H. C. Deb. 3s. June 8 1885 col. 1436. Real property was exempt from Probate Duty. It was liable for the Succession Duty introduced by Gladstone in 1853, but on terms more advantageous than the Probate Duty on personal property. For a contemporary and clear discussion, Sidney Buxton and G. S. Barnes, *A Handbook to the Death Duties,* John Murray, 1890.

92 Dunbabin, 'The politics of the establishment of county councils'; R. Taylor, *Lord Salisbury,* Allen and Unwin, 1975; P. Marsh, *The Discipline of Popular Government: Lord Salisbury's Domestic Statecraft 1881-1902,* Hassocks, Harvester Press, 1978; R. F. Foster, *Lord Randolph Churchill; a Political Life,* Oxford, Clarendon Press, 1981; R. Jay, *Joseph Chamberlain,* Oxford, Clarendon Press, 1981.

93 The Annual Reports of the Local Taxation Committee in the 1890s show the number of MPs subscribing to have fallen to between thirty-five and forty.

94 J. A. Thomas, *The House of Commons 1832-1901,* Cardiff, University of Wales Press, 1939; M. Ransome, 'Some recent studies of the composition of the House of Commons', *University of Birmingham Historical Journal,* VI, 1958, pp. 1132-1148; J. P. Cornford, 'The parliamentary foundations of the Hotel Cecil', in R. Robson (ed.) *Ideas and Institutions of Victorian Britain,* G. Bell & Sons, 1967.

95 Of 59 seats in London, the Conservative Party took 36 in 1885 and 47 in 1886. Craig *British Parliamentary Election Results.*

96 *The Times* 22 June 1888 p. 9; 23 June p. 9; 3 July p. 9 and 6 July p. 8.

97 *First Report from the Royal Commission on the Housing of the Working-classes,* 1884-5 (C. 4402) XXX p. 41.

98 Speech of Salisbury at Newport, *The Times,* 8 October 1885 p. 7.

99 303 H. C. Deb. 3s. 23 March 1886 col. 1463.

101 *Reports of the Select Committee on Town Holdings;* especially evidence of Lord Farrer and S. Webb in favour of the division of rates; Farrer for a municipal death duty; and Charles Harrison for a reversion duty, in 1890 (341) XVIII, 1 and J. Moulton Fletcher for site value rating, in 1890-1 (325) XVIII 15.

101 Memoranda to Chancellor of Exchequer, 21 December 1885 and 1 March 1886, Hamilton Papers, PRO T 168/82.

102 *Memorandum to Cabinet on the County Council Bill* from A. J. Balfour, 8 January 1886, PRO CAB 37/17.

103 Churchill to Salisbury, 6 November 1886, Salisbury Papers.

104 Salisbury to Churchill, 30 July 1886, *ibid.*

105 *Ibid.*

106 Balfour to Salisbury, 1 August 1886, *ibid.*

107 Churchill to Salisbury, 31 July 1886, *ibid.*

108 Walter Long, *Memories,* Hutchinson, 1923, p. 96.

109 Salisbury to Churchill, 7 November 1886; Salisbury to Hicks Beach, 26 November; Salisbury to Hicks Beach 29 November; Salisbury to Hicks Beach 1 December; Hicks Beach to Salisbury, 21 December, Salisbury Papers. Cranbrook to Salisbury, 23 November, quoted Lady Gwendolen Cecil, *Life of Robert, Marquis of Salisbury,* Hodder and Staughton, 1922-31,

III, p. 326; Salisbury to Cranbrook, 25 November, *ibid.* p. 327.

110 Salisbury to Churchill, 19 December 1886, Salisbury Papers.

111 Details construed from above correspondence, corroborating details of Churchill's proposed Budget in W. S. Churchill, *Lord Randolph Churchill,* Odhams, 1905, pp 539-556.

112 Salisbury to Churchill, 19 December 1886; Churchill to Salisbury, 20 December 1886, Salisbury Papers.

113 324 H. C. Deb. 3s. 26 March 1888 col. 268; *Statement of the Proposed Financial Arrangements in Connection with the Local Government Bill, 1888,* 1888 (C. 5344) LXXXVI 65.

114 *Ibid.* col. 295.

115 Under the Metropolitan Poor Law Act, 1867 (30 & 31 Vict. c. 6 s. 69) indoor relief administered by poor law authorities in the Metropolis was charged to the Metropolitan Common Poor Fund to which they contributed on the basis of their rateable values.

116 324 H. C. Deb. 3s. 9 April 1888 col. 730. Formally withdrawn 331 H. C. Deb. 3s. 28 November col. 485.

117 328 H. C. Deb. 3s. 3 July 1888 col. 214.

118 *Ibid.*, col. 245.

119 *Ibid.,* col. 220-1.

120 *Statements as to the Licence Duties, Probate Grant and Existing Parliamentary Grants Dealt With by the Local Government Bill 1888,* 1888 (C. 5424) LXXXVI 71; *Statement as to the Proposed Distribution of Probate Duty Grant amongst the Counties of England and Wales under the Local Government Bill 1888,* 1888 (C. 5475) LXXXVI 117. The Treasury's estimates of the amounts which would have been received under the population and rateable value criteria are in PRO HLG 29/43.

121 328 H. C. Deb. 3s. 6 July 1888 col. 597.

122 *Ibid,.* 3 July 1888 col. 260.

123 *Ibid,.* 9 July col. 763; Lady Gwendolen Cecil, *Life of Robert, Marquis of Salisbury,* Hodder and Stoughton, 1922-31.

124 Salisbury to Balfour, 6 February 1889, Salisbury Papers; Cecil, *Robert Marquis of Salisbury* IV 402; for background, Marsh, *The Discipline of Popular Government,* pp. 163ff; James Cornford, 'The transformation of Conservatism in the late nineteenth century', *Victorian Studies,* VII, 1963, pp. 33-66.

125 341 H. L. Deb. 3s. 25 February 1890 col. 1142.

126 335 H. L. Deb. 3s. 13 May 1889 col. 1829; 337 H.L. Deb. 3s. 9 July 1889 col. 337; 346 H. C. 10 July 1890 col. 1310.

127 Goschen to Chaplin, 6 May 1889; Chaplin to Goschen 7 May 1889; Goschen to Chaplin 8 May 1889, PRO CAB 37/24. Memorandum to Goschen [from Local Taxation Committee], 11 May 1889, *ibid.*

128 343 H. C. Deb. 3s. 17 April 1890 col. 692.

129 346 H. C. Deb. 3s. 26 June 1890 col. 77; 347 H. C. Deb. 3s. 14 July 1890 col. 342.

130 Chaplin to Balfour, 25 December 1891, A. J. Balfour Papers, Add. Mss. 49772.

131 23 H. C. Deb. 4s. 16 April 1894 col. 469.

132 Salisbury to Balfour, 31 December 1892, A. J. Balfour Papers, Add. Mss. 49690; Chaplin to Balfour, 17 December 1894, *ibid.*, Add. Mss. 49772; Balfour to Chaplin, 17 January, 1895, *ibid.*

133 *Second Report of the Royal Commission on Agriculture,* 1896, (C. 7981) XVI 413.

134 *Ibid, Minutes of Evidence and Appendices,* 1896 (C. 7400) XVII I, Evidence of Sir Alfred Milner, Qs. 63,071-63,520; *ibid,* Appendix A, Statements XXXIII and XXXIV.

135 Papers on Agricultural Rates Bill 1896, December 1895, PRO HLG 29/53.

136 *A Reply to the [Treasury] Memorandum of 7 January, ibid.*

137 *First Report of the Departmental Committee Appointed to Inquire into the Sufficiency of the Clerical Staff and Secretariat of the Local Government Board,* 1898 (C. 8731) XL 429. The evidence was not published, see *Minutes of Evidence taken before the Local Government Board Inquiry Committee,* PRO MH 78/1, evidence of F. Stevens and C. N. Dalton.

138 Correspondence and papers on the Agricultural Rates Act Continuance Bill, 1901, PRO HLG 29/68.

139 *Ibid;* and correspondence and papers on the Continuance Bill 1905, 1904-5, PRO HLG 29/85.

140 *Final Report of the House of Commons Select Committee on Town Holdings,* 1892 (214 Sess. I) XVIII 613.

141 Ken Young and Patricia Garside, *Metropolitan London: Politics and Urban Change, 1837-1981,* Edward Arnold, 1982, pp. 59-104; Avner Offer, *Property and Politics 1870-1914,* Cambridge University Press, 1981.

142 351 H. C. Deb. 3s. 13 March 1890 col 934; 2 H. C. Deb. 4s. 4 May 1892 col 66; 31 H. C. Deb. 4s. 8 March 1895 col. 700; 42 H. C. Deb. 4s. 24 June 1896 col 2; 66 H. C. Deb. 4s. 10 March 1899 col. 522.

143 *Report of LCC Local Government and Taxation Committee to LCC,* 21 May 1889; *Report of LCC Local Taxation Committee,* 3 May 1891. *Report of Town Holdings Committee,* evidence of Lord Farrer and S. Webb.

144 *Report of Town Holdings Committee,* evidence of Lord Farrer; Costelloe to Harcourt, 24 October 1892, Harcourt Papers Box 187.

145 *Annual Report of the Council of AMC for 1895,* PRO 30/72.24. The protagonist corporations were Hull and Crewe. The opposition included Liverpool.

146 Minutes of AMC Council meetings, 21 October 1903, PRO 30/72.33; 4 February 1904, 17 March 1904, PRO 30/72.34. *Report of Deputation from AMC Council and representatives of the Conference on Ground Values Taxation* *to President of LGB and Home Secretary* (n.d. 1904), *ibid.*

147 Ken Young, *Local Politics and the Rise of Party: the London Municipal Society and the Conservative Intervention in Local Elections, 1894-63,* Leicester University Press, 1975, chapters 2 and 3; Young and Garside, *Metropolitan London,* pp. 59-104.

148 *Report of the Rt. Hon. H. H. Fowler, President of the Local Government Board to the Treasury on Local Taxation,* 1893-4 (C. 168) LXXVII 233.

149 London (Equalisation of Rates) Act, 57 & 58 Vict. c. 53. On electoral considerations in London, Shaw Lefevre to Harcourt, 19 April 1894, Harcourt Papers, Box 91.

150 *First Annual Report of County Councils Association,* 1890-1; Minutes of meeting of Executive Council, 25 January 1896 and 28 October 1896. 11 H. C. Deb. 4s. 21 April 1893 col. 896; 33 H. C. Deb. 4s. 2 May 1895 col. 293; 37 H. C. Deb. 4s. 2 March 1896.

151 9 H. C. Deb. 4s. 24 February 1893 col. 335; 11 H. C. Deb. 4s. 27 April 1893 col. 1307; 12 H. C. Deb. 4s. 18 May 1893 col. 1266; 46 H. C. Deb. 4s. 23 February 1897 col. 965; 47 H. C. Deb. 4s. 23 March 1897 col. 1224; 145 H. C. Deb. 4s. 18 April 1905 col. 449; *ibid.* 5 June 1905 col. 705; 154 H. C. Deb. 4s. 22 March 1906 col. 629; 170 H. C. Deb. 4s. 12 March 1907 col. 1430; 171 H. C. Deb. 4s. 20 March 1907 col. 944.

152 *Memorandum on Exchequer Grants,* from Lord Welby, ordered to be printed by Local Government and Taxation Committee of LCC, 13 May 1898. Copy in Hamilton Papers, PRO T 168/82.

153 *Memorandum on Questions to be dealt with in Final Report,* by E. W. Hamilton and G. H. Murray, 15 October 1898, Hamilton Papers PRO T 168/82, and *Memorandum on Imperial Relief, on Local Burdens, and on the System of Imperial and Local Taxation,* by Sir E. W. Hamilton, March 1897, *ibid.*

154 *Memorandum on Questions to be dealt with in Final Report* by C. N. Dalton, n.d., *ibid.*

155 *Final Report of the Royal Commission on Local Taxation* 1901 (Cd. 638) xxiv 413.

156 Long to Salisbury, 3 November 1901, Salisbury Papers.

157 'Separate Report on Urban rating and Site Values', *Final Report of Royal Commission on Local Taxation,* 1901.

158 'Separate recommendations by Lord Balfour of Burleigh' *ibid.*

159 'Report by Sir E. W. Hamilton and Sir G Murray', *ibid.*

160 *Memorandum to Cabinet on Tithe Rent and Agricultural Rates Act Renewal,* from Walter Long, 12 December 1904, PRO CAB 37/79.

161 A. J. Balfour to Hicks Beach, 9 June 1902, A. J. Balfour Papers, Add. Mss. 49695; *Memorandum to Cabinet on Financial Prospects,* from Hicks Beach, October 1901, PRO CAB 37/58; *Memorandum from Ritchie to Cabinet,* 31 December 1902, PRO CAB 37/63; *Memorandum to Cabinet on the Financial*

Situation, from Austin Chamberlain, 8 December 1903, PRO CAB 37/67.

162 Papers on Agricultural Rates Act Continuance 1900-1 and 1904-5.

163 *Minutes Taken Before the Local Government Board Inquiry Committee,* 1898, evidence of C. N. Dalton.

164 *Suggestions for a Unionist Fiscal Policy,* unsigned, 25 March 1905, Gerald Balfour Papers, PRO 60/44.

165 *First Report of Royal Commission on Local Taxation* (on valuation and rating), 1899 (C. 9141) XXXV 733, and *Second Report of Royal Commission,* (on tithe rent charge: valuation and rating), 1899 (C. 9142) XXXV 795.

166 Memorandum to Cabinet from W. H. Long, PRO CAB 37/57.

167 Valuation Bill, 1904 (166) iv 631.

168 145 H. C. Deb. 4s. 17 April 1905 col. 328.

169 Urban Site Value Rating Bill, 1902 (3) iv 541; Land Values (Assessment and Rating) Bill 1903 (3) ii 397; Land Values (Assessment and Rating) Bill 1904 (3) ii 481.

170 John Burns *Diary,* 31 May 1907, 24 October 1907, 28 December 1907, Burns Papers, Add. Mss. 44325; *Memorandum to Cabinet on Valuation,* from John Burns, December 1908, PRO CAB 37/90.

171 Kenneth D. Brown, *John Burns* Royal Historical Society, 1977, pp 111-133.

172 Bernard Mallet, *British Budgets 1887-8-1912-13,* Macmillan, 1913, pp 283-286.

173 4 H. C. Deb. 5s. 29 April 1909 col. 472.

174 Minutes of the meeting of the Council of the AMC, 8 July 1909; Minutes of the Autumn Meeting of the AMC, 27 October 1909; Minutes of the meeting of the Council, 18 November 1909. PRO 30/72.39.

175 11 H. C. Deb. 5s. 27 September 1909 col. 934.

176 *Ibid.,* col. 937.

177 Report of Deputation to the Chancellor of the Exchequer, 8 July 1909, bound in AMC minutes 1909-10 PRO 30/72.39.

178 18 H. C. Deb. 5s. 30 June 1910 col. 1910.

179 *Final Report of the Departmental Committee on Local Taxation,* 1914 (Cd 7315) xl 537.

180 *Ibid.*

181 62 H. C. Deb. 5s. 4 May 1914 col. 56.

182 Bentley B. Gilbert, 'David Lloyd George: the reform of British land holding and the Budget of 1914', *The Historical Journal,* XXI, 1978, pp. 117-141.

183 CCA *Official Circular,* May 1910, p. 69.

184 Minutes of AMC Council Meeting, 15 February 1906, PRO 30/72,36.

185 The origins of the CCA are described in an unsigned typewritten note kept with the early minutes of the association in the offices of the Association of County Councils. See also, K. Isaac-Henry, *The Association of Muncipal Corporations and the County Councils Association: a study of influences and pressures on the reorganisation of Local Government,*

1945-72, unpublished PhD. thesis, University of London, 1980, Chapter 3.

186 Rt. Hon J. J. Hibbert. MP for Oldham, 1862-4 and 1877-86, was Parliamentary Secretary, LGB 1872-4 and 1880-3 and held junior ministerial office at the Home Office and Treasury, 1883-5. He was Deputy-Lieutenant, Lancashire County Council and Chairman Lancashire County Council and became President of the CCA in the 1890s.

187 Henry Thring was Parliamentary Counsel and Head of the Office of the Parliamentary Counsel from 1868-1886. In retirement he became a member of Surrey County Council, and was active in the CCA becoming Vice President in the 1890s.

188 Sir John Dorington was Chairman of Gloucestershire Quarter Sessions and Gloucesershire County Council. He was elected to Parliament for Tewkesbury in 1886, becoming prominent on the country wing.

189 Henry Hobhouse was a Parliamentary draftsman in the 1880s. He became MP for Somerset E. in 1885 and was a member of Somerset County Council and Quarter Sessions. He was Chairman of the CCA's Parliamentary Committee and subsequently of its Education Committee. In 1900, he became a member of the Consultative Committee of the Board of Education.

190 Sir Albert Rollit was a solicitor and shipowner from Hull and was prominent both in its local government and in the national association of chambers of trade. He was MP for Islington N from 1886 until his defeat on the free trade issue in 1906.

191 *Report of the Joint Select Committee of the House of Commons and House of Lords,* 1903 (270) vii I.

192 Report of Deputation to Long, 29 November 1901 filed with Annual Report of AMC for 1901-2, PRO 30/72.32.

193 Speech to Annual Meeting of AMC, 21 October 1903, PRO 30/72.33.

194 Harmood-Banner was a member of Liverpool City Council from 1894. He was President of the Institute of Chartered Accountants 1904-5. He was elected for Liverpool, Everton, in 1905.

195 The Education Codes were issued annually, often with amended provisions. The changes which provoked most hostility were: the Code for teacher training, 1903; the new Elementary Education Code of 1903; the Secondary School Regulations of 1905 and 1907 (which were accompanied by higher rates of grant in 1905-6; the review of school accommodation in 1908; and, especially, the new Code of 1909 announced in Circular 709 of the Board of Education, March 1909. References to these changes are in the Annual Reports of the Board of Education.

196 6 Edw. VII c. 57, (provision of school meals); 7 Edw. VII c. 43 s. 13, (medical inspection); 10 Edw. VII & 1 Geo V c. 37, (employment); 4 & 5 Geo V c. 45 (epileptic and defective children).

197 Both AMC and CCA minutes record a series of deputations to the Local Government Board, the Board of Education, The Chancellor of the

Exchequer and the Prime Minister, between 1902 and the War, which are too extensive to list in detail.

198 vote taken 162 H. C. Deb. 4s. 31 July 1906 col. 838.

199 172 H. C. Deb. 4s 11 April 1907 col. 331.

200 171 H. C. Deb. 4s. 20 March 1907 col. 975.

201 Presidential Speech by H. E. Haward to Institute of Municipal Treasurers and Accountants, *Proceedings,* 1909.

202 *Annual Report* of Executive Council, 1910-11, *Annual Report,* 1912-13; Sir Robert Morant to Lloyd George on finance of the National Insurance Act, 22 May 1913, Lloyd George Papers, HLRO C/6/2/2.

203 Lloyd George to Henry Hobhouse, 31 July 1913, in LGB Circular 11 to County Councils, 1911-12.

204 55 H. C. Deb. 5s. 22 July 1913 col. 1907.

205 *Annual Report of the Executive Council* to CCA, 1911-13.

Chapter Three
Local loans and local debt

The attitude of central government to local loans and local debt reflects a profound ambivalence towards the process of local public capital accumulation; their growth was at the same time a source of congratulation and of political embarrassment to the centre. It provided the most measurable indicator of the local authorities' compliance with the spirit of the public legislation of the emerging instrumental state. But it was also the most reliable pointer to the growing burden on the ratepayers. In consequence, capital investment by local authorities was by no means uncompromised, but was subject to political, economic and administrative constraints which became more powerful in periods when the financial and economic costs of borrowing increased. The period demonstrates, therefore, no consistent or steady growth in capital expenditure: there were sustained periods – in the 1880s and 1900s – when the level of capital spending fell (Figure 3).

The contemporary perception – held by officials at the LGB – was that, in the early part of our period, the development of local capital was hindered by its finance; that is by problems in securing local loans in easily managed form, at a reasonable price. Until the 1890s, at least, the Local Government Board pressed for easier access for local authorities to the money market and to public works loans. In the eyes of the Treasury, however, the growth of local debt was an unwelcome complication in the management of the national debt, and a threat to the credit of the nation. The Treasury therefore attempted to pursue a strategy on local loans similar to its strategy on local expenditure – to protect the Exchequer from local demands and to separate their management from the Imperial finances – and the LGB came under pressure to use its loan sanction powers primarily to impose financial discipline

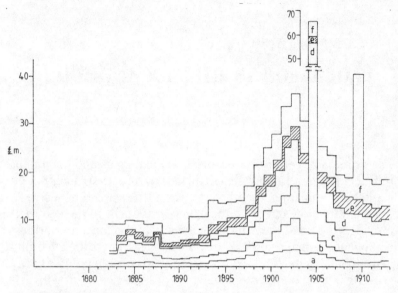

Fig. 3 Local Authority expenditure from loans, 1883-1914, on workhouses, lunatic asylums and hospitals (a); highways (b); sewers and waterworks (c); utilities (d); education (e); and others, to make aggregate (f)
Source: Local Taxation Returns

and restraint on local authorities.

Until the 1890s, most local authorities borrowed separately in respect of each capital project: they had no general power to consolidate loans. With limited powers to invest sinking funds and limited administrative capacity to manage maturity loans, local authorities generally sought facilities for annual repayment.[1] Repayment periods of loans taken out under the sanction of the central government were limited by statute: although the Education Act of 1870 and the Public Health Act, 1875 (which became the model for all legislation regulating district councils) allowed a maximum of fifty and sixty years,[2] the Local Government Board granted this term only for land, so that most loan sanctions were for fifty years or less.[3] Boards of Guardians, municipal corporations and county councils were limited to thirty years.[4] That is, local authorities borrowed by fixed period, fixed interest, non transferable loans – terminable annuities, instalment loans, mortgages or bonds – secured either on their property or on their rate funds.

With the partial exception of bonds, local authority loans were consequently an unattractive proposition for the private or trust investor, and they were not tradeable on the money markets. The official and local authority evidence to the Royal Sanitary Commission in the late 1860s and to the Select Committee on Public Works Loan Bills in 1875, showed that most investment in public health capital was financed by insurance companies, and a rather smaller proportion by the Public Works Loan Board, at rather high and inelastic interest rates.[5] Moreover, fixed terms prevented Treasurers from exploiting shifts in the price of money. But at the same time, until 1875, there was comparatively little effective regulation of the local authorities' capital accounting: there was no general statute requiring local authorities to keep separate capital and revenue accounts, or to make returns showing the application of loan moneys and their repayment. In smaller places, the local banker often acted as Treasurer to the authority, providing illegal and therefore uncontrolled overdraft facilities.[6] The reputation of local government outside the very biggest towns was such, therefore, as to discourage easy lending.

The strategy of the Local Government Board in the period after 1870 was aimed at increasing the credit of local government, and at creating tradeable, consolidated, more advantageously managed securities. It also attempted, at least in the early years, to use public works loans as an inducement to increase the rate of local capital expenditure. It was here, particularly, that it came directly into conflict with the Treasury.

The Public Works Loan Commissioners had been established in 1817, to provide finance for secure but unmarketable loans required for projects which were deemed by statute to be in the public interest.[7] Since 1848, local authorities had borrowed either from their general funds or from special funds established under particular Acts, for example the 1870 Education Act.[8] Although the Commissioners were doubtless a welcome source of funds for local authorities, the Commissioners' terms were not particularly easy: under the Public Works Loans Act of 1853,[9] loans were allowed only for twenty years, and they were repaid (either by express provision of the enabling statute or by administrative requirement of the PWLC) on the instalment system, which bore especially heavily on the ratepayers in the early years of the loan.[10] Despite an Act of 1853, which gave the the Treasury discretion to vary the rate for public loans above a minimum three and a half per cent,[11] the Treasury set in October 1859 a standard rate of interest of five per cent, a rate calculated to provide a margin for administration and bad debts. This rate was understood to be independent of the condition of the money market: the 1859 Minute stated clearly that 'the Government is not a competitor with other money lenders, and... makes advances in order to assist desirable public objects, which cannot be obtained by the ordinary operations of the money market'.[12]

The case for easier and cheaper public works loans was one aspect of sanitary reform on which public health reformers and the local taxation lobby could agree. In 1871, the Royal Sanitary Commission pressed the Treasury for lower rates and longer periods on local loans.[13] By the early 70s, moreover, several precedents existed of public works loans being authorised at a special cheap rate where the public interest overrode financial orthodoxy: for example, loans taken out for the special public works programme in Lancashire during the cotton famine in 1863, for 'harbours of refuge' on hostile coasts in the interests of marine safety; and by farmers hit by the cattle plague, were available at a minimum of three and half per cent.[14]

As we have seen in Chapter Two, the financial package which Stansfeld negotiated with Lopes, to allow the Public Health Bill to make progress in the summer of 1872, acknowledged the case for special public loans for local sanitary administration, and s. 44 of the Bill was also amended to allow the LGB to sanction loans at three and a half percent.[15] But although it was made with their agreement, this offer was frowned on by Gladstone and Robert Lowe, his Chancellor. They regarded cheap loans as hidden grants, and believed that the PWLC had made loans without due regard to the financial security of borrowers, particularly for harbours.[16] Gladstone therefore emphasised that the concession did not imply that the Treasury would cease to have discretion to manage the rate.[17]

Moreover, the Treasury and the Public Works Loan Commissioners disapproved strongly of the implication of s. 44 – that the centre had acknowledged a duty to support local improvements. They were, consequently, obstructive in its implementation. The evidence given to the Select Committee of 1875 by J. G. Hubbard MP, the Chairman of the PWLC, shows that he continued to hold to the view expressed in the 1859 Minute. 'The State has no business to be a money lender at all', he asserted. 'It is only from exceptional necessity that the existence of such a Board as that over which I preside can be tolerated'.[18] The 'normal' rate, he argued, should be five per cent, to be regarded as 'a rate of refuge for applicants if they cannot get the money more easily elsewhere'.[19] Hubbard was, however, only following liberal economic orthodoxy. Fawcett, for example, held forcefully that moneylending by the state would pervert the operation of financial markets, and that special rates for favoured projects and authorities amounted to arbitrary discrimination by the centre between different localities.[20]

Once the Public Health Act 1872 was safely on the statute book, the Board requested the Treasury to issue a general instruction to the PWLC for loans to be made at three and a half per cent for purposes covered by the Act,[21] The Treasury declined to do so, stating that

> advances by way of loan out of the Consolidated Fund are now authorised by Parliament to an extent which materially affects financial arrangements. It is therefore most important that the Treasury should not surrender powers which enable it to watch over and in some degree control the issue of Public Money, and on this ground my Lords do not think it desirable that a general authority such as the Local Government Board suggest should be given to the Public Works Loans Commissioners.[22]

In January 1873, the Treasury informed the Board that it intended to impose a limit of thirty years on the repayment of three and a half per cent sanitary loans: local authorities would be charged three and three quarters for loans up to forty years, and loans for the maximum period stipulated in the Act, that is fifty years, would bear a rate of four per cent.[23] Its justification was that the Exchequer stood to lose on long loans if the cost of borrowing to fund them rose sharply before they were redeemed, and that authorities must be encouraged to keep their borrowing short. The

Board could only point out to the Treasury that they had no statutory power to refuse to sanction loans for fifty years.[24] John Lambert's diffidence stemmed from an uncomfortable awareness that
the Board could not guarantee the financial probity of the local
authorities whose loans they sanctioned, and he was prompted to
reissue instructions to the engineering inspectors that they were
to take account not only of the durability of the project but also
of the authority's total debt structure in their reports on loan
sanction applications.[25] He also urged on Stansfeld the need for a
government audit of corporation accounts, including loan
accounts.[26]

More fundamental conflict between the Board and the Commissioners broke out in the summer of 1874, and centred on the
scope of s. 44. Lambert's view was that in 1872 Parliament had
indeed conceded a form of capital grant.[27] The Board therefore
began to recommended all improvement projects it sanctioned to
the PWLC for three and a half per cent loans.[28] In June, however,
the PWLC notified the Treasury that it considered that Parliament
intended s. 44 only for works having 'an immediate and direct
connection with the salubrity of the district and the health of the
inhabitants' and that it would refuse cheap loans for other improvement purposes.[29] The Board pointed to the absence of restriction
in the wording of s. 44 and asserted that 'the object of s. 44. was
not only to promote works of sanitary necessity but to enable Local
Authorities to undertake works of improvement without unduly
increasing the existing burdens of local taxation'.[30] As a compromise, the Board agreed to draw up a classification of works
which were henceforth to be considered ineligible for cheap loans,
and to consult the Treasury in doubtful cases.[31] This was acceptable
to the Treasury, but not to the Commissioners, and the Treasury
declined to press the Commissioners on the grounds that they
were an independent body.[32] The Commissioners were also, as witnesses to the 1875 Local Loans Committee did not fail to point
out,[33] a politically irresponsible body attempting to restrict the
terms of a public statute, but the Local Government Board could
do nothing except point out, pertinently, that 'It is no less an interference with the money market to grant loans for purposes which
the Treasury approves as it is to grant money for those they do

not'.[34]

The attitude of the Treasury and the Commission to public works loans are explained, however, not only by the financial orthodoxy of the period, but also by very real fears that the growth of public loans would seriously undermine the management of the government's debt. The Treasury's obvious worry that public works loans would become a normal source of borrowing, rather than a last resort, was not an unreasonable one in the political climate of the early 1870s. In 1870, a potentially massive demand for public works loans was created by the Education Act and, in 1873, the Treasury's fears that the 1872 concession would be used as a precedent to wedge open the state's lending powers seemed to be confirmed when the local taxation lobby pressed for cheap loans for 'national' purposes, especially police stations and lunatic asylums.[35] In 1874, therefore, the Treasury announced a fundamental review of public works loans.[36] For the Treasury had clearly decided that the method by which public works loans were financed severely exacerbated the problems of their management, and that the Public Works Loans Commission must be placed on a new financial footing.

Until 1875, the Public Works Loans Commissioners were authorised to lend whenever an application was received, subject to the sanction of the appropriate department, but subject to no effective top limit.[37] The Exchequer was required to fund loans on demand and the Treasury was obliged, if the flow of repayments was sluggish, to go into the money market regardless of its condition. Doubtless, also, its sense of financial vulnerability was heightened by the threatened insolvency in 1874 of the National Debt Commissioners, who had been relending too cheaply to cover the interest payable on savings banks deposits.[38]

In 1875, therefore, after minimal consultation with the Local Government Board,[39] the Treasury proposed a package of measures designed to increase control over local loans, and to bring political pressure to bear to contain the growth in local indebtedness.[40] Departments were henceforth to take an annual vote in Parliament for their public loan requirements in a Public Works Loan Bill, and Northcote asked Parliament for a fixed rate of interest – five per cent – for public loans, to protect the Treasury from the importuning of departments.[41] He also proposed a Local Loans Act,[42] to empower local authorities to issue marketable securities, under strict central regulation. By these two measures, local loans would be rationalised and the indebtedness of local authorities consequently more open to public accountability. The Local Loans Bill was intended to impose the district audit on local authority loan accounts, to require authorities to make returns showing their annual repayments, and to give the LGB powers to compel local Treasurers to make good deficiencies discovered in their sinking funds. The local authority returns, together with the annual estimates of borrowing requirements, would form the basis of an annual 'local budget' on the occasion of the Public Works Loan Bill.

However, under pressure from the Association of Municipal Corporations and from Joseph Chamberlain, acting as the spokeman for a 'large number' of borough members of Parliament,[43] Northcote retreated from the state audit of municipal accounts. The Local Government Board's inability to obtain full, certified returns, and chronic delays in its Statistical Department, rendered the 'local budget' statement of limited value, and merely provided an embarrassing and public platform for the Local Taxation Committee and orthodox economists to air their grievances about the burden of the growing local debt and the PWLC.[44] The local budget was discontinued after three years, and, despite sporadic pressure from the Local Taxation Committee, it was never resurrected.

Nor was the drafting of the Acts adequate for the regulation of local capital finance. Prompted by the Board's officials,[45] amendments had to be made in the early 1880s to compel authorities to make good deficiencies discovered in their schedules of repayments,[46] to keep separate loan accounts[47] and to regulate the maintenance of sinking funds.[48] But the most telling indictment of the 1875 legislation was that it failed in its main objective, to open up new avenues of local authority borrowing. The view of Cornelius Dalton[49] – who became Inspector of Local Loans and Acts at the Board in 1878 – was that the Local Loans Act was so useless that it was beyond amendment and needed to be repealed. In his opinion, it did not permit local authorities to do what they most needed to do, to consolidate a mass of small loans, with a multitude of due dates, into large loans, and to reborrow to exploit shifts in interest

rates. Dalton believed that constant forced renewal of unconsoli-
dated, short-term loans, especially at a time when local indebtedness was rising, severely increased the costs of borrowing for local
authorities, and was a source of insecurity in the whole system of
local finance.

The Local Loans Act provided for the issue of negotiable
annuities, debentures and debenture stock. A limited volume of
debentures was issued under the Act, but the Act restricted the
issue of debenture stock to those few authorities who had already
taken private stock powers, and no stock issues were sanctioned
under this Act. In the late 70s, Birmingham, Nottingham and Liverpool Corporations acquired powers – after some resistance from
the officers of the House of Lords who objected to private powers
that exceeded the scope of public statutes – to consolidate their
loans in a stock issue, and to borrow to lend to smaller authorities
within their boundaries,[50] a power which the Metropolitan Board
of Works had possessed in London since 1869.[51] Dalton was convinced that these were powers which should be made generally
available to the larger provincial authorites in a public statute, and
in 1881-82 proposed a Local Authorities Stock Facilities Bill to Dodson.[52] In 1884, the Royal Commission on Working Class Housing
commended the principle of local authority stock, and pointed out
that the MBW and Birmingham were borrowing at a rate lower than
the cheapest PWLC loans.[53]

Dalton's proposal was was not taken up immediately, and local
authorities did not receive general legislative powers to issue stock
till 1888, when a clause for county council stock was inserted in
the Local Government Act.[54] However, by the late 1880s, some fifty
to sixty million pounds' worth of municipal stock had been been
authorised by private act of Parliament, and model stock clauses
for private acts were agreed in 1889.[55] In 1890, the Board therefore
took a general power, to sanction the issue of stock by urban local
authorities.[56] It appears, however, that the urban stock regulations
of 1891 were more restrictive than the Board's officials wished.
Owen and Dalton (now Permanent Secretary and Assistant Secretary) were still pressing for the consolidation and amalgamation of
loans, both to meet the needs of the local authorities and to reduce
the work of sanctioning loans.[57] They believed that the consolida-

tion of loans enhanced public accountability for local debt, by
promoting the simplification of returns and accounts. But they
were also agreed that the marketability of urban stock depended
upon its being classed with municipal stock; it must therefore be
issued under similar terms. They therefore consulted with the parliamentary officers in charge of private bill business. We must
assume that it was pressure from this source which led to the
requirement to earmark local authority loans to separate projects
and enterprises. '... this earmarking', commented one of the
Board's own auditors in his treatise on local authority accounts
after the Great War, 'has occasioned so much unnecessary borrowing, and such heavy losses to local funds, in addition to great complication of the accounts'.[58] He could also have added that it
occasioned much extra work in the Board in sanctioning reborrow-
ings and reissues.

Such an attitude was, however, altogether in line with the
policy of Parliamentary officers towards borrowing by private acts.
When we discuss private bill procedures in Chapter Six, we will
see that in the 1880s the line between controls designed to ensure
the financial probity and creditability of local authority debt
management, and those designed to discourage the expansion of
local authority borrowing had been clearly breached. For the
growth of local authority debt, from the late 70s onwards, alarmed
both ratepayers and those charged with the management of the
national debt, especially when viewed against the policy of successive Chancellors to reduce the burden of the national debt (Figure
4). Nor were the arguments of the municipal collectivists reassuring
to those who believed the floodgates might open. Joseph Chamberlain was pressing in the late 1870s for municipal powers to consolidate loans.[59] But Chamberlain was also arguing for significantly
longer loan periods, for land to be classed as an asset justifying
the creation of a permanent loan, and for other radical changes in
controls on borrowing.[60] Moreover, Birmingham appeared to be
setting precedents for the creation of a vast, uncontrolled municipal debt: in 1877 and again in 1878, to the indignation of the
Treasury,[61] the corporation took unprecedented public works loans
of a million pounds a time to finance its town improvements and
slum clearance.

Meanwhile, opinion had moved significantly against the corporations' position. The Local Taxation Committee, which in the mid 70s had pressed for cheap loans to relieve ratepayers now,

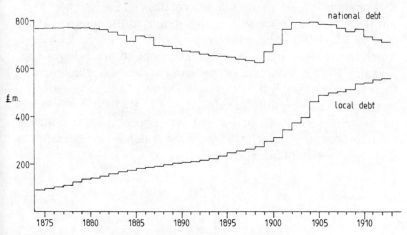

Fig. 4 Changes in the National and Local Debt, 1874-1913
Sources: Annual Reports of Local Government Board and Returns of the National Debt Commissioners

in the 1880s, blamed easier access to capital finance for the growing rate burden.[62] Nor was the Liberal Government entirely sympathetic to Chamberlain's position: while endorsing the public spirit of self-government and municipal enterprise – and, indeed, erecting them as models for the reform of county and parish government – the Liberal Party leadership was not fully sympathetic to their aspirations. 'I presume that while the system of municipal corporations is excellent', Gladstone told a dinner in 1885 for the jubilee of the Municipal Corporations Act, 'the danger of the bigger ones is to attempt too much and to be too ready to lay burdens on their successors, and of the smaller to indulge in something of jobbery'.[63]

Fears for the growth of local debt stemmed not just from the ratepayer lobbies. Statements drawing attention to the worrying growth of local debt became a routine part of budget speeches from the late 70s onwards. For the difficulties of financing local loans had placed too much of the capital development in public health and education on public works loans, and demand began

regularly to outstrip repayments of old loans, a situation exacerbated by the fact that, since 1875, the interest paid on public loans
had been redirected into the public revenue accounts, leaving only
the capital payments in the accounts of the PWLC,[64] Northcote was
unwilling to finance local loans by adding to the funded debt, a
process which would have undermined both the New Sinking Fund,
which he had created in 1875,[65] and the long term strategy of the
Treasury for the reduction of the national debt. Local loans were
therefore increasingly financed by Exchequer bills and bonds, and
by the new Treasury bills introduced in 1877. By 1880, the Treasury
calculated,[66] local loans had added over fifteen million pounds to
the unfunded debt, which was already swollen by the demands of
Disraeli's foreign policy (Figure 5).

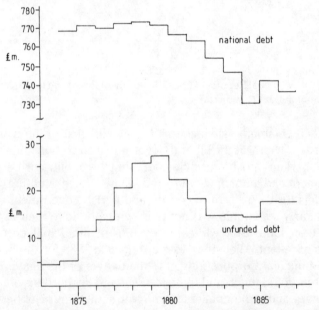

Fig. 5 Changes in the Unfunded Debt and the National Debt, 1874-1887
Source: Returns on the National Debt Commissioners

In 1879, the Treasury therefore took steps to make public works
loans less attractive to the local authorities by proposing, in the
annual Public Works Loans Bill, to remove the discretion created

in 1875 to allow authorities to repay by the annuity system rather than by the less advantageous instalments system, and to reduce the repayment period for loans at the cheap tariff from thirty to twenty years. The rate for cheap thirty year loans would henceforth be four per cent, on the grounds that three and a half per cent left 'too small a margin over the average rate at which the Treasury can borrow in Consols to create a sufficient security against bad debts'.[67] So far as public works loans were concerned, this cancelled the concession of 1872 and a similar concession in the 1875 Artisans and Labourers Dwellings Act.[68] In response to the Birmingham loans, Northcote also proposed a limit of £100,000 on the loans which any one authority could take from the PWLC in a single year.

But the bill did not pass as drafted. Caught between the obstruction of the borough members, and the fact that the PWLC were about to run out of funds,[69] Northcote was forced to make concessions to pass the Bill. The annuity clause was withdrawn, and it was agreed that, in place of a fixed statutory tariff, the Treasury would have a discretion to fix the rate.[70] Chamberlain failed, however, to secure the withdrawal of the borrowing limit. After the amended bill received the Royal Assent, the Treasury imposed the tariff originally proposed in the bill,[71] and gave the LGB to understand that the PWLC should normally be repaid by instalments, unless a special case was made by a local authority for the annuity system. 'The reasoning of the Chancellor of the Exchequer about bad debts', grumbled Lambert, 'is altogether unsound'.[72]

After 1880, the National Debt Commissioners were empowered, under Treasury guarantee, to put the savings banks deposits to the funding of Public Works Loans; between 1880 and 1887, eleven million pounds was contributed from this source.[73] Nevertheless, in 1887, the unfunded debt still carried some twelve million pounds for local loans.[74] Goschen believed that local loans damaged the credit of the state by being counted as part of the state's liabilities.[75] He therefore resolved to separate national and local loans.

What specially irritated Treasury officials was that the Exchequer was being used to make hidden grants: that is, they believed that Parliament had sanctioned cheap loans without taking responsibility for the financial consequences.[76] It was their opinion that a three and a half per cent rate represented a precariously small margin over the costs of financing local loans and, as short term bills, Treasury bills were more expensive than Consols. But the Treasury also expected the public works loan rate to cover general losses in the accounts of the National Debt Commissioners, including current losses on the Friendly Society deposits.[77] They calculated that the relatively high cost of financing public works loans, coupled with political pressure to lend cheaply for a wider range of functions, had contributed, by the mid 1880s, to a twelve per cent loss on the capital advanced through the PWLC.[78]

In 1887, therefore, Goschen devised a scheme[79] to separate the funding of local loans from the management of the unfunded debt and established procedures by which Parliament would be confronted with the effects of its local loans concessions. Henceforth,[80] a separate Local Loans Fund would be maintained by the National Debt Commissioners, and would be financed by repayments of loans and by a local loans stock, issued with the full backing of the state. An income and expenditure account would be kept, and Parliament would be required to make up any deficiency by a vote. Deficiencies in the Local Loan Account would therefore come into the budget statement. 'The Chancellor of the Exchequer trusts', the Treasury minute reads[81] '... the review of Parliament of any loss which may occur, will produce the result of increased caution in the extension of the local loan system'.

There is an element of paranoia in these statements. The twelve per cent loss on public works loans was an historic figure, representing an accumulation from 1792, and included Irish investments made in the 1850s which had always been recognised to be gifts not loans. By common consent, local authority defaults in repayments, particularly in recent years, were minimal. But we may speculate that, in addition to the pressures of loan management, Treasury officials were feeling politically vulnerable on the issue of loans, because of a recent defeat on the question of finance for working class housing.

The Report of the prestigious Royal Commission on the Housing of the Working Classes, which was established under the Chairmanship of Dilke in response to the exposés in the early 1880s of housing conditions in London and other cities, shows clearly the complex issues which were thought to be involved in the problem.[82]

Underpinning all their recommendations, the Commission forcibly declared, was the unsatisfactory nature of local government finance, including local authority capital finance. Strong representations were made, by Torrens and others, for cheaper, longer loans for housing[83] and, against strong Treasury advice,[84] the Commission recommended a rate of three and an eighth per cent. 'The State', they declared,' should lend at the lowest rate possible without loss to the national exchequer and... in making the necessary calculations, ancient losses should not be brought into account'.[85]

Salisbury's 1885 Housing Bill accordingly provided for public loans at this rate (though it made no statement about the length of loans).[86] The Treasury put its objections on record to the Local Government Board: the Act would be taken as a precedent; the big city councils and the Metropolitan Board of Works should be encouraged to go to the money market leaving public works loans for the smaller authorities; and three and an eighth could be borne only if the Treasury reneged on its commitments to find a home for savings banks deposits and put local loans on the funded debt.[87] The Board's officials took some pleasure in reminding the Treasury that the Bill was not a Government measure,[88] and the Treasury's objections did not prevail.

In general, however, the political and financial environment remained difficult for those who wished to facilitate local authority capital accumulation, particularly in pursuit of social legislation. It is a measure of the shift of political pressure by the 1880s, (as well as of the perceived financial aggression of certain towns) that whereas school boards and district sanitary authorities were allowed sixty years maximum loan periods, under the 1870 and 1875 Acts, the far more prestigious municipal corporations were allowed only thirty years under the 1882 Municipal Corporations Act.[89] Goschen and Ritchie proposed sixty years for the new County Councils in 1888, but were forced to amend this to thirty years, and to remove a clause for county councils to consolidate the loans of minor authorities in their area.[90] In 1897, however, the LGB successfully proposed to Parliament that poor law loans should be extended to sixty years,[91] in line with public health loans. But poor law authorities were relatively insignificant investors.

The main feature of the history of local debt in the 1890s is the sharp and accelerating growth of local government investment as the century came to its close. This resulted from a conjunction of several factors: it was clearly led by infrastructure development, especially roads and electric trams, and by other municipal enterprise, especially electricity generation and supply: it reflects, therefore, technological and industrial change. To a lesser extent it also reflects changing attitudes to social policy and the specialisation of social policy and educational provision. But above all, the beginning of the sharp rise in capital expenditure coincided in the mid 1890s with the availability of cheap and plentiful funds seeking relatively secure placement, manifested in the high price of Consols.[92] In consequence, the dependence of local authorities on public works loans waned and the Treasury's problems in managing public works loans, therefore, temporarily changed. The PWLC were embarrassed by the loss of revenue from new local loans, and the Treasury by an influx of money from local authorities repaying old loans early to go into the money market for better terms. Buoyant savings banks deposits also required to be placed.[93] The Treasury reduced the public works loans rate in 1897 to two and threequarters, and repealed the limit on advances to a single borrower.[94] The Cabinet was, however, too nervous of offending the 'friends of the ratepayers' to impose a suggested premium on early repayment.[95]

After 1898-9, however, the supply of funds for local loans became tighter, and borrowing became more expensive, as the Government's own demands increased and colonial securities came onto the London money market in direct competition for funds. Figures 8 and 9 in Chapter Six indicate that local authority applications for borrowing powers began to fall in 1900: we must therefore assume the peak in capital expenditure in 1902 represents a lag while projects already in the system were completed. And, as the revenue effects began to be felt in a harsher economic climate, the 'boom' in local investment at the end of the century generated much tension in the financial relations of central and local government, leading to renewed pressure for easier loans, and to new demands for capital subsidies. This pressure focussed particularly on the difficulties of urban improvements, rural housing and education.

Local authorities were first permitted to build houses by the 1890 Housing of the Working Classes Act, Part III.[96] This Act did not however authorise cheap public loans: housing loans were therefore subject to the standard Treasury rate. The length of loans was sixty years for land and forty for building, usually composited to fifty. The LCC complained continually through the 1890s about the costs of building in London, and their campaign received public endorsement by Liberal spokesmen, especially Rosebery and Asquith, in the approach to the 1900 general election.[97] After 1900, housing achieved high political salience, in Parliament and out, as a result of the activities of labour, professional, municipal and Unionist housing lobbies, and of public health lobbies who used housing to focus wide ranging grievances about urban environmental conditions.[98]

As we have seen, the AMC had been arguing since the 1870s that land purchased for public health purposes should be deemed an asset to the authority, securing a permanent loan. Now under pressure from towns with acute housing difficulties like Plymouth and Hull, the AMC began to press its case more urgently.[99] In April 1900, a conference of London boroughs called for hundred year loans for housing[100] and the London Progressives promoted a bill, which received much public attention, proposing loans at two and a half percent, and permanent loans for housing land.[101] The calculation of the Local Government Board was that longer loans would only marginally relieve the rates,[102] and its officials feared that a concession on loans could not be restricted to housing.[103] The furthest they would go was the extension of loans for Part III only to eighty years.[104] Given the general salience of local indebtedness as a political issue at the turn of the century, Chaplin preferred in 1900 to take up secondary proposals made by the LCC, to allow local authorities to take land in the suburbs, and to hold land banks. This of course was too little to satisfy either the AMC or the LCC.[105]

Under further pressure in 1902, Walter Long, who replaced Chaplin at the Board in 1900, conceded a departmental inquiry on the Repayment of Loans, in the expectation that it would recommend eighty years for housing loans.[106] This the committee duly delivered, but with the proviso that the interest of ratepayers must be protected by repayment under the instalment system.[107] This proviso, the Permanent Secretary calculated, would make loans more expensive to service in the first eighteen years than sixty year loans under the annuity system.[108] The power to sanction eighty year loans was nevertheless written into the Housing Act of 1903.[109] But the Treasury refused to amend the terms of Public Works loans to match, and refused to contemplate local authority borrowing for land banks. Its view was that the pressure of the national debt in the early 1900s and the falling price of Consols, which had already obliged the Chancellor to restrict the operations of the PWLC, should prompt the Board to discourage rather than encourage borrowing by local authorities.[110] Nevertheless, urged on by Noel Kershaw, the Assistant Secretary in charge of housing, Gerald Balfour and then John Burns continued to press the Treasury for cheaper loans and longer periods.[111]

In 1906, the Select Committee on the rural housing bill promoted by the National Housing Reform Council, recommended strongly that the Treasury's long standing practice of charging higher rates for longer loans should cease,[112] a proposal which Kershaw immediately took up with Burns.[113] The Board's pressure was renewed in 1907, when work began on Burns' great housing measure. Asquith eventually conceded that public works loans for housing should be made at the cheapest rate (then three and a quarter per cent) for sixty years. The concession was understood to be strictly limited to housing loans.[114] So far as public works loans were concerned, the Treasury had effectively reversed the 1903 concession.

The 1909 Housing and Town Planning Act nevertheless provided for a maximum of eighty years for public works loans.[115] However, demands that central government support the capital costs of housing did not die away. In 1911 and 1912, the influential Unionist Social Reform Committee on housing, chaired by Sir Arthur Boscowan, introduced a private members' bill proposing *inter alia* public works loans for housing at two and three quarters per cent, and capital subsidies worth some half million pounds a year.[116] The Local Government Board brief for Burns dismissed loans at this rate as totally impracticable, and spelt out the Board's long-standing objections to grants for housing construction, namely that housing was a specially local issue, that grants would discriminate against those authorities who had undertaken construction without subsidy, and that they would interfere with the housing and land markets.[117] And a Memorandum from the Treasury, which the officials noted had received the explicit approval of Lloyd George, castigated the proposed grant as a 'dole', a direct gift to the ground landlord, and an instrument for the pauperisation of the workman who would be charged less than the economic rent for his house.[118]

Nevertheless, Kershaw and Dickinson, the Board's new Comptroller of Housing (appointed to administer the 1909 Act), recommended Burns to readjust the Board's policy on housing subsidies. Kershaw was convinced that local authorities would only build if they had capital grants and argued that the Board badly needed positive inducements in its handling of localities, not just in relation to housing but in public health in general.[119] Dickinson was also clear that the talk of grants stirred up by the Unionists had blighted local authority construction: no authority would now build without a grant when the prospect of a subsidy had been so publicly mooted.[120] But, above all, they agreed that a negative reaction from Burns would merely play into the hands of lobbies who wished to remove the functions of the increasingly unpopular Local Government Board to other agencies.

> The risk seems to be that finding from the debate on Friday that the idea of a grant is generally popular in the House of Commons it may be adopted in some form or another as part of a scheme emanating from the Treasury in providing further social reforms, from the administration of which the Board will be as far as possible excluded, and duplicate an expensive machinery on the lines of the Road Board to do what is this Board's work and work from which a certain amount of solid credit can be derived.[121]

They were not, however, able to persuade Burns to moderate his opposition to subsidies. He ignominiously failed in 1912 to prevent a Second Reading,[122] and courted much adverse publicity for a 'very ill-advised, ill-tempered and reactionary speech'[123] in committee in June. 'The net result', commented the Observer in a press-cutting pointedly filed by the Board's officials, was 'tantamount to a vote of censure on the present administration of the Local Government Board'.[124]

The history of the housing issue suggests that officials in the sanitary division of the Board were prepared to exploit political pressure to press for financial concessions to stimulate local provision. But neither the Board or the Treasury saw even the small relaxation of terms for housing loans that ocurred in the 1900s as more than exceptional treatment for a special case. In general, the Board continued to hold rigorously to the principles of loan sanction laid down in the 1870s. This created special conflicts in education.

When education was transferred to the local education authorities in 1902, the Local Government Board reduced the period for school building loans from sixty years (the limit imposed on School Boards) to thirty years (the general limit imposed on counties and county boroughs), producing a predictable outcry from the local authority associations.[125] The Board of Education inserted a clause for sixty year loans in the 1907 Education Act[126] and in March 1909, a deputation of LEAs to the President of the Board of Education and Prime Minister was promised that the periods sanctioned for school building would be extended.[127] Nevertheless, despite strong pressure from Asquith and the Cabinet in 1908 and 1909 to redeem this pledge,[128] Burns refused to move, privately contemplating resignation if forced.[129] Although more obstinately pursued and more rigidly sustained, Burns's attitudes to loans were not out of step with his officials or with the views of previous holders of his office. Their attitudes to local borrowing arose from a number of considerations that became more, not less, salient after 1900.

There had been much discussion during the proceedings of the Select Committee of the House of Commons on the Repayment of Loans and of the Joint Committee on Municipal Trading in 1902 and 1903 about the durability and obsolescence of capital works. Noel Kershaw told the Select Committee that, given the lack of central supervision over construction and operation, the Board could not assume that all authorities were capable of extracting the maximum life from their capital works,[130] and supplied the committee with a list of projects where the loan periods had outstripped the life of the works.[131] The representative of the Board of Education was forced to admit that part of the problem of securing a modern education system was that local authorities were reluctant to invest in more suitable modern accommodation till their old loans expired.[132] Likewise, Chaplin liked to cite loans that were still being paid off on the superceded poor law 'barrack' schools in London, in response to Parliamentary pressure.[133] That is, the view was that long loans inhibited responses to changing methods and new circumstances, and this was endorsed by the 1902 Committee.[134]

But the officials of the Board also understood that there were political and financial limits to the capacity to fund the capital demanded for rising standards. Their view at the turn of the century was that the marked increase in local debt reflected not temporary economic circumstances but an inexorable process of local capital accumulation, largely independent of central policy but fed by technological development and changing aspirations.[135] At the least it demonstrated that there was no administrative barrier to local investment, or any reason to suppose that it could not be sustained. The role of the central authority was, therefore, to regulate borrowing in the interests of lenders and the money markets, and to ensure that the burden of inherited debt did not overwhelm future generations. The duty of the Board to act as a 'trustee for posterity' became a favourite maxim of politicians.[136]

At the beginning of the twentieth century, then, the Local Government Board and the Treasury became convinced that the problem of local capital accumulation was not a failure of local demand for funds, but rather one of supply. And this was reinforced by experience in the early 1900s. The depressed price of Consols, the higher interest rates of the 1900s, and, in 1904-5, difficulties in finding a response to the local stock issue,[137] convinced successive Chancellors of the fragile capacity of the money market to support the borrowing needs of the state, and stern warnings about the impact both of independent trading by local authorities and of demands on the PWLC became a ritual part of annual Budget statements. In 1904, the Treasury increased the PWLC rate[138] and the Chancellor warned the House that public works loans would be restricted to small authorities only. 'It is not tolerable', he said 'that after they have spoiled the money markets by their own large demands, [local authorities] should be in a position to force the state into the money markets so spoiled'.[139] In 1905, therefore, the

PWL Bill provided for a vote to cover urgent demands only, to obviate the need to go into the market.'[140] If we have to come into the Market with large issues of Local Loans Stock', Asquith warned Burns privately in 1907, 'the terms on which we can borrow (and, as a result the terms on which we can lend also) are bound to suffer, to say nothing of our credit'.[141]

The tighter financial environment of the 1900s points up sharply the essential contradiction in the Local Government Board's roles. On the one hand, officials with sponsoring responsibilities for particular areas of policy – especially housing – bemoaned the meanness and lack of energy of local authorities in providing for the needs of their localities. But the Board was also conscious that it mediated their demands on ratepayers and moneymarkets, and stood sponsor for the financial reputation of local government. And there is a contrast here with departments with unambiguous service interests. 'The Board of Education', Walter Long told an AMC deputation pressing for longer education loans, 'had no regard to local indebtedness, economy or considerations of that character, their only desire being to promote the building of schools'.[142]

Hence, we can see the Local Government Board as a 'Treasury' for local government, moderating spending demands generated by central bureaucrats with service orientations in the interest of the wider conspectus of local finance. Indeed, the desirability of maintaining a single department with powers to regulate local spending, especially loan sanction powers and the district audit, became, after 1911, a major argument deployed by the Board against the exclusion of general local government matters from the projected Ministry of Health. The acceptance of this argument meant that the Ministry of Health established in 1919 inevitably turned out to be a new local government ministry.

If the Local Government occupied conflicting roles, then the question is in whose interests those roles were performed. The Local Government Board served (and mediated between) a number of interests, which its controls were developed to protect; namely the individuals possessing statutory rights under the growing volume of legislation; the ratepayers and property holders whose purses and property were disturbed by the emerging administrative state; and the national Exchequer. Their interests were recognised by an extensive system of quasi-judicial powers exercised by the Board as the central administrative authority. At the same time, many central officials nurtured a paternalistic ambition to teach the localities to share the ethos and practices of their own more developed administrative systems. It is the tensions between legalism and tutelage, worked out within the financial and ideological constraints of the late nineteenth century system of central-local relations, that explains the style and organisation of the Local Government Board, which we will explore in the next Part.

NOTES TO CHAPTER THREE

1 The Poor Law Amendment Act of 1834 (4 & 5 Wm IV c. 76 s. 124) required Boards of Guardians to repay by equal instalments of capital, plus interest (the instalment system), over not more than ten years. The 1848 Public Health Act (11 and 12 Vict. c. 63 s. 107) allowed local authorities to repay by the instalment system; by equal sums of capital and interest together (the annuity system), over not more than thirty years; or to establish a sinking fund for repayment in the same period. The 1869 Poor Law Amendment Act (32 & 33 Vict c. 45 s. 5) allowed Poor Law authorities to adopt the annuity system.

2 Treasury to LGB, 24 February 1887 and LGB to Treasury, 20 April 1887, PRO MH 19/217

3 33 & 34 Vict. c. 75 s. 57; 38 & 39 Vict. c. 55 s. 233.

4 The maximum period for poor law loans was extended to thirty years under s. 5 of the 1869 Act. The 1882 Municipal Corporations Act (45 & 46 Vict c. 50 ss. 112 and 113) provided for thirty years. Likewise the 1888 Local Government Act, 51 & 52 Vict. c. 41 s. 69(5).

5 *First Report of the Royal Sanitary Commission,* 1869 (C. 4218) XXXII 469. Evidence of William Willink, Secretary to the PWLC, Qs 1681-3; Joseph Heron 2379-2384; C. W. Johnson 2957-2960; R Johnson, 3185-92; H Davy 3049-51; W. Winkley 3789-3790; J. Ponsonby 3962-7; T. J. Dyke 6361; *Second Report of the Royal Sanitary Commission,* 1871 (C. 281-II) XXXV 555, III, evidence of Robinson Latter, Qs. 11384-7; *Special Report from the Select Committee of the House of Commons on the Public Works Amendment Acts Amendment Bill,* 1875 (358) XIV I, evidence of J. Lambert, Q 672, 718.

6 This practice accounts for a significant number of surcharges imposed by the District Audit on the accounts of local authorities; *Selections from the Correspondence of the Local Government Board,* I-IX, 1877-1912, PRO HLG 46/127-135, *passim.* The persistence of the practice in many towns

was made possible by the fact that most municipal corporations did not come under the District Audit. *Report of the Select Committe of the House of Commons on the Repayment of Local Authority Loans,* 1902 (239) viii I para. 13.

7 57 Geo III c. 34. This Act required repayment by instalments. An outline history of the Public Works Loan Board is in *Ninety-Third Annual Report of the PWLB,* 1967-8, 1969 SBN 10 222768.3, Appendix D.

8 11 & 12 Vict. c. 63 s. 113; 33 & 34 Vict. c. 75 s. 57. The separate funds were consolidated in 1874, *Report of Select Committee on Public Works Loans,* 1875, evidence of Willink, Q. 153.

9 16 & 17 Vict. c. 40 s. 1.

10 The higher burden of repayments in the early years of the instalment system was assumed to imply a more responsible attitude to the loan by the borrowers. *First Report of Royal Sanitary Commission,* evidence of Willink, Q. 1596. *Report of Select Committee on Public Works Loans,* 1875, evidence of Lambert, Q. 745.

11 16 & 17 Vict. c. 40 s. 3.

12 Treasury minute 26 October 1859, quoted in Treasury to LGB PRO MH 19/209.

13 *Second Report of Royal Sanitary Commission,* 1871, I, pp. 68-70.

14 Harbours and Passing Tolls Act, 1861, 24 & 25 Vict. c. 47 s. 3(2); Public Works (Manufacturing Districts) Act, 1863, 26 & 27 Vict. c. 70 s. 3(5); Contagious Diseases (Animals) Act, 1866, 29 and 30 Vict. c 110 s. 4(2).

15 35 & 36 Vict. c. 70. s. 44.

16 Gladstone to Lowe, 4 July 1873, Gladstone Papers, Add. Mss. 44302.

17 213 H. C. Deb. 3s. 1 August 1872, col. 277.

18 *Report of Select Committee on Public Works Loans,* 1875, evidence of J. G. Hubbard, Q. 388.

19 *Ibid.,* Q. 423.

20 e.g. Fawcett's questioning of Lambert before the 1875 Select Committee, *ibid.,* Qs 712-714.

21 LGB to Treasury, 20 September 1872, PRO MH 19/190.

22 Treasury to LGB, 6 November 1872, ibid.

23 Treasury to LGB, 11 January 1873, PRO MH 19/208.

24 LGB to Treasury, 11 March 1873, *ibid.*

25 *Ibid.,* and *Instructions to Engineering Inspectors,* 26 March 1873, *ibid.*

26 Lambert to Stansfeld, 24 January 1873, *ibid.*

27 *Report of Select Committee on Public Works Loans,* 1875, evidence of Lambert, Q. 712.

28 Treasury to LGB, 30 June 1874, PRO MH 19/209.

29 Enclosure, *ibid.*

30 LGB to Treasury, 28 August 1874, *ibid.*

31 LGB to Treasury, 11 July 1874, *ibid.*; LGB to Treasury, 28 August 1874, *ibid.*

32 Treasury to LGB, 5 December 1874, *ibid.*
33 '... it is scarcely satisfactory for a body wholly irresponsible like the Public Works Loan Commissioners to put whatever construction they do on an Act of Parliament without a power of appeal', *Report of Select Committee on Public Works Loans,* 1875, Q. 407.
34 LGB to Treasury, 18 December 1874, PRO MH 19/209.
35 218 H. C. Deb. 3s. 5 May 1874 col. 1674.
36 Treasury to LGB, 27 January 1875, PRO MH 19/210.
37 222 H. C. Deb. 3s. 11 February 1875 col. 217; *Report of Select Committee on Public Works Loans,* 1875, evidence of Willink.
38 222 H. C. Deb. 3s. 9 March 1875 col. 1486.
39 *Report of Select Committee on Public Works Loans,* 1875, evidence of Lambert, Q. 701; LGB to Treasury, 5 February 1875, PRO MH 19/210.
40 222 H. C. Deb. 3s. 11 February 1875 col. 217.
41 38 & 39 Vict. c. 89.
42 38 & 29 Vict. c. 83.
43 *The Times,* 19 June 1875, p. 6.
44 e.g. speeches of Fawcett, Rathbone and Hubbard, 225 H. C. Deb. 3s. 4 July 1876 cols. 960-973; speeches of Rathbone and Sewell Read. 233 H. C. Deb. 3s. 23 April 1877 cols. 1724-1731; speeches of Sewell Read, Paget and Hankey, 239 H. C. Deb. 3s. 4 April 1878 cols. 609-619 and 12 April 1878 col. 1252.
45 Correspondence of LGB with Treasury, January 1878, PRO MH 19/212; *Memorandum on Defective Provisions in the Public Health Act, 1875, Relative to Loans and their Repayment,* 1881, PRO MH 19/91 and *Memorandum on Proposed Amendments in the General Law,* March 1882, PRO MH 19/92.
46 Public Works Loans Act, 1881, 44 & 45 Vict. c. 38 s. 8.
47 Public Works Loans Act, 1882, 45 & 46 Vict. c. 62 s. 8.
48 Local Loans Act 1875 Amendment Act 1885, 48 & 49 Vict. c. 30.
49 Cornelius Dalton, *Memorandum on Defects in the Local Loans Act, 1875,* undated, and *Memorandum on Proposed Amendments in the Law by means of which Local Authorities might Obtain their Loans on Better Terms than they can at Present in the Open Market,* revised March 1881, PRO MH 25/33.
50 *Ibid.*
51 32 & 33 Vict. c. 102.
52 *Memorandum on Proposed Amendments; Draft of a Bill to Facilitate Raising of Local Loans by Issue of Stock,* 1882, Monk Bretton Papers, Box 55; *Memorandum Prepared for the President on Private Bill Legislation,* n.d. (probably 1881) *Ibid.,* Box 51.
53 *First Report of Royal Commission on Housing of Working Classes,* 1885, I pp. 37-40.
54 51 & 52 Vict. c. 41. ss. 69 and 70.
55 Biddell to Dalton, Autumn 1890, PRO MH 19/167.

56 53 & 54 Vict. c. 59, Part V.

57 Internal LGB papers, Winter 1890 to Spring 1891, in PRO MH 19/167.

58 Arthur Carson Roberts, *Local Finance and Administration*, Harrison & Sons, 1930, p. 135.

59 239 H. C. Deb. 3s. 4 April 1878 col. 601. *The Times*, 6 April 1878, p. 9.

60 223 H. C. Deb. 3s. 23 April 1877, col. 1726; *The Times*, 25 April 1877, p. 10.

61 Speech of Sir Stafford Northcote at Birmingham, *The Times*, 22 October 1878, p. 4; 223 H. C. Deb. 3s. 23 April 1877 col. 1717; 239 H. C. Deb. 3s. 4 April 1878 col. 547; *First Report of Royal Commission on Working Class Housing*, 1885, evidence of E. R. Spearman, Q. 11185. The Birmingham loan was paid off in 1880.

62 261 H. C. Deb. 3s. 23 May 1881 col. 1084; 278 H. C. Deb. 3s. 17 April 1883 col. 238.

63 Agatha Ram (ed.), *The Political Correspondence of Mr Gladstone and Lord Granville, 1876-1886*, Oxford, Clarendon Press, 1962, II, pp. 400-1.

64 Treasury Minute, *The Establishment of a Local Loans Budget*, 23 May 1887, 1887 (166) XLIX, 289, para. 8.

65 Until 1874, the figures presented to Parliament in the annual estimates of expenditure and revenue were based on the previous year's figures: any surplus that resulted was put to paying off the national debt. From 1874, the figures were based on estimates of predicted outcome: this meant that a decision had to be made annually about the sum to be devoted to redeeming debt. In 1875, Northcote announced a New Sinking Fund to which twenty eight million pounds a year would be routinely dedicated. Rather than interrupt this arrangement, he created in 1877 a new class of Bill, the Treasury Bill, to provide for greater flexibility in short term borrowing, to finance the deficits of the late 1870s.

66 Treasury Minute, *Local Loans Budget*, para. 9.

67 Treasury to LGB, 14 February 1879, PRO MH 19/213.

68 Artizans and Labourers Dwellings Act, 1875, 38 & 39 Vict. c. 36 s. 22.

69 249 H. C. Deb. 3s. 4 Aug 1879 col. 64.

70 *Ibid.*, 9 August 1879 col 601; *ibid.*, 11 August 1879 col 743.

71 Treasury Minute, 16 August 1879, PRO MH 19/213. The tariff set by this Minute was:

For 3½% max. 20 years
3¾% max. 30 years
4% max. 40 years
4¼% max. 50 years

On 15 May 1885, the tariff was eased:

For 3½% max. 35 years
3¾% max. 40 years
4% max. 50 years

(From *Statement of Rates of Interest Permitted by the Treasury*, with

Memorandum by N. Kershaw, 18 July 1907, PRO HLG 29/1908-9, Papers on Housing and Town Planning Bill.)
The calculations behind these tariffs are discussed in *First Report of Royal Commission on Working Class Housing,* II, evidence of Sir Reginald Welby, Q. 11384.

72 Lambert to Sclater Booth, filed with Treasury Minute, 16 August 1879.

73 Treasury Minute, *Local Loans Budget,* para 9.

74 *Ibid.*

75 313 H. C. Deb. 3s. 21 April 1887 col. 1444.

76 Treasury Minute, *Local Loans Budget,* para 5.

77 *Ibid., passim,* and *First Report of Royal Commission on Working Class Housing,* II, evidence of Welby, Q. 11376.

78 Treasury Minute, *Local Loans Budget,* para. 4.

79 313 H. C. Deb. 3s. 21 April 1887 col 1418.

80 National Debt and Local Loans Stock Act, 1887, 50 & 51 Vict. c. 16.

81 Treasury Minute, *Local Loans Budget,* para 29.

82 *First Report of Royal Commission on Working Class Housing,* I, p. 41.

83 *Report of the Royal Commission on Working Class Housing,* I, p. 33.

84 *First Report of the Royal Commission on Working Class Housing,* II, evidence of Welby.

85 *Ibid.* I. p. 40.

86 48 & 49 Vict, c. 72 s. 6.

87 Treasury to LGB, 15 July 1885, PRO MH 19/216.

88 LGB to Treasury, 23 July 1885, *ibid.*

89 45 & 46 Vict. c. 50 s. 112 and 113; 51 & 52 Vict. c. 41 s. 69(5).

90 328 H. C. Deb. 17 July 1888 col. 1533.

91 Poor Law Act 1897, 60 & 61 Vict. c. 29 s. 1.

92 The price of Consols rose from 93.3/4 in 1890 to a high of 114 in 1896. It began to fall in mid 1898. The Treasury's perception of the changing money market in these years is in *The Price of Consols,* by J. Bradbury, Lloyd George Papers, 14 July 1910, HLRO c/14/1.

93 *Local Loans Fund,* Memorandum to Cabinet by E. W. Hamilton, 2 October 1895, PRO CAB/40.46 and *Local Loans Fund,* Memorandum to Cabinet by E. W. Hamilton, 17 March 1896, PRO CAB/41.17.

94 Public Works Loans Act, 1897, 60 & 61 Vict. c. 51; 56 H. C. Deb. 4s. 21 April 1898 col. 679.

95 Hicks Beach to Balfour, 31 October 1895, Balfour Papers, Add. Mss. 49695.

96 53 & 54 Vict. c. 70 ss. 65-67.

97 *The Times,* 14 November 1899, p. 4; *ibid.* 15 November 1899, p. 13. The LGB papers in response to this pressure are in PRO HLG 29/66. This file also contains cuttings and summaries of the coverage in the London, national and local government press, and a summary of representations received.

98 The major pressure groups were the Workmen's National Housing Council, dating from 1898, representing trades union, trades council and Labour Party affiliates. Lansbury, Bentinck and McKinnon-Wood were prominent Parliamentary spokesmen: and the National Housing Reform Council, formed in the early 1900s as an umbrella organisation, sponsoring and developing the voluntary, professional and municipal housing movements.

99 *Annual Report of AMC Council for 1899-1900,* PRO 30/72.29; Minutes of Annual Meeting of AMC, 31 March 1900, *ibid; Report of Law Committee of AMC on Housing of Working Classes Bill, 1900,* Minutes of AMC Council Meeting, 31 January 1901, PRO 30/72.30.

100 93 H. C. Deb. 4s. 7 May 1901 col. 948.

101 *Report on Housing of the Working Classes Bill,* 1900, PRO HLG 29/66.

102 Provis to Chaplin, 17 February 1900, *ibid.* The response of the LCC is in LCC to LGB, 1 May 1900, *ibid.*

103 LGB to Treasury, 16 February 1900, *ibid.*

104 *Ibid.*

105 Report of deputation of members of LCC to President of LGB and Chancellor of the Exchequer, 15 June 1900, *ibid.*

106 *Statement to Deputation of AMC,* 29 November 1901, PRO HLG 29/80. Also in Minutes of Council meeting of AMC, 28 November 1901, PRO 30/72.31: 101. H. C. Deb. 4s. 17 January 1902 col. 227.

107 *Report of the Select Committee on the Repayment of Loans,* para. 68.

108 Provis to Long, April 1903, PRO HLG 29/83.

109 3 Edw VII c. 39 s. 1.

110 Treasury to LGB attached to Provis to Long, 28 July 1903, *ibid.*

111 *Memorandum on Presentation of Estimates 1905-6,* Gerald Balfour Papers, PRO 30/60.55; LGB to Treasury, 10 May 1906, and associated papers, PRO HLG 29/96.

112 *Special Report of Select Committee on Housing of the Working Classes Acts Amendment Bill, 1906,* 1906 (376) iv I, Pt. IV.

113 *Report on the Report of the Select Committee,* 18 January 1907, PRO HLG 29/96.

114 Asquith to Burns, 28 February 1907, *ibid.*

115 9 Edw VII c. 44 s. 3.

116 1911-12 (385) II 639; 1912-13 (4) II 759.

117 *Memorandum on the Housing of the Working Classes Bill, 1911,* by Baines, n.d. and accompanying Memorandum by Kershaw, 15 December 1911, PRO HLG 29/106.

118 Memorandum from Treasury, 17 April 1913, *ibid.*

119 *Memorandum on Grants in Aid,* n.d. Spring 1912, *ibid.*

120 Memorandum on the Housing of the Working Classes Bill, 1912, Spring 1912, *ibid.*

121 *Memorandum on Exchequer Grants,* by N. Kershaw, 12 March 1912, *ibid.*

122 35 H.C. Deb. 5s. 15 March 1912 col. 1482.

123 *Morning Post,* 7 May 1912, from cutting in LGB file, *ibid.*

124 *The Observer,* 17 March 1912, *ibid.*

125 Minutes of Council of AMC, 30 April 1903. PRO 30/72.33; Minutes of Autumn Meeting of AMC, 21 October 1903, *ibid;* Report of Deputation to LGB, 4 February 1904, PRO 30/72.34; Minutes of Autumn Meeting of AMC, 19 October 1904, *ibid.;* Memorial to LGB on repayment of loans, filed in Minutes of Council meeting, 23 November 1905, PRO 30/72.35; Minutes of Annual Meeting of AMC, 15 May 1906, PRO 30/72.36; Report of Deputation to Chancellor of the Exchequer and President of the Board of Education, 15 March 1907, filed in Minutes of Council meeting, 21 March 1907, PRO 30/72.37; Report of Deputation of LEAs to Prime Minister, 18 March 1909, in Minutes of AMC Council, 26 May 1910, PRO 30/72.40. *Annual Report of Executive Council of CCA for 1904-5; Annual Report of Executive Council of CCA for 1905-6.*

126 7 Edw VII c. 43 s. 3.

127 *Annual Report of EC of CCA for 1908-9.*

128 Asquith to Burns, 20 June 1910, Burns Papers, Add. Mss. 46282; Burns, Diary, 10 March 1908, Burns Papers, Add. Mss. 46326; also entries for 1 Jan 1909, Add. Mss. 46327; 26 March 1909 *ibid.*; 30 March 1909, *ibid.*; 31 March 1909, *ibid.*; 28 April 1909, *ibid.*

129 Burns, *Diary,* 9 May 1909, *ibid.*

130 *Report of the Select Committee on the Repayment of Loans,* evidence, Qs 17-18.

131 *Ibid.,* Appendix 29.

132 *Ibid.,* evidence, Qs 458-60.

133 82 H. C. Deb. 4s. 10 May 1900. col. 1333.

134 *Report of Select Committee on Repayment of Loans,* para. 42.

135 *Ibid.,* evidence of Noel Kershaw.

136 e.g. 65 H. C. Deb. 4s. 8 August 1898 col. 575; 187 H. C. Deb. 4s. 2 June 1899 col. 229; 97 H. C. Deb. 16 July 1901 col. 646.

137 *The Financial Outlook of 1904-5,* Memorandum to Cabinet from E. W. Hamilton, 11 February 1904, PRO CAB 37/68.

138 On 7 August 1897, the rate for thirty year loans was reduced to two and threequarters per cent, the lowest permitted under the 1897 Public Works Loans Act. On 2 November 1899, thirty year loans were raised to three per cent, and again to three and a quarter on 18 June 1900. Thirty year loans were raised to three and three quarters per cent on 3 March 1904, three and a quarter per cent being allowed only for twenty year loans.

139 133 H. C. Deb. 4s. 19 April 1904 col. 536.

140 151 H. C. Deb. 4s. 4 August 1905 col. 306, and 8 August 1905 col. 379

141 Asquith to Burns, 28 February 1907, PRO HLG 29/96.

142 LGB Notes of statement of President to deputation from AMC on education loans, Gerald Balfour Papers, 1905, PRO 30/60.53.

Part Two

The organisation and techniques of the Central Authority under local possessive pluralism

Chapter Four
The Local Government Board: organisation and culture

There is no modern, comprehensive academic study of the Local Government Board. Nevertheless, it has a decided reputation amongst students of the history of social and public administration, who have perceived the Board to have acted as a repressive and retarding influence on the development of social policy. This part explains its reputation in this respect, in that it argues that the style and organisation of the Board was the product of an explicit strategy for central-local relations which was publicly explored by the Royal Sanitary Commission in the late 1860s and endorsed at the highest levels within Government in the Board's formative years. This strategy was evolved for the conduct of internal diplomatic relations by a central authority which was significantly constrained both by the conventions of local possessive pluralism and by the unresolved tensions generated by the fiscal problems of the emerging administrative state, and which was obliged to operate without a coherent national structure of financial support for local government. That is, the Local Government Board had few positive financial inducements to offer the localities and operated in a climate in which neither the political will or the local capacity to fund the local services of the state could be assumed.

The deference accorded to local fiscal and property interests encouraged and legitimised a marked diffidence in the centre's handling of local authorities, expressed as a constitutional notion of local self-government. It also determined the nature of the central controls that were developed. For while the Local Government Board became chronically overladen by a massive volume of work, its business was primarily directed to enforcing local financial discipline and stewardship, and to mediating the tensions between collective action and private property rights. The culture of the

Board, therefore, reflected the values appropriate to an essentially quasi-judicial and bureaucratic business, heavily tempered by a pragmatism derived from its political constraints.

The immediate stimulus for the establishment of the Royal Sanitary Commission was pressure in the mid 1860s from the British Medical Association and Social Science Association. Representations of the SSA to the Privy Council in 1866 called for a comprehensive system of sanitary authorities, large enough to employ whole time qualified officers, with peremptory powers to enforce the public health laws. The local authorities were to be directed by a strong central authority with full powers to coerce defaulting localities.[1] These views were developed in memorials and resolutions drawn up in 1867 and 1868 by a Joint Committee of the BMA and the SSA.[2] By 1869, the BMA and SSA Health Department were referring with some confidence to a central Ministry for the 'supervision and regulation of the public health'.[3] However, the precise nature and organisation of the central authority was not an issue to which the Joint Committee gave much detailed attention.

Before 1871, the local powers of the state in relation to health were administered by a variety of local authorities, supervised by three distinct central authorities. Under the Public Health and Local Government Acts of 1848, 1858, 1861 and 1863,[4] Local Boards of Health (usually town councils or local Improvement Commissions established under private acts) exercised, in urban areas only, powers relating to water supply, sewerage, drainage, cleansing, food and housing. The central authority was, until 1858, the General Board of Health and thereafter the Local Government Act Office of the Home Office. The Sewage Utilisation Acts of 1865 and 1867, together with the Sanitary Acts of 1866 and 1868,[5] imposed on parish vestries in rural areas the duties of supplying water to and sewering rural places, and extended to rural places powers given to urban places in 1848 and 1858 to take lands and to borrow money. The administration of these powers was also supervised by the LGAO.

In 1855, the General Board of Health was authorised to appoint a Medical Officer,[6] and he was transferred to the Privy Council when the General Board was abolished in 1858.[7] It was his Department of the Privy Council which supervised local nuisance authorities (along with other medical functions, including the regulation of the medical profession). The Nuisances Removal Act of 1855[8] imposed a duty on nuisance authorities to appoint sanitary inspectors and to compel the removal of nuisances. The nuisance authority was the Local Board; where there was no Board it was the town council or the Improvement Commission. In rural areas the nuisance authority was the Highways Board, or, in places without Highway Boards, a committee of the parish vestry or the Guardians of the Poor. Medical relief for the pauper sick and public vaccinations were administered by local poor law authorities, under the supervision of the Poor Law Board.

Of the three central authorities, the Poor Law Board was the only independent ministerial department. It was also the only department with a locally resident district inspectorate. The Poor Law Inspectors conducted systematic, routine inspection of poor law institutions; by contrast, the medical inspectors of the Medical Department and the engineering inspectors of the LGAO acted primarily as technical advisers to their departments. They were based in London and, except for the routine inspection of vaccinations by medical inspectors under the 1867 Vaccination Act,[9] visited localities on an ad hoc basis only; the medical inspectors conducted local investigations into epidemics under the Diseases Prevention Acts; the engineering inspectors conducted local public inquiries under the Local Government Act and Sanitary Acts (mainly for purposes of loan sanction and boundary readjustments).

The BMA and the SSA inferred from the very nomination of the Royal Sanitary Commission that the case for the consolidation of the central authority had been accepted, and that the new authority would be in effect a Health Department, dominated by medical professionals working under John Simon, the Medical Officer to the Privy Council. Simon made no secret of his own aspirations, and was working to expand his empire independently of the proposed Commission. 'I do not think', he wrote to the Privy Council in June 1868

> there would be any advantage in referring to such a Commission any questions as to central sanitary consolidation. The Ministers of the

> Departments concerned will, I presume, settle that matter. The main
> question apparently will be as to giving the holder of my office a much
> increased sphere of action.[10]

On the basis of his recent experience in government, Simon had
every reason to suppose that he would be able to persuade Ministers to deliver a Health Ministry. Lambert has described Simon's
considerable success in the 1860s in mobilising political support
to build up the Medical Department.[11] And in 1869, he persuaded
Home Secretary Bruce to approve a 'Concordat' to assimilate the
operations of the Medical Department and LGAO.[12] This envisaged
that the medical inspectors would become the authoritative chan-
nel of communication with the local authorities on health matters,
with the engineers of the LGAO becoming, in effect, their tech-
nicians. By 1870, Simon was confidently pressing for an increase
in his salary on the grounds that

> the arrangement makes me Medical Officer of a second sanitary depart-
> ment, and establishes by anticipation in work though not in pay, one
> of those extensions of my office which consolidators propose to enact
> ... regularly and irregularly, my office has been undergoing conversion
> into that of a Superintendent-General of Health.[13]

In their evidence to the Commission, both Simon and Tom Taylor,
the Secretary to the LGAO, chose to assume that the Commission
would endorse the merger of the LGAO and Medical Department.[14]
Simon's main preoccupation was to achieve the Commission's recognition of his *de facto* role as the Home Office's Medical Officer,
and a guarantee of direct access to Ministers in the new Department. However, although several local Medical Officers of Health
and sanitary reformers emphasised the necessity for a consolidated
central authority, only Dr Rumsey, a leading figure in the BMA/SSA
Joint Committee, argued explicitly for a Ministry of Health.[15]
Perhaps more damagingly to Simon's position, only one local wit-
ness categorically stated that the Poor Law Board would be unacceptable as a central authority for public health.[16]

As the Commission took its evidence, however, it became clear
that a merger with the Poor Law Board could hardly be avoided,
for in the poor law medical service and the vaccination administration, the PLB supervised the only comprehensive local health

machinery. For every sanitary reformer or MOH who asserted the professional basis of state medicine, there was a local guardian arguing for the exploitation of the medical services of the poor law in the fight against squalor and disease. Simon himself emphasised how closely his Department worked with the Poor Law Board: although he presumably wished to establish that they functioned adequately as contingent departments, the representatives of the PLB on the Commission were not slow to point to the alternative conclusion. Arthur Helps, the Secretary to the Privy Council, sealed the fate of Simon's health ministry by raising problems about the veterinary services of the Medical Department.[17] Clearly, they were inappropriate for a Health Department, but could not be left free standing in the Privy Council. And so it was agreed to transfer only the local government functions of the Council's Medical Department to a local government department, to include the supervision of the poor law.

If Simon failed to establish the case for a central health authority, it cannot be said that he failed to elucidate a clear strategy of central-local relations. Simon shared many of the assumptions of the Millite model of central-local relations. Action and discretion, he held, belonged to the locality. But he asserted less equivocally than Mill that the primary national importance of public health justified the coercion of the locality by the centre. His scientific mind taught him, however, that coercion could be legitimised only by demonstrable need and default: where this was not established, the centre had no authority to influence the locality.

> Rather indeed, in the present divided state of opinion on the subject, Government ought primarily to endeavour that responsibility for choice of means should rest, as unreservedly as possible, upon the shoulders of the Local Authority. Let each authority get for itself what skilled advice it thinks best ... and let it within its legal rights act accordingly. Government in its coercive relations has not to insist on anything but results.[18]

Insisting on results, however, requires standards by which outcome can be measured. What Simon proposed was systematic, comprehensive, comparative enquiry into local conditions to produce the statistical information to elucidate the connection between disease and its causes. The central health authority was therefore to be placed at the apex of a system of local MHOs and in a reporting relationship with the registration authorities, so that standards could be authoritatively established. In contrast he believed that the General Board of Health and Local Government Act Office had relied on a commonsense empiricism, which had come across to the local authorities as confused and arbitrary and had damaged the cause of public health, both scientifically and politically.[19] The authority of the centre should now be placed on the sure ground of demonstrable, scientific principle.

Simon therefore argued that coercive powers against default-ing authorities should be set in motion only on the advice of pro-fessional officers of the central authority. He envisaged a Medical Officer with direct access to the Minister, supported by trained medical inspectors and by regular reports from a network of quali-fied local MOHs. That is, he looked to a formal, impersonal relation-ship between centre and locality, founded on the authority of scientific laws and mediated by experts. What he overlooked was that this scheme would completely by-pass the elected members of local authorities. Against Simon, officers from the PLB and the LGAO argued for relations with local authorities to be based on the exploitation of personal influence and empirical demonstra-tion, reinforced by patterns of social deference and authority. Arnold Taylor, the Engineering Inspector, argued, for example, that legal qualifications were an acceptable alternative to engineering qualifications for the engineering inspectorate, but above all the inspector must be a gentleman.[20] Robert Weale, a long-standing Poor Law Inspector, argued that technical qualifications were irrelevant: a central inspector could not hope to carry out local sanitary inspection in the way a Poor Law Inspector could visit a workhouse, because nuisances were so scattered. A local authority would be obliged to employ its own professional experts. Therefore, the central inspector need not be an expert, but he should be able to judge the quality of officers and to gain influence over an author-ity.[21] Both Poor Law and Engineering Inspectors produced much anecdotal evidence to confirm that personal influence together with judicious use of example and statistics, rather than technical expertise or coercive central powers, secured local compliance. Here, for example, is Robert Rawlinson's account of his experience as an Engineering Inspector on the public works programme in the Lancashire cotton famine:

> ... it was only by conciliatory conversation and persuasions that we got the Local Authorities started, and then principally by referring them to places that had been some time under the operation of the Local Government Act ... and after the favourable replies from these and some other places, we induced them to proceed ... My whole life's experience goes to this, that you cannot compel unwilling men ... you cannot put intelligence into an unwilling community.[22]

We can see in the Commission's evidence, therefore, a direct clash between a political-diplomatic approach to central-local relations, adopted by the officers of the Poor Law Board and the LGAO, and a technical-bureaucratic approach, prescribed by Simon and the professional lobbies.

By the former I refer to a strategy directed by general guidelines which are not so much task objectives as parameters for the long term exploitation of influence and for the conduct of negotiations. Within those guidelines, agents seek movement rather than achievement, an acceptable outcome rather than the technically correct solution. Their aim is to minimise error and avoid the breakdown of relations, rather than to maximise performance. A political-diplomatic approach is, therefore, characterised by flexibility, discretion and influence. In contrast, a technical bureaucracy seeks consistency and clarity: it works by explicit rules determined by technical requirements: it depends on formal procedures rather than informal negotiation, and is results oriented rather than relationship oriented. Paradoxically, it postulates a centre which is both more authoritarian and more liberal than that envisaged by the diplomatic model: it insists on the undisputed authority of scientific principle, but subjects the locality to more limited and predictable controls.

It is on this last ground that Simon subsequently argued that his approach was the more compatible with English constitutional doctrines of local government:

> It is not in the English theory of local government that local authorities, even of the weakest sort, shall permanently have to be pinafored by central *bonnes:* and the authority which is not confessedly in the nursery-stage, is understood to be in active duty. If in this stage, central

assistance is needed (as no doubt it very largely is) the need almost invariably is technical; and also ... it is almost universally from a technical basis that supervision of the discharge of duty has to be exercised.[23]

The blueprint for the Local Government Board was put to the Royal Sanitary Commission in a special memorandum prepared in October 1870,[24] and it is this document, rather than the Report itself, which seems the clearest pointer to the organisation of the new central authority. The memorandum envisaged a single ministry, organised into six specialist departments, with a single district inspectorate based on the Poor Law Inspectorate. The specialists – engineers, lawyers and doctors, together with occasionally appointed technical consultants – were to be on tap rather than in the direct line of communciation with the local authorities. The major benefit which this scheme was said to possess was economy: it would enable the new department to be formed with very few extra staff. (It should be said that Weale and the President of the Poor Law Board, the Earl of Devon, explicitly refuted this statement in their evidence.)[25] The merger would concentrate all sanitary information in one place, and make available the skills and expertise of the officers of the several departments for the full range of public health functions.

The Final Report of the Royal Sanitary Commission was published in 1871, and is a masterpiece of ambiguity, allowing the competing factions to read into it their own versions of the new central authority. The Report finds 'irresistible' the case for the consolidation of the central sanitary authority with the central poor law authority, and looks to 'an united superintendence and single responsibility'.[26] But it recommends the establishment of two sub-departments under one Minister, one for the poor law and one for health. Moreover, though '... efficiency demands their final reference to one chief Minister, his title should clearly signify that his charge is of two distinct, though correlative departments'.[27] That is, the Report appears to recommend a federal arrangement, under one politically responsible Minister. John Simon subsequently asserted that the 'Sanitary Department' of the Local Government Board was intended to be placed under a Medical Officer directly responsible to the Minister,[28] but John Lambert, the LGB's first Secretary who was a member of the Commission, consistently stated that the integration of the staff of both departments under a single Secretariat was understood to be the necesary corollary of a single Ministerial head.[29]

The Report is clearer about the organisation of the department's field officers, and recommends unambiguously the establishment of a 'general body of central inspectorate'. 'We deprecate', the Commissioners wrote, 'the maintenance of parallel inspectorates of sanitary and poor law administration under the same chief Minister, not only on the grounds of waste of powers but still more of probable conflict'.[30] But even here, Simon was given some ground on which to assert that the Commission had endorsed his views. There is a recognition that for 'specific' purposes, 'a variety of officers will be requisite', and the Report concludes rather lamely, 'Experience alone can determine how far the same inspector can act for sanitary and poor law purpose'.[31] Discussing the special inspectors, however, the Report envisages '... some with medical knowledge who would be the agents of the chief Medical Officer in the central department and bring him into relationship with the four thousand medical officers already attached to the local authorities in the kingdom'.[32]

The Local Government Board Act of 1871[33] left formally open the nature of the Department, but it is clear that Gladstone, his Chancellor, Robert Lowe, and the new LGB President, James Stansfeld, had already agreed, on general grounds of efficiency, economy and good discipline, that the new Board was to be a unitary rather than a federal department, working to a unified Secretariat whose members alone of the Board's officers would be authorised to sign its Orders.[34] The Medical Officer was clearly destined, therefore, to work to the Secretaries rather than direct to the Minister. The Act specified that there were to be sanitary inspectors with the same powers of inquiry as the Poor Law Inspectors: it was left open whether Poor Law Inspectors could be appointed to these posts. The issue was settled by Parliamentary pressure: the local taxation lobby was suspicious that the new Department was to be the agent of an aggressive spirit of centralisation, foisting expensive works on local authorities and imposing a hefty charge on the civil estimates.[35] Stansfeld felt obliged to give assurances that the Board was to be the means of simplifying and envigorating local self government, but the argument that Adderley, the Chairman of the Royal Sanitary Commission, seems to have thought most reassuring was that the new rural sanitary authorities were the familiar lay Guardians, and the new central authority was the old Poor Law Board rather than a ministry of doctors. He made a point, too, of stating that

> ... an economy of officers would also increase efficiency – for instance, the united central authority would have one set of inspectors for all local government instead of having a variety of inspectors under various Acts. The machinery of the Poor Law Board would be sufficient in carrying out this work[36]

These assurances were accepted, and the bill passed.

The man who created the organisation of the new Board and determined its business methods was John Lambert.[37] He developed a unitary Secretariat through which, for consistency's sake, all papers requiring the decision of the Board were to pass.[38] The Secretariat was supported by clerical departments, into which the clerks from the Poor Law Board, Local Government Act Office and Privy Council Medical Department were assimilated, though they generally continued to work at their old tasks. There was, therefore, little integration at the clerical levels as a result of the merger. The clerks registered, recorded, filed and, at the more senior levels, prepared drafts of correspondence and memoranda for scrutiny by the Secretaries, who, in turn, prepared recommendations and minutes for the President. The Secretaries and the President called, at their discretion, upon the advice of technical officers. The Architect's Department of the PLB, the Medical Inspectors of the Privy Council and the Engineering Inspectors of the LGAO formed technical departments and retained only that clerical support which was necessary for the direct servicing of their professional activities: correspondence with local authorities was handled by the appropriate clerical department. The Board's personal relations with the local authorities were conducted through the General Inspectors who superseded the Poor Law Inspectors as the locally resident district officers of the Board.

The technical staff visited localities only as necessary, to conduct public inquiries or special epidemiological inquiries or to visit institutions, but Lambert envisaged that their instructions would come from the clerical departments. Their reports and recommendations would be made to the Board through the Secretariat, and they were under instructions to inform the General Inspector when they visited his district.[39] The Architect and Poor Law Medical Inspectors of the Board were forbidden to inspect workhouses except in his company.[40]

This is a classical model of a civil service department based, both in its headquarters organisation and in its field administration, on the predominance of the generalist. As has been well documented elsewhere,[41] its implementation in the first half of the 1870s in the Local Government Board caused much conflict between the Secretaries and John Simon. Simon's view was that the Poor Law Board's notoriety in the matter of the sick poor, which had so badly damaged its reputation in the 1860s, had been largely due to its 'signal capacity for mismanagement of medical matters ... its extreme unwillingness to make full and frank use of skilled co-operation, its unwillingness to be served by technical knowledge except at such respectful distance as must make the knowledge practically useless',[42] and he believed that the LGB was going the same way.

Despite its political tribulations, the Poor Law Board – with some reason – considered itself to be the most efficient and advanced of the three offices which were merged into the Local Government Board. It was relatively large and it possessed a relatively complex clerical organisation through which it carried out the bureaucratic routine of central-local relations. Following Treasury inquiries in 1853 and 1866[43] it had adopted the separation of 'mechanical' and 'intellectual' business, and open competition. Above all, its political salience had instilled into its staff a keen sense of political circumspection. In contrast, both the Local Government Act Office and the Medical Department of the Privy Council had been specialist organisations, much more marginal within their respective offices, and consequently their Heads had enjoyed considerable day to day autonomy. And they were administratively simple: Simon brought with him a clerical staff of four (two of whom had been appointed under limited competition only after the expansion of work under the Concordat of 1870); Taylor brought five clerks (including a Chief Clerk), none of whom had

Chart 1 The structure of the Poor Law Board, 1869

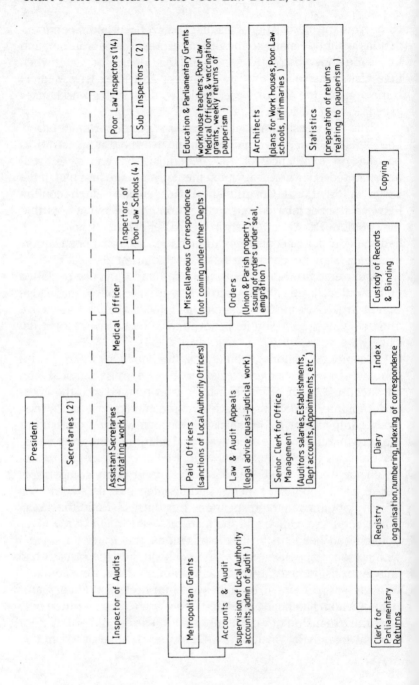

been appointed under open competition. The Local Government Act Office had no legal support but Simon had enjoyed the services of a legal assistant, J. F. Rotton, since 1870.[44]

The arguments used by the Secretaries and General Inspectors against Simon's position were based on assumptions about the effective maximisation of authority and the minimisation of conflict in dealing with local authorities, and on certain prejudices about the nature of local government. The evidence of PLB and LGAO officials to the Royal Sanitary Commission was predicated, like Mill's discussion of local self government, on a significant disjunction of cognition and values between centre and localities. Moreover, they could not assume, in the early 70s, that contemporary theories and technologies of environmental health were undisputed or widely disseminated; and they did not perceive that they were dealing with men trained to defer to the pedagogy of abstract principles or scientific theory. 'Guardians at least in the country districts are for the most part un-educated or half-educated men, whom it is impossible to move by reason' reported Inspector Murray Browne in the mid 1870s.[45] And his colleague, Baldwyn Fleming asserted that '... my experience of the Poor Law leads me to the conclusion that generally speaking such shortcomings as may be observed are due to want of intelligence and purpose in administration by the Local Authorities'.[46]

The diplomatic approach to central-local relations was geared to the long term promotion of greater consistency of understanding and practice between central bureaucracy and local authorities, and hence to the development of a kind of partnership. It was founded on a perception that the centre could offer tutelage to localities, but also that the localities did not always seek it and possessed the political resources to resist it. The Board's primary concern was therefore to develop and protect its precarious authority.

Lambert's first concern was that, above all, the centre must be seen to speak with one voice. One of the main themes of the Report of the Royal Sanitary Commission was the need to unify the central administration: its members had been regaled with embarrassing tales of inspectors from two or three different offices investigating the same district, giving conflicting advice or, worse,

allowing local people to play one department against another.[47]
Hence Lambert insisted that the whole of the Department work to
a common Secretariat, using common files. 'In order to secure the
unity of policy and action in the transaction of the business of the
Board', ordered Stansfeld, in what was the definitive Minute on this
point, 'I am of opinion a. that all correspondence must pass through
the general Secretariat b. that the inquiries of the medical inspectors must in each case be authorised and directed by the Board'.[48]

The Board's conventional wisdom also warned of the dangers
of technical officers dealing with local authorities without adequate
legal and administrative guidance. Local witnesses to the Royal
Sanitary Commission complained of engineers advising them to
take measures for which they had no powers,[49] and this impression
was reinforced when the new Board found that it had been committed by the LGAO's inspectors to positions which rested on highly
dubious law and financial doctrine.[50] The administrators were
specially wary of allowing specialists to get involved in local conflicts about the relative merits of rival sanitary inventions and
methods. A general view was that the protagonism and partiality
of its technical men accounted in large part for the local resistance
encountered by the General Board of Health, and for its failure to
survive,[51] and there continued, after 1870, to be occasional rows
when Engineering Inspectors allowed themselves to be drafted as
advocates in battles between competing interests in local improvement projects.[52] The prejudices of the Poor Law Board officials
coincided with those of the ratepayer lobbies and local officers:
technical inspectors, they assumed, were prone to recommend ill
founded or unreasonable schemes. Their fear was that the narrow
technical perspective taken by specialists would involve the central
authority in unwinnable conflicts with local authorities which
would merely damage its authority. Here is Inspector Wodehouse,
a General Inspector of the Board:

> Having regard to the existing condition of sanitary science, to the dif-
> ferent opinions entertained even by those best qualified to form a judge-
> ment on the subject as to the most efficient machinery for sanitary
> administration, and to the comparatively short period during which the
> question has been prominently before the public mind, I do not think
> it is to be wondered at, that the sanitary authorities should be of many

minds upon the subject, and should hesitate to adopt at once that particular arrangement which the Local Government Board or the Inspector of the district may recommend.[53]

The prevailing opinion, then, was that the central authority should remain aloof from professional disputes, to concentrate on procedures and machinery, and to insist that local authorities seek their own technical advice, a view which reinforced the constitutional objection to Simon's scheme, that positive supervision of local professionals by central professionals was incompatible with the responsiblities of elected local authorities:

> ... as the questions which will arise will be of opinion quite as much as of fact differences between the local and central authorities will prevail and cause endless controversies ... I am sure that the less the Board is an inquisitional and enquiring body and the more it is administrative the more it will be respected and the less it will enter into conflict on debatable questions[54]

This theme is one which ran through the Board's discussions of its methods for a decade or more. Baldwyn Fleming, the Inspector in the North Midlands, complained after ten years of the Board's administration, that it had still not got a grip on the technical inspectors, to the detriment of his relations with his authorities.

> It may be questionable, under existing circumstances and with existing powers, whether it be advisable that the Reports of the Board's Medical Officers should conclude with a series of specific recommendations. It might be better that the Report should clearly describe the evil and that the remedy should be left entirely within the responsibility of the local authority ... Recommendations have sometimes been made which local authorities could scarcely be expected to entertain ... Every recommendation made by the Board and allowed to remain inoperative must tend to weaken the Board's influence and to lead local authorities to think that the Board's views need not be acted upon.[55]

Above all, independent action by the technical inspectors was held to be incompatible with their status as servants of a ministerial department of growing political salience. Henry Fleming, formerly Secretary to the Poor Law Board and Joint Secretary to the Local Government Board, warned Stansfeld in May 1873 that Simon's claims threatened the President's responsibility, because they amounted to the formation of '... a branch department, independent nominally and officially of the Secretaries, and substantially of the President too. What control could the President exercise under such circumstances? Absolutely none'.[56] And Stansfeld's successor, Sclater Booth, in the Minute which finally precipitated Simon's resignation in 1876, told him firmly that his claims could not be granted to any officer not directly or personally responsible to Parliament. 'The whole of your proposals seems to me inconsistent with the cardinal features of our English system of Government'.[57]

Lambert proceeded with the assimilation of the three offices from which the Board had been formed in two directions: he needed to integrate the business of the new Board and to establish a common grading structure for its staff. The establishment of common grades based on the three classes used in the Poor Law Board was substantially achieved by 1874,[58] though, to Lambert's chagrin, the clerical staff had to be re-organised again into first and second divisions after the report of the Playfair Committee in 1876.[59] Lambert also used the departmental structure of the Poor Law Board as the framework for organising the LGB's business.

In 1872, the Board was enlarged by the transfer from the Home Office of the administration of the Turnpike and Highways Acts, the Metropolitan Water Act and the Alkali Act, which became the subject of new administrative departments and a technical department. In 1874, the Local Government Act Office was dismantled and its clerks formed into a new department for sanitary administration (K Department), leaving the Engineering Inspectors as a separate technical inspectorate supported by their personal clerk, John Haile.[60] K Department received its papers from the General Correspondence Department, which conducted all correspondence with local authorities.

The assimilation of the Medical Department was, however, far more fraught. Simon enjoyed an independent professional reputation; he continued to act (conjointly with his appointment to the Local Government Board) as the Medical Officer to the Privy Council; he drew a higher salary than Lambert;[61] and he bitterly resented the dominance of the Secretariat. Moreover, his dispute with the Board was carried on in a very public manner. The BMA and SSA continued to campaign for a Ministry of Health and were happy to exploit stories emanating from the Board of Simon's ill treatment and Stansfeld's indifference to public health.[62]

In 1871, the Poor Law Board's vaccination duties were transfered to the Medical Department. Lambert stipulated that business relating to legal contracts, appointment of local officers, the construction of vaccination stations, and the collection of statistics must be referred to the appropriate clerical departments, that is the Legal, Paid Offices, Orders, Statistics or Metropolitan Departments, and that the correspondence of the Medical Department with local authorities on all matters must be channelled through the General Correspondence Department.[63] But it was not until Simon's retirement in early 1876, that this could be enforced and that an administrative department for public health was created. K Department was then split into two divisions: one (K1) based on the administrative work of the LGAO (which included not only sanitary administration but matters relating to local acts and to local government); and one based on the Medical Office's public health functions (K2). At the same time, correspondence relating to public health was transfered from A to K. The Medical Officer's Department became a technical department and Rotton was transfered to the Secretariat.[64]

A common complaint about the Local Government Board is that it was dominated by the poor law: certainly, in so far as the Medical Department and the LGAO were assimilated into a ministerial department founded on the Poor Law Board, this is true. But the Board's subsequent reorganisations, and the career patterns of its top officials, shows that the local government, sanitary and public health business remained largely untouched by officials with roots in the poor law, and there was little co-ordination and crossflow of business. That is, the Board was never organised for the integration of public health and poor law policy; rather, it was organised to secure the minimum overlap of responsibilities and the maximum clarity of authority.

Following the death of Henry Fleming in 1876, the Secretariat was reorganised, and Lambert became the sole Secretary to the Board. At the same time, the number of Assistant Secretaries was increased from two to four, and clear specialism began to emerge between them.[65] 'In order to ensure uniformity in administration',

Chart 2 The Local Government Board, 1876-85

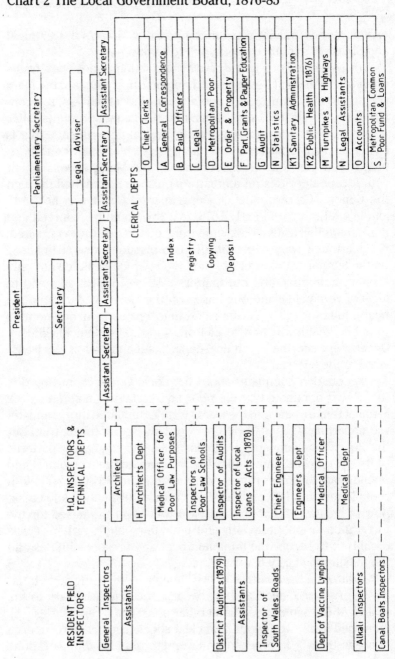

President

Parliamentary Secretary

Secretary

Legal Adviser

Assistant Secretary — Assistant Secretary — Assistant Secretary — Assistant Secretary — Assistant Secretary — Assistant Secretary

CLERICAL DEPTS

Index
registry
Copying
Deposit

O Chief Clerks
A General Correspondence
B Paid Officers
C Legal
D Metropolitan Poor
E Order & Property
F Parl Grants & Pauper Education
G Audit
N Statistics
K1 Sanitary Administration
K2 Public Health (1876)
M Turnpikes & Highways
N Legal Assistants
O Accounts
S Metropolitan Common Poor Fund & Loans

H.Q. INSPECTORS & TECHNICAL DEPTS

Architect
H Architects Dept
Medical Officer for Poor Law Purposes
Inspectors of Poor Law Schools
Inspector of Audits
Inspector of Local Loans & Acts (1878)
Chief Engineer
Engineers Dept
Medical Officer
Medical Dept

RESIDENT FIELD INSPECTORS

General Inspectors
Assistants
District Auditors (1879)
Assistants
Inspector of South Wales Roads
Dept of Vaccine Lymph
Alkali Inspectors
Canal Boats Inspectors

wrote Lambert to Gladstone in 1880, (revealing the balance of work in the Board), 'one assistant secretary takes all Poor Law cases, and another deals with those which pass through the Legal Department; whilst the local government and sanitary and other papers are disposed of by the two remaining assistant secretaries'.[66] Until 1885, most of the Board's administrative departments were organised on the principles of the PLB, that is according to the type of powers they exercised rather than by the service or type of local authority to which they related. This arrangement meant, however, that, with the exception of A, the clerical departments still worked to more than one Assistant Secretary.

Following an inquiry set up by the Treasury in 1885[67] in response to persistent requests for more staff, the number of administrative departments was reduced to increase the responsibilities of the principal clerks who acted as heads of department. This was in line with the Treasury's general policy requiring more delegation to the Civil Service First Division. The Highways Department(M) was amalgamated with K1, Parliamentary Grants(F) with Office Mangement(OC), Alkali Acts(N) with Public Health(K2) and the work relating to London was no longer separated from provincial business in the Metropolitan Department(D). The work of K1 on local acts and loans was transfered to S and there was a redistribution of work between K1 and K2, so that K2 acquired the public health business and K1 became a department mostly concerned with district and (after 1894) parish administration (including main roads and housing). The Committee also recommended the amalgamation of S (Metropolitan Common Poor Fund and Loans) with G (Audit) but, although this was formally implemented, the two branches remained separate for all practical purposes, and a new Department(S) was constituted in 1892 to deal with Local Loans and Acts.[68]

These changes confirm two trends in the organisation of the Board. The first is the specialisation – almost isolation – of policy interest within the clerical structure: the second is that, with the partial exception of A, K1 and K2, the Board's administrative departments were engaged in the work of supervising the procedural, legal, statistical, and financial aspects of local government and ensuring its probity, legality and formal accountability, rather than

Chart 3 The Local Government Board, 1885-98

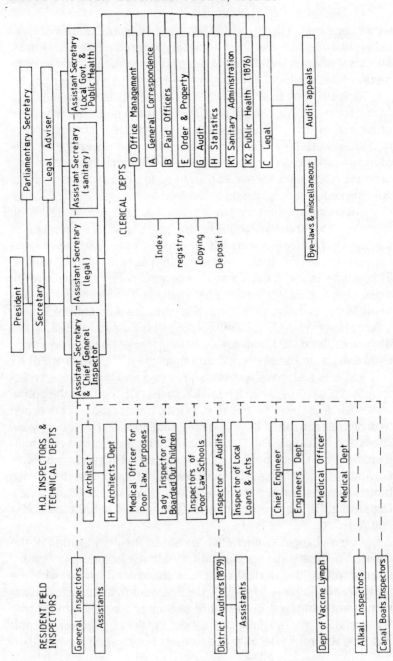

the development of its services or with policy issues. A continued to be the corresponding department with the poor law authorities, and thus became the sponsor of the poor law; Kl with district government and the sanitary functions of the state; and K2 with its public health functions. The business of all three consisted of much routine correspondence, issuing of sanctions and documentation of inspection and inquiry work, but they nevertheless also acknowledged a developmental function. The head of A told the 1898 Committee of Inquiry into the Board's organisation that his department existed primarily to get the local authorities to spend money.[69]

The trend towards specialisation was completed in the major re-organisation of 1898 which – with the additions of the Housing and Pensions Departments as new departments of the Board in 1909 – fixed its structure till its dissolution in 1919. It was based on the recommendations of the 1898 Local Government Board Inquiry Committee, and established a much clearer relationship between the Assistant Secretaries' responsibilities and the clerical departments, by organising business into five major divisions.

The Poor Law Paid Officers work was amalgamated with the Correspondence Department in a new Poor Law Division. Similarly, the Paid Officers business for sanitary and public health officials was transfered to the Public Health Department, which formed a second division together with Local Loans and Acts. A third division was based on the Audit, Local Taxation and Statistics work. The fourth was composed exclusively of K1, and the Legal and Order Departments (together with Office Management) formed Division Five, bringing together the major centres of the Board's legal work.

Lambert and his successor, Hugh Owen, believed in promotion on merit rather than seniority, and in senior officials having experience in the work they directed. Indeed, Lambert's reservation about open competition was that it would bring into the office's First Division men with no knowledge of its business,[70] and, on his retirement in 1882, he pressed hard for his successor to be appointed from within the Board.[71] The result of this principle was that officials in the Local Government Board were promoted to responsibilities in or contingent with their own departments. The five divisions established in the late 1890s enjoyed, therefore, a high degree of experiential autonomy.

Chart 4 The Local Government Board after 1898

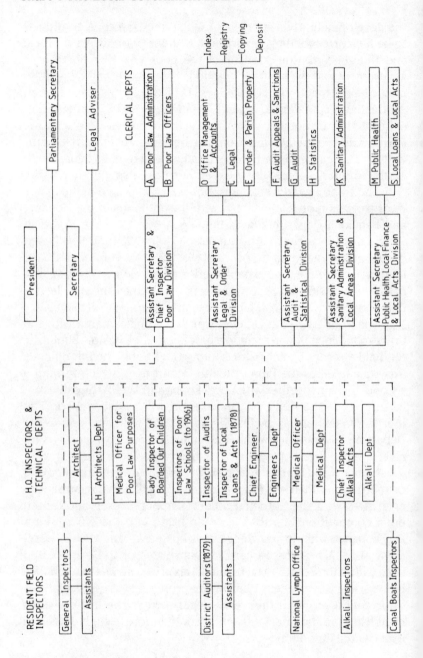

The establishment of upper division clerks allocated to the new divisions reinforces the initial impression that a very considerable proportion of the Board's energy was now devoted to local authority administrative, legal or financial issues. The Poor Law Division was to have six upper divison clerks from a total of fifty-six; the Public Health and Local Loans Division, twelve. The single largest division was to be the Legal and Order, with an establishment of fifteen.[72] That is, far from being by the turn of the century a Poor Law Department or even a Department for Social Policy, the Board was what its name suggested, a *Local Government* Board.

From the late 1880s, a relatively large number of middle class Oxbridge graduates entered the Board through open competition,[73] and this coincided with an increasing number of private secretaryships as the work of its permanent and political heads expanded. A small stream of high flyers (including Owen's successors as Secretary, Samuel Provis and Horace Monro) enjoyed comparatively rapid promotion to Assistant Secretary, by way of the private office. However, they shared with other members of the Secretariat a common characteristic, and this was the possession of a legal qualification, experience in the legal work of their specialist branch, or (as in the case of all Secretaries after Lambert), experience in the Legal Department or as a legal assistant. Lambert was a qualified solicitor; Hugh Owen, Samuel Provis and Horace Monro were barristers.

The pattern of promotions in the 1890s and 1900s shows both the continuing practice of promoting within divisions, and the continuing dominance of the legally-minded. The new Public Health and Local Finance Division was given in 1898 to Alfred Adrian, a qualified lawyer who began his career in the Legal Department of the Poor Law Board, and subsequently specialised in the law of public health in the Board's Legal Department. In 1899 he became the Board's Legal Adviser, and was succeeded by John Lithiby who joined the Medical Department of the Privy Council in 1870, qualified in law and served the Board in the Public Health Department. Thomas Pitts, who took Statistics and Audit, entered in 1876 as a third class clerk in the Audit Department and served as Head of the Legal Department (though he was not qualified in law). Noel Kershaw became the Assistant Secretary for the Sanitary Division;

he entered by open competition from the Post Office in 1891, and served in K.l and in the private office: he was succeeded in 1911 by F. J. Willis, a barrister, who entered by open competition in 1891 from the Board of Trade. He served in the Sanitary Department, and, from 1906, as the Inspector of Local Loans and Acts. Provis, who had begun life in the Board in 1872 as a legal assistant, took the Legal and Order Division.

The exception to this pattern is the Poor Law Division. In 1886, during a brief second Presidency, James Stansfeld began the practice (which survived till the appointment as Assistant Secretary of Aubrey Symonds in 1913) whereby the Assistant Secretary for the Poor Law held office jointly as Chief General Inspector. Stansfeld wanted an Assistant Secretary with field experience[74] but this practice underlined the reality, that the General Inspectors were effectively poor law inspectors. Unlike the other divisions, the Poor Law Division did not, therefore, send its papers to an Assistant Secretary with a legal-and-administrative background, and it did not develop self-sufficiency in law within its administrative staff. The Poor Law Division was the only department to use the Legal Department for legal advice: the Legal Department therefore dealt mainly in the technical work of checking by-laws, examining bills and revising regulations.

The influence of lawyers in the Local Government Board reflects much about its duties and its methods. Just as local authorities in Britain were (and are) the instrument for the exercise of multifarious statutory powers, rather than subordinate governments enjoying a general competence for their territories, so the Local Government Board was a department established by statute to exercise the powers of the central authority under a (growing) medley of public and private acts, most of which regulated the relations of local authorities with ratepayers, property owners and other bodies. The Local Government Board, wrote the contemporary authorities 'is a Board of controls ... not a Board of control'.[75] The consequence was that the tutelary role to which its officers aspired, could be pursued only as a by-product of and was limited by its formal statutory duties.

The statutory duties of the Local Government Board can be grouped in four analytical categories. Firstly, the Board had a duty

Chart 5 The Local Government Board, 1917

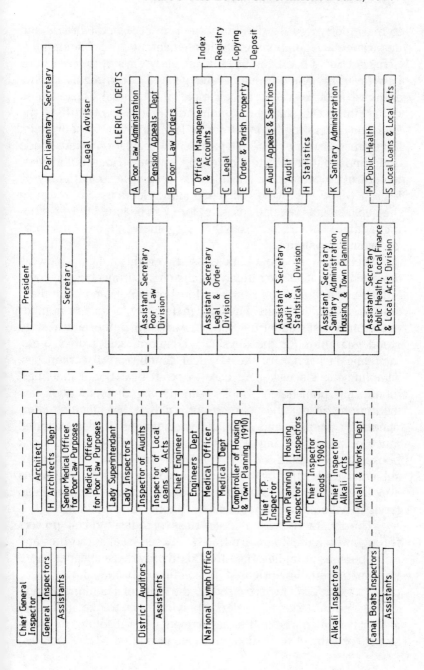

to make delegated legislation in the form of General Orders and departmental regulations for the implementation of public statutes. General Orders had been used in the early days of the New Poor Law to bring named Unions under general codes regulating the administration of relief, for example, the General Consolidated Order (for the regulation of Unions and their officers) in 1847, the Outdoor Relief Prohibitory Order of 1844, and the Outdoor Relief Regulatory Order of 1852. Departmental regulations were made under most public statutes conferring powers on local authorities, to control procedures for levying rates, keeping accounts, applying for sanctions, employing staff, conducting elections, and so on. In the departmental regulations, therefore, can be found the developing administrative code for the late nineteenth century local government system.

Secondly, the Board possessed certain policing powers designed to protect the ratepayers and clients from abuse by local authorities and their officers, and local officers from undue pressure from local interests. The former specially includes a number of statutory tasks under the Poor Laws, by which the central state stood guarantor for the physical and moral safety of paupers, including inspection of the physical conditions of workhouses, sampling the discussion of case-work at local Board meetings, monitoring punishment books, sanctioning diets in poor law institutions, inspecting boarded-out children, investigating complaints by paupers and sampling vaccinations. It also included much detailed checking of poor law officers' accounts and stock books. Appointments of officers under the 1834 Poor Law Act were subject to ratification by the Board, and poor law officers and MOHs appointed under the 1872 grants enjoyed security of tenure in so far as they could not be dismissed without LGB sanction.[76]

Thirdly, there was a large class of quasi-judicial powers through which the Board arbitrated between local authorities and other persons or bodies. Here the Board provided a cheaper, more flexible, more policy-oriented jurisdiction than the courts. These powers were formally exercised by the issue of sanctions or individual Orders (that is, Orders applying only to the individual authority) which were either departmental (or absolute) or provisional (or subject to Parliamentary confirmation). They included adjudication between different local authorities – for example, on questions of poor law settlement or the disposal of corporate property when local boundaries were changed – or between local authorities and private interests, for example when the Board responded to default complaints under the Public Health Acts or arbitrated the price of land purchased by authorities. The Board also disposed of appeals against disallowances and surcharges made by the district auditors.

And fourthly, the Board ensured the public accountability of local government. The most important of these functions were the collation of annual returns under the 1860 Local Taxation Returns Act;[77] the preparation of the occasional extraordinary returns called for by Parliamentary motion; and the certification by the district auditors of local authority accounts. The Board was also required to certify that the necessary procedures had been completed by local authorities applying for powers under private acts of Parliament or provisional orders.

Policy emerged at the Local Government Board mainly through case work generated by the exercise of its statutory duties: the Board's distinctive method for handling its business was the case paper method: precedents and policy evolved through the disposal of applications submitted by local authorities. Most of the officials' work was, therefore, reactive rather than proactive, and much of it was detailed, particular and laborious. An important consequence of the case method was that the only systematic statements of policy were the precedents recorded in the private working files of the Board. Neverthless, information seeped through the local government system, in several ways.

Formal casework was supported, from the 1880s onwards, by the growing practice of informal consultations with local officers. This latter particularly made the Board's professional expertise more widely available, if in a somewhat unsystematic fashion, though it added immeasurably to the burden on officials.[78] More systematic dissemination of approved practice was possible where local authorities were subject to routine inspection: the regular contacts with guardians and poor law officers by the General Inspectors provided the opportunity for tutelage in orthodox poor law doctrines, and the yearly audit of local accounts gave district auditors a lever on the accounting and financial practices of treasurers.

Formal, explicit statements of policy are to be found in the circular letters regularly sent by the Board to authorities and inspectors: these were advisory only, but they spelt out the Board's interpretation of statutes and the principles used in casework, and announced shifts in practice and emphasis. The Board occasionally issued model by-laws and clauses[79] and published model plans, though these activities tended to be interrupted or delayed by pressure of work. Much of the systematic, technical information which provided the common, professional thread holding the late nineteenth system of local administration together was disseminated either by private enterprise or by the emerging professional bodies. But here again, we can note the domination of the legal mind in the Board: the Local Government Board followed the practice of the Poor Law Board of selling guides to the developing law of local government, and its officials published the standard legal texts.[80] In contrast, the texts on municipal engineering, accounting, sanitary inspection, and so on, were prepared by local practitioners, often through the aegis of the professional institutions.[81] With the exception of the Medical Officers of Health[82] and the partial exception, in the early years, of the Municipal Engineers,[83] the Board's professional officers, including the auditors, did not participate in the relevant professional bodies, which performed, therefore, a limited role in connecting the central and local administrative systems.

The Board placed much faith in the demonstration value of the statistical information published in bluebooks and its annual reports. However, apart from financial statements and the six monthly statistical returns of pauperism, the only information systematically collected by the Board was the annual reports on their districts made by the General Inspectors: but these almost exclusively concerned social (not environmental) conditions and the state of the poor law. Lastly, of course, the Board's officials made a significant contribution to policy and legislative change, through their extensive work on public legislation, their reports on private bills and by means of their participation in the many Parliamentary and official inquiries held into aspects of local authority administration and social policy.[84]

The importance of all this activity in defining, recording and moulding late nineteenth century administration should not be underestimated. But a lot of it is policy development by a 'dripping tap method': that is, its effects were designed to be cumulative rather than quick or spectacular. The Board was a conservative department but it was certainly not, at least until the early 1900s, a reactionary department. The first generation of officials included several who were steeped in the reformist culture of post-Chadwick social administration.[85] But they had a profound scepticism about the capacities of the local government system and a long time scale for change. They regarded their task to be the building of a hearts and minds consensus around the principles of sound administration, particularly in the poor law, not just the mechancial imposition by coercive techniques of superficial compliance with the letter of the law.

In any case, the officials of the Board lacked space to develop a more proactive or strategic role: under chronic pressure of business, the priority was the disposal of statutory cases. It is clear from MacLeod's work that successive governments were never prepared to face the establishments implications of the Board's duties,[86] and the overload of its staff is well documented in the reports of the Inquiries of 1885 and 1898. The latter shows particularly clearly the high regular overtime worked by the First Division and long arrears of business, especially in the formal statutory work.[87]

But the overload of the Local Government Board was not just a product of the volume of paper passing through its office. It was also a function of the nature of its powers, and of the Board's understanding of how they should be handled. That is, it would be a mistake to infer from the dominance of lawyers that the Board worked its cases in a rigid, mechanistic way. In line with its diplomatic strategy, the Board was flexible and pragmatic, knowingly tolerating a great deal of variation in local practice, even against clear statutory prescription. That is, though the Board was apparently dominated by a legal culture, we find a reluctance to pursue technical requirements unmediated by political judgement. Indeed, the imperatives of diplomacy became stronger as fiscal tension heightened, and the political constraints under which both central and local government operated more powerful.

Local authorities were elected by ratepayers and we have seen that ratepayers had an effective voice in Parliament. The Board's officers also perceived that there was no general consensus behind many of their legal powers. For example, when pressed by the 1898 Inquiry Committee to explain the Board's attitude to the modern poor law, Owen confessed that its officials sympathised with many reforms favoured by advanced opinion. But he strongly resisted the view that these improvements should be made compulsory, repeating thirty years on the points made in evidence to the Royal Sanitary Commission:

> My view is that if the Board were to proceed on lines such as these, they would in a short time be in hopeless condition. Guardians are representatives of the ratepayers, and are reluctant to go far in advance of the views of their constituents. The Board proceed by persuasion and pressure through their inspectors and by correspondence and it is by means such as these that they have secured the success they undoubtedly had in obtaining improved arrangements ... the action which the Board take is by way of advice, persuasion and pressure, and this action subsequently lays the foundation for more stringent regulations.[88]

He then went on to make a general statement about the nature of the Board's external relations, compared with departments who managed employees of the state, who dealt with private individuals, or who (like the Home Office in relation to the police) held the purse strings through a system of conditional grants. The LGB, he argued, was dealing with members of local authorities who were unpaid, voluntary and who mostly spent ratepayers' money, a state of affairs which 'specially requires tact, judgement, discretion ... they have to rely more on advice, persuasion and pressure than on compulsory action'.

> It also has to be borne in mind that all the matters with which the Board deal have relation to the daily life, practically, of every member of the community. We are also always acting under the light of public criticism ... It is of the greatest importance that all mistakes should be avoided in consequence of the publicity which would be given to any unfortunate communication. What might pass unnoticed in the case of a communication by a public department to a private individual has a very different

complexion when addressed to a local authority. It is also the case that any departure from the ordinary practice of the Department becomes known in a most remarkable way, and is pressed on the Board subsequently as a precedent ... Of course, great care and judgement are necessary in the case of all departments, but I think that for the reason I have mentioned they are specially required in connection with this.[89]

Owen's perception of the potential for controversy in the handling of individual cases was justified by three developments during his career at the Board. The first is that from the 1870s onwards, a set of national associations for different classes of local authority came into existence: one important effect of which was that a mechanism was created by which general issues might be extrapolated from a single individual case.[90] The second is the building of communication networks between local authorities by the development of a local authority press.[91] Thirdly we have already noticed that the officials of the Board worked to a minister who was answerable to Parliament; if the number of Parliamentary Questions addressed to the President indicates the parliamentary salience of its casework, then it remained high, decade by decade.[92]

The consequence was that the Board insisted on maintaining a discretion in the management of its cases, and often declined to insist on compliance to the letter of the law. Rather, its officials exercised judgement as to how far an individual authority should be pushed. There was, therefore, a tendency to pass cases up the hierarchy, from from junior clerks to principal clerks and from heads of departments to the Secretaries, and the Board experienced great difficulty in conforming to Treasury policy – which was nevertheless reflected in its establishment – to delegate more business. An important cause of the overload of work was therefore the pressure on the senior levels. The Secretariat, Cornelius Dalton told the 1898 Committee, 'had a horrible life',[93] and a chronic bottleneck developed at the Assistant Secretary level, causing lengthy arrears in the dispatch of business. The case put forward in the 1900s for the Board to be raised to the status of a department of a Secretary of State rested partly on the view that its staff required political sensitivity of as high an order as was needed in the Offices which were obviously engaged in 'high politics': the essential difference, however, was that their expertise lay in internal diplomacy.[94]

If the Board was conducting internal diplomacy with its local authorities, then the General Inspectors were intended to be the ambassadors. However, in practice, the role of the General Inspectors did not significantly expand from that of the old Poor Law Inspectors, and they continued to act primarily as inspectors of the indoor poor. Indeed, the general inspectorate replicates many features of the Board's headquarters' staff, for the same sorts of reasons. That is, the field services for the poor law and public health remained largely unintegrated and unco-ordinated; their development functions were subordinated to routine bureaucratic procedures which were designed to guarantee individual rights rather than to respond to collective policy needs; and they were chronically understaffed, even for such limited functions. For the same reasons, it is difficult to place the General Inspectors within current academic classifications of inspectorates. Rhodes[95] has distinguished between 'efficiency' inspectors, concerned with maintaining or improving standards, and 'enforcement' inspectors, concerned with compliance with statutory provisions. He has noticed, historically, a relative decline of the first in favour of the second, and classes the poor law inspectorate as a typical example of an efficiency inspectorate. The *purpose* of the general inspectorate was clearly to promote efficiency: their *tasks,* however, were essentially the monitoring of the Orders and regulations of the central authority. However, they lacked powers to enforce these Orders through the courts; the Local Government Board relied on the district audit as the major sanction against illegal practices, and on its powers to dismiss unsatisfactory officers.

The General Inspectors were the descendents of the Assistant Poor Law Commissioners, who had been formed into a Poor Law Inspectorate when the Poor Law Board replaced the Poor Law Commission in 1847. Two factors immediately cast doubt on whether the change of nomenclature in 1871 signalled a real change of role. The first was that the personnel of the new inspectorate was that of the Poor Law inspectorate, and the new assistants appointed in 1872 (to provide relief from routine duties while the General Inspectors negotiated the implementation of the new Public Health Act with the local sanitary authorities) were very obviously cast in their mould. The second was that neither the 1871 Local Government Board Act or the 1872 Public Health Act extended routine inspection into the municipal corporations or the Local Boards (which became the urban sanitary authorities): the only formal duty imposed on inspectors continued to be the twice yearly inspection of poor law institutions and and the yearly visit to Boards of Guardians, originally prescribed under the Poor Law Board. Nor was the inspecting role of the medical or engineering inspectors enlarged in the new Board. It was the practice in the Board for the Secretariat to seek the advice of the General Inspectors on the diplomatic – but not the medical or technical – aspects of handling difficult authorities in their districts in matters of sanitary administration, and General Inspectors occasionally sat with the technical inspectors conducting local inquiries under the Public Health Acts. But the General Inspectors' statutory and routine duties related to poor law administration, and as the years passed, it became clear that their best energy was used in this direction. The consequence was that in health and sanitary administration – especially in the urban areas – the frequent personal contact and influence predicated by the Board's diplomatic strategy of central-local relations did not occur.

Like all the Board's inspectors, the General Inspectors were exempt from open competition; throughout the whole period appointments were by the patronage of the President. But appointment to the general inspectorate was no sinecure: the Board enjoyed a relatively low status, the work was arduous, the inspectorate chronically understaffed, and the inspectors were obliged to conform to demanding bureaucratic routines.

In the absence of more tangible instruments to encourage local authorities to comply with central policy, much emphasis was placed upon the appointment of men who would develop maximum personal influence in their districts. The Treasury Report on the Poor Law Board in 1853[96] recommended that the inspectors should be worldly and experienced in life; apprenticeship to the inspectorate at an early age was to be discouraged and appointments were to be made at a salary level which attracted gentlemen: a post as inspector was not conceived as being a career opportunity for the regular bureaucrat. This how Stansfeld explained his strategy in 1872:

> I do not believe in harmonious relations between bodies of men conducted by correspondence ... It seemed to me ... more than necessary that I should be able to rely on my negotiators, and that the local boards should be able to feel that there was some one person with whom they could have oral communication, and who should represent the policy of the Local Government Board. I therefore determined to make the Poor Law Inspectors the local government inspectors for all purposes between this department and the local bodies, including boards of guardians. I wanted men of experience and of tact, accustomed to deal with men, knowing the boards of guardians and having their confidence.[97]

In the early years of the Board, especially, appointments were made from the minor branches of landed political families or from the gentry: of forty general inspectors in the employment of the Board between 1869 and 1880, eighteen came from families listed in Burke, and another four had clear family connections with politics.[98] That is, they appear to have been recruited from backgrounds similar to those who staffed the civil service, particularly its less glamourous, more hard worked departments before open competition. Some partisan appointments were made, but some knowledge of the poor law was also required: several inspectors had backgrounds as Chairmen of Boards of Guardians, as auditors, or a family connection with the Poor Law Board.

After 1880, it is more difficult to trace the backgrounds of the twenty-four inspectors appointed, which suggests a tendency to appoint from less well connected backgrounds. A small but significant number (six) came from landed backgrounds and four were appointed from the first division of the Local Government Board to ease the promotion blockage which had become acute by the 1890s. There were also two promotions from the District Audit. Apart from the civil servants, none were Oxbridge graduates and there is, therefore, no longer the obvious community of background with the Secretariat who, by the late 1890s, were increasingly meritocratic, open competition entrants.

The relatively large gentlemanly contingent which characterised the inspectorate until after the turn of the century reflects assumptions about the nature of political and social authority, more obviously suited to the less heavily urban areas. If the General

Inspectors were chosen for their natural social authority, it seems difficult to see why a country gentleman from Gloucestershire or an ex-colonial diplomat should be thought to be specially able to sway the tradesmen of Manchester or Sheffield.[99] Indeed, only the particularly evangelical or careerist, or those most in need of a job, would go to the 'populous' areas of Yorkshire and Lancashire, where historically the Poor Law was most sensitive, and workhouse accommodation remained generally deficient, and in 1886 a special increment had to be paid to induce an experienced inspector to take on the 'distinctly disagreeable' Unions of West Yorkshire when James Davy secured a more congenial district near London.[100]

Apart from a few especially well connected men who held office only for a few months till a better job was found, inspectors generally held office for thirty or forty years, and, in that time, took no more than one or two districts. Although there was some disparity of opinions between the inspectors, the Guardians of a district were subject, therefore, to some consistency of influence. But this pattern of office-holding meant that there were in the 1890s a few inspectors who had become quite out of sympathy with changing ideas of poor law administration. James Davy, of whose influence Beatrice Webb was so censorious,[101] held to strict 1834 principles learnt when he was a new inspector in the early 1870s – 'the hanger-on should not be so well cared for as those on whom he hangs'[102] – which were by no means typical of the attitudes of his colleagues. By the 1890s a majority of inspectors acknowledged what the LGB's statistics obscured,[103] that the 'able-bodied malingerers' made up a very small proportion of the workhouse population, and that the Poor Law mainly dealt with those who were disabled, from extreme youth, age or infirmity, from participating in the labour market, rendering less eligibility a redundant concept. They argued (along with many Guardians) that the majority of deserving poor should not have to suffer the company and regime of those of bad character and anti-social habits.[104] That is, in most districts by this time, the barrier to specialised treatment was shortage of accommodation and of Guardians willing to spend money, not central dogma. By the 1900s most inspectors held views on the poor law close to that of the Majority Report. The basic framework of the Poor Law was not questioned, but there was an acknowledgement that changes in opinion, social structure and methods of treatment made a strict interpretation of 1834 politically impossible and administratively undesirable. That is, the General Inspectors probably represented a fair cross-section of informed opinion in their class at that time.[105]

The inspectors were required to report twice yearly on each poor law institution; to make inquiries into complaints by inmates of workhouses or cases of fraud by officers; to discuss plans for new buildings with local officers and the Board's Architect; to submit annual reports on the economic and social condition of their district; and to advise the Board in its dealings with their local authorities. Inspectors were also consulted regularly by letter on general poor law issues raised in Parliament or other political arenas, and they were asked occasionally to supply information about places of particular distress. The immediate concern of governments during severe winters and trade depressions was whether the fabric of the poor law could survive intact, and it is this stark question with which many of the reports are concerned. Throughout the period, the inspectors were used, as Stansfeld had intended, as the 'eyes and ears' of the Government on social questions and their status in the Board, between principal clerk and the Secretariat to whom they directly reported, reflected the weight which their views were intended to carry.

The major constraint on the development of a wider role by the inspectorate was the lack of resources: during a period of constant change in domestic policy, and despite the considerable proliferation of specialised institutional poor law provision, the inspectorate did not expand significantly. The Local Government Board inherited from the Poor Law Board thirteen General Inspectors (including a Medical Inspector for the Poor Law) and a sub-inspector: Lambert then negotiated twelve assistant inspector posts to support the implementation of the Public Health Act and the wider responsibilities of the new inspectorate.[106] However, because the Treasury refused to make these posts permanent, the districts of the General Inspectors could not be reorganised, and each of the full inspectors continued to supervise, sometimes with an assistant, a district of some fifty or so Unions. In 1875, six of the assistants were dispensed with, and the establishment became seventeen inspectors (of whom one was the Chief) and two assistants.[107] The number of districts was reduced again in 1892 to thirteen, and the number of full inspectors to fourteen (excluding the Chief, who had become a member of the Secretariat in 1886 but again including the Medical Inspector), with four assistants.[108] The inspectorate remained at fourteen, with between three and five assistants, until 1914.

The inspectors worked under several pressures – physical and emotional; legal and moral; and political – which combined to encourage them to a reactive rather than proactive role, a life of routine reporting and careful inspecting. The most obvious pressure on a Local Government Board inspector was time; they had large districts – organised according to the layout of the railway system and with an eye to the location of the staple industries[109] – often spread over several counties, and a considerable programme of visiting and supporting paperwork. One of the most rigid rules imposed by the Board was that the inspector took up residence near an appropriate railway station, from whence he could depart on his ceaseless travels and to which a bag of papers could be regularly despatched from London.[110]

The formal requirements imposed on the inspector were demanding enough, but most inspectors found that their routine would be interrupted by the pressure of *ad hoc* inquiries, by outbreaks of disease, or by special distress arising from industrial disputes or severe weather. In August 1896, Murray-Browne of the South Midlands District calculated that the inspectors in the 'ordinary' districts (by which he meant the districts outside London and the manufacturing districts of Lancashire and Yorkshire) inspected an average of forty-eight Unions with 64.8 institutions and 10,371 indoor poor, but complained bitterly that he was unable to get on with the inspection of his own eighty-two institutions because a month had been taken by special inquiries.[111] The pressures in the manufacturing districts were even greater. In 1895, Jenner Fust of Lancashire inspected ninety-one institutions (of which only forty-one were general workhouses), many requiring, he alleged, several days to inspect thoroughly.[112] But what worried Fust was the rate of growth of institutions in the 1890s as provision for the indoor poor became more specialised: some forty of his institutions, he calculated, were less than five years old. In response to Fust's complaints, the Board relaxed his formal obligations, and asked him to visit annually.[113] By the early 1900s all inspectors were formally inspecting on an annual basis.[114] But the expansion of provision for the indoor poor also made other demands on the inspectorate. Changes in central policy and in the climate of opinion manifested by the mid 1890s, required inspectors to make many informal visits to Unions, to confer with chairmen and officers on building programmes and on changing institutional management.

The fiscal and political climate under which the Board operated kept any question of a substantial expansion of the general inspectorate off the parliamentary agenda. The successive reductions in the number of full inspectors, and the increasing geographical size of poor law districts, reflects a policy which the Treasury had consistently pursued since the 1850s in relation to the field staff of central departments, and there was little countervailing political pressure in the case of the General Inspectors. Grumbles about the numbers of government inspectors of all kinds (and their expenses), usually accompanied by complaints about 'centralisation', were a regular feature of supply debates in the 1870s and 1880s, and the citation of conditions in poor law institutions or questions about occasional scandals led much more frequently to censorious remarks about the qualifications and efficiency of the inspectors than about the resources devoted to their work. The public health lobbies wanted not more lay inspectors but an expanded role for the Medical Inspectors, and there was little support for the general inspectorate from pressure groups active on poor law questions. For the approach to central-local relations taken by the inspectorate was at odds with that of the three main poor law lobbies, all of whom wanted much stronger central direction of the poor law than the General Inspectors were able or prepared to implement.

These lobbies were, firstly, the 'dispauperisers', who argued for the abolition of the poor law, and who, in the 1870s, began to put forward the case for compulsory national insurance to compel individuals to make provision for themselves against economic misfortune.[115] Secondly, there were the 'poor law zealots', whose views were focused by the Poor Law Conferences movement,[116] and who secured control over a few unions in the 1870s – Atcham in Shropshire, Brixworth in Leicestershire, and Manchester[117] – which became models of strict administration where rates of pauperism fell dramatically. The Poor Law Conferences had significantly overlapping membership with the charity organisation movement and the Local Taxation Committee, and favoured the introduction of new legislation or new Orders enforcing a more rigid application of less eligibility. Third, there were various 'specialist' lobbies, especially those for extending the practice of boarding-out pauper children[118] and improving the treatment of the sick poor.[119] They pressed the Board to take a stronger line to accelerate the modernisation of accommodation and practice.

Most inspectors favoured a rather more relaxed approach to the local authorities. Partly, this was from jealousy of their freedom to deal with their authorities in their own way: the implication of the role defined for them by Stansfeld as the Board's 'negotiators' implied some discretion to adjust central policy to local circumstance. There was also a profound anxiety in the Board that a too rigid insistence on the letter of the poor law would merely provoke a reaction in the country. If the poor law was essentially an agency of control, then the main priority was to preserve its legitimacy and acceptability, not so much amongst the lower classes, but amongst those who were charged with its local administration. This meant that the central authority was ultimately obliged to defer to local judgement as to how far to take a strict application of the law, and it made the Board chary of bringing in new Orders or regulations which would fail to secure local support.[120]

But partly, many inspectors found that the generalisations of orthodox poor law doctrines were not always easily applied to the complexities of the social conditions they found in their districts, especially in the industrial areas. Although one finds in the inspectors' reports some easy, censorious, moral judgements about the want of thrift of the working classes and the evils of trade unionism and strikes, there is also evidence that some (though by no means all) inspectors made efforts to know their districts, acquainting themselves with life outside the Boardroom and workhouse, and were genuinely shocked and surprised by the conditions which they found. Thus Knollys reporting (as Chief Inspector) on conditions in the North East during the Durham Miners' strike in April 1892, declared himself appalled by the squalor in the workmen's homes, and was forced to the conclusion that wages in the iron industry, where men had been laid off, were too low for them to save against unemployment.[121] However, he continued to take a tough line in public, and his sympathy did not extend as far as the strikers or the workmen who refused a cut in wages to keep their works open with imported coal. Bircham's report from the Welsh manufacturing districts in 1890 excuses the extent of out relief in Wales (which was frequently commented on by the poor law zealots):

> I often think that some of our English critics at Poor Law Conferences and elsewhere would modify their opinions on the subject of the Poor Law in Wales if they were more conversant with the traditions and habits of the people and with the features of the Country generally.[122]

But there is also the simple fact that inspectors had little power to insist on good practice, or the capital investment on which it increasingly depended. Herbert Preston Thomas, who was inspector in East Anglia and then in the South West in the 1890s, stated bluntly that the only remedy he possessed to deal with inadequate practice was the sledgehammer of sacking the officers.[123] Likewise, the Board possessed only negative controls over capital investment: indeed, loan sanctions and building standards, though not rigidly enforced, presented hurdles over which inspectors had to drag unwilling local authorities. Here is Inspector Kennedy venting his frustrations in 1897:

> There is no Alladin's lamp in the hands of a Local Government Board inspector to conjure up workhouse buildings of the most approved types as the occasion may arise; indeed I think that if I were asked to devise a system which should wear a fair appearance, as if framed in a progressive spirit, but which should really make it as difficult as possible to get new buildings erected, or old ones improved, I could not suggest any more effectual scheme that the one with which it has been my melancholy duty to make way during the last eleven years.[124]

In general, the Board was more rigorous in the control of non-capital than capital expenditure. This partly follows from the fact that, in the District Audit, the central government had created an instrument which, once established, ran under its own steam: the auditors had little discretion over the disallowance of illegal expenditure. But the relatively greater rigidity in matters of current administration compared to development, reflects the Board's direct responsibility – political and moral – for individual paupers. That is, the poor law can be seen as a statutory framework of rights possessed by those who qualified for relief by the test of destitution. The Board and its inspectors accepted on behalf of the state the duty of guaranteeing that those rights and regulations were fulfilled. Explaining to the Royal Commission in 1909 'why it is more necessary to centralise the administration of the Poor Law than any other branch of local administration', Chief Inspector, James Davy, pointed out that

> ... the destitute man, has, in this country, what is practically a right to relief, but his right is not a complete right, for the necessary sanctions are lacking, that is to say, he cannot sue for his relief or move the courts to compel the Guardians to give him his relief: therefore it is the duty of the state to see that he gets his rights.[125]

The regulations and orders of the Board were the code through which that duty was implemented. But it meant that the Board was obliged to take more direct action over defaults in the performance of detailed obligations to existing paupers, than on general policy. And it was easier to control (through the district audit) the details of expenditure on workhouse diets, or (through loan sanction powers) the areas of bedspaces in dormitories, than positively to influence a Board of Guardians' general approach to indoor relief.

When coupled with the greater flexibility in matters of capital development, the detail of its regulation of day to day administration left the Board open to the accusation that it was preoccupied with trivia at the expense of strategy. Doubtless, this was exacerbated by the inflexibility of the district audit and the preoccupation with protecting its authority from challenge: the Board preferred to let things ride than to issue an Order that would be defied. The inspectors were an important source for such judgements: new Orders or Circulars were habitually issued only after time consuming surveys of inspectors' opinions,[126] or after the definitive statement of policy by an official inquiry. That is, in its formal declarations of policy, the Board followed rather than led local opinion.

This implied enormous dependence on the General Inspectors' ability to exert informal influence to mould that opinion: it also meant that they enjoyed few sanctions with which to support it.

The conception of the New Poor Law as a statutory framework regulating the relief of paupers accounts for the Board's preference for institutional solutions to pauperism. Simply, paupers could be protected more easily where they could be inspected, and where their environment could be controlled. Most inspectors strongly favoured reforms which improved classification and specialist institutional provision. What they disliked was sending children or imbeciles, for example, to institutions beyond the Guardians' control, or the extension of outdoor relief for vulnerable paupers. The consequence was that there was much greater unanimity amongst inspectors for reforms of institutional practice – most particularly for the establishment of professionally staffed infirmaries for the sick[127] – than for reforms which dispersed paupers to less conveniently 'inspectable' environments, and this accounts for the hostility of many inspectors to the emigration of poor law children and to boarding-out[128] and their suspicion of cottage homes for children or the aged.[129]

The principles of central supervision required the inspection of every institution or home to which paupers were sent by guardians, including the individual inspection of children boarded away from their Unions, but these inspections were annual only, and they were immensely time consuming. In 1885, a lady inspector was appointed to take over the inspection of boarded-out children from the General Inspectors. Miss Mason also interpreted her task to be the disseminating of inspectorial techniques: she worked hard to establish and guide local ladies' committees to supervise boarding-out. But she also favoured very rigid central rules, which she helped to draft.[130] Her work epitomises the problems of the Board's approach to central-local relations. The duty of the Board to guarantee individual statutory rights, coupled with the belief in personal leadership by inspectors, implied highly particularistic, detailed work which, even in a by-way of the nineteenth century poor law, placed enormous personal strain on the inspector. In relation to the general administration of indoor, and especially outdoor relief (which was hardly touched by these arrangements), it was unsustainable.

The inspectors also acted as policy advisers to the Board. However, the general inspectorate failed to develop as a coherent source of policy because it remained a cadre of individual field agents, unorganised and unable to develop a corporate stance on the important issues of contemporary poor law administration; the treatment of vagrants, the education of poor law children, the treatment of 'harmless' imbeciles, the sick poor, and the treatment of the aged. Evidence to the series of official inquiries on aspects of the poor law in the 1890s and 1900s reveals that there were almost no arrangements for co-ordinating the work or thinking of inspectors; they had little common socialisation, no formal training and only haphazard opportunities for apprenticeship (through the sporadic use of assistant inspectorships). Conferences of inspectors in London to discuss policy with the President and Secretaries ceased in the 1870s.[131] Nevertheless, it is possible to overstate the isolation of inspectors: the Board addressed frequent circulars to them setting out its latest thinking; they had access to the published papers of the Board, including each other's annual reports; they conducted a frequent correspondence through the Chief Inspector; and they saw the Board's papers on their unions. The status of the General Inspectors ensured them ready personal access, on visits to the Board, to the Secretaries and Ministers, and they could call on the Chief Inspector in difficult cases. The Chief Inspector carried out no systematic monitoring or visiting of the inspectors or their districts, however: his field work was limited to the occasional special inquiry, and his communications with his staff were mainly by correspondence.[132]

There was thus some opportunity for the individual inspector to understand the mind of the Board. What was entirely missing were arrangements for the inspectors collectively to formulate a view on issues. The annual and special reports returned by the general inspectors are lengthy and detailed. They contain much statistical information on local pauperism (though this reflects the structure of statistics formally required from authorities by the Board, and, as the inspectors and headquarters officials knew full well seriously misrepresents the pattern of nineteenth century pauperism). And there is voluminous, discursive, impressionistic information about local conditions. But all this information had to be digested by a clerk before it could be passed onto the Secretaries or President. That is, the advice from the inspectors was raw and unaggregated advice, and the potential for the inspectorate to form a consolidated pressure group within the Board remained undeveloped. So the evidence of individual inspectors to official inquiries could be only personal opinion.

Some inspectors, at least, were aware of this deficiency. In 1898 they met to formulate their evidence to the Inquiry Committee, but failed to find a common voice. A few, represented before the Committee by Bircham,[133] hankered after the role envisaged by Stansfeld, regretting their detachment from the public health and local government work, and resenting the role of auditors and engineers within the Board. But the majority, represented by Jenner Fust and Baldwyn Fleming,[134] made no secret of the fact that their interest lay in the poor law. They advocated the appointment of assistants to relieve them of routine work so that they might acquire a more policy oriented role, a role, that is, of greater political influence. This proposal was echoed by the Majority Report of the Poor Law Commission in 1909, which also recommended the institution of qualifications and apprenticeship for poor law inspectors, and the institution of investigative inquiries to develop policy.[135] The Minority Report recommended the specialisation of the inspectorate according to the different client groups within the Poor Law, and an end to the concept of a 'general' inspector.[136] It was especially concerned by the almost complete neglect of the outdoor poor by the rules under which the inspectors worked.

Some reorganisation and regrading of the inspectorate was envisaged in 1914, in response to the Majority Report. The Board proposed to develop a hierarchically differentiated inspectorate: the number of districts was to be reduced to eight, and each would henceforth be worked by an general inspector, a lady inspector and an assistant, and it was specially intended that this would free the general inspectors from much of their routine business, to allow a more policy oriented role to emerge. The assistants' posts were to be reserved for the Second Class Clerks of the Board, to ease the promotion blockage and to bring keen young men into the inspectorate.[137] This scheme was agreed in principle in 1915, but evidently not implemented before the dissolution of the Board in 1919. In 1924 a departmental committee of the Ministry of Health[138] was forced to report that the burden of detailed administration, and the more or less exclusive connection of the general inspectorate with 'the taint of the poor law', had seriously damaged their influence and effectiveness.

It can be seen, then, that the culture and organisation of the Local Government Board – both at headquarters and in the field – was adapted much more successfully to a role of the state as the guarantor and arbitrator of private interests and individual rights, than to the development of collectively consumed services. In the general inspectorate, the Board failed to develop a body of men and women able to contribute collectively and authoritatively to policy-making. The physical pressure of work on the inspectors confined them largely to the inspection of the indoor poor, and their role as mediators between the centre and locality largely consisted of personal pressure on Guardians and the personal assessment of local opinion on the shifting issues of the day. This limited role reflects a central authority with few political, limited organisational and almost no financial resources with which to dominate either the process of policy formulation or its implementation.

The controls of the Board over local authorities were largely negative, and those that were effective were financial. That is, they were directed to controlling expenditure, both revenue and capital. The penetration of inspection rested ultimately not on any powers of enforcement possessed by inspectors, but on the threat of surcharge by the district auditor. Likewise an unfavourable report of a sick ward inspection counted much less than the power of the Board to reject an application for a loan to renew it. The Board's powers over expenditure were developed, however, because the administrative needs of the central bureaucratic authority coincided with demands from elsewhere in the political system, namely the organised interests of ratepayers, of property holders, and the Exchequer. However, as we will see in the next two chapters, the audit and loan sanction powers were essentially reactive and negative, not positive and strategic: and the central bureaucracy operated compromised, partial and pragmatic controls, which largely failed to secure a grip on local policy.

NOTES TO CHAPTER FOUR

1 Memorial and deputation to Privy Council 2 April 1866, following resolution of Council of SSA, in 'Report of Tenth Annual Meeting', *Transactions of the National Association for the Promotion of Social Science,* 1866.
2 Memorial from Joint Committee to Privy Council, Home Secretary and Poor Law Board, 22 May 1867; Reports of Joint Committee 1867-8 and 1868-9, *Transactions,* 1868 and 1869; H. W. Rumsey, 'Memorandum on state medicine', *First Report of the Royal Sanitary Commission,* 1869, II, Appendix 6.
3 'Report of Health Department of SSA', *Transactions,* 1869.
4 11 & 12 Vict. c. 63; 21 & 22 Vict. c. 98; 24 & 25 Vict. c. 61; 26 & 27 Vict. c. 17
5 28 & 29 Vict. c. 72; 29 & 30 Vict. c. 90; 30 & 31 Vict. c. 113
6 18 & 19 Vict. c. 115.
7 21 & 22 Vict. c. 97.
8 18 & 19 Vict, c. 121.
9 30 & 31 Vict. c. 84.
10 John Simon, *Memorandum on Appointment of Royal Sanitary Commission,* 17 June 1868, PRO PC 8/143.
11 R. J. Lambert, *Sir John Simon 1816-1904 and English Social Administration,* Macgibbon and Kee, 1963.
12 John Simon, *Suggestions for Amending the Present Disorderly State of Parts of the Central Health Administration,* reprinted with the evidence taken for the Royal Sanitary Commission, 1871, III, at Q. 9479.
13 Simon to Treasury, 27 January 1870, PRO PC 8/164.
14 Simon gave evidence three times and Taylor, four times. Simon's evidence is at *First Report,* Q,1789 and *Second Report,* III. Q. 9694 and Q. 9927; Taylor's at *First Report,* Q.2 and *Second Report,* III, Q. 8511, 8669 and 12379.
15 *First Report,* Q. 4298.
16 *Second Report,* III, evidence of Robert Druitt, Q. 9095.
17 *Ibid.,* Q. 9921.
18 Simon, *Suggestions for Amending the Central Health Administration.*
19 *First Report,* Q. 1855.
20 *Ibid.,* evidence of Arnold Taylor, Q. 884.
21 *Second Report,* III, evidence of Robert Weale, Q. 10802.
22 *First Report,* evidence of Robert Rawlinson, Q. 702.
23 Simon, *English Sanitary Institutions,* fn. p. 388.
24 *Memorandum on the Duties of Central Inspectors of Public Health,* prepared by some members of the Royal Sanitary Commission, 18 October 1870. *Second Report,* II.

25 *Second Report,* III. Q. 10644 and 10851.

26 *Second Report,* I. p. 31.

27 *Ibid.,* p. 32.

28 Simon, *English Sanitary Institutions,* p. 329 asserts that the Chairman and other members of the Commission wanted the more forceful scheme put forward by Sir Charles Adderley in his Public Health and Local Government Bill, 1871 (269) V. 5 ss. 66-87.

29 e.g. Lambert to Stansfeld, 17 May and 26 May, 1873, PRO MH 78/87.

30 *Second Report,* I. p. 33.

31 *Ibid.*

32 *Ibid.*

33 34 & 35 Vict. c. 70.

34 It is clear that although Fleming was appointed Joint Secretary with Lambert, against Lowe's wishes, this was intended to be a temporary arrangement to last only till Fleming retired. Stansfeld to Gladstone, 29 August, 1871, Gladstone Papers, Add. Mss. 44428; Lowe to Gladstone, 6 September 1871, Gladstone Papers, Add. Mss. 44301.

35 208, H. C. Deb. 20 July 1871, col. 78ff.

36 *Ibid.,* col. 80.

37 John Lambert was a solicitor and sanitary reformer from Salisbury. He was appointed Poor Law Inspector in December 1856, and subsequently promoted to Inspector of Audits. Lambert undertook much of the special legal and administrative work involved in setting up the Public Works programme in Lancashire during the cotton famine, carried out for Gladstone the psephological and topographical calculations preparatory to the Parliamentary Reform Bill and was sent to report on conditions in Ireland in 1870. The creation of the LGB and his appointment to it, was seen by Conservatives as a partisan act by Gladstone, and Lambert believed that this was an important reason for the relative low status of the Board during the Disraeli administration, which weakened Sclater Booth in fighting for parliamentary time for his measures. Lambert to Gladstone, 17 April 1880, Gladstone Papers, Add. Mss. 44235. The correspondence of Lambert and Gladstone in the 1860s is also in this volume. Lambert's personal file is at PRO MH 32/30.

38 The following statement has been compiled from knowledge of the methods of the Board from its working files, and from the principles stated in the correspondence of Lambert, Simon and Presidents Stansfeld and Sclater Booth in PRO 78/44. The printed formal minutes arising from this correspondence, governing relationships of officials in the Board, are collected in PRO MH 78/169 and 78/87.

39 Circular from Sclater Booth to Medical and Engineering Inspectors, 24 May 1876, MH 78/135.

40 Circular from Sclater Booth to General Inspectors, 9 April 1874; Minute of

21 December 1875 on role of medical and architectural staff, PRO MH 32 67 and PRO MH 32/67; correspondence between Sclater Booth, Salt, Lambert and Inspector Mouat, June and July 1877, PRO MH 32/51; Minute of Sclater Booth to General Inspectors and Inspector Mouat, 23 October 1878, PRO MH 78/135.

41 Brand, *John Simon and the Local Government Board Bureaucrats;* Brand, *Doctors and the State;* Lambert, *John Simon,* Part V.

42 Simon to Sclater Booth, 10 November 1875, PRO MH 78/87.

43 'Report on the Poor Law Board', 20 July 1853, *Reports of Committees of Inquiry into Public Offices* 1854 (1715) XXVII 33; *Report to Treasury on the Poor Law Board,* by G. W. Hunt, 13 November 1866, PRO MH 19/180.

44 *The Imperial Calendar and Civil Service List, 1869, 1870 and 1871.*

45 Report on outdoor relief in his district, from Thomas Murray-Browne, March 1873, PRO MH 32/97.

46 Baldwyn Fleming, *Observations on the Poor Laws and Sanitary Laws,* 7 November 1872, PRO MH 32/99.

47 *First Report of Royal Sanitary Commission,* evidence of Tom Taylor, Q. 17 and 56; T. J. Dyke, Q. 6302 and J. Clegg, Q. 724; *Second Report,* III, evidence of W. J. Mawle, Q. 11170 and Augustine Batt, Q. 10458.

48 Stansfeld to Simon, 23 June 1873, PRO MH 78/87.

49 *First Report of Royal Sanitary Commission,* evidence of E. J. Hayes, Q. 2572.

50 e.g. the case of Sudbury Local Board, 1871-2, PRO MH 12/12028; and of Billericay Guardians, 1871-2, PRO MH 12/3359.

51 *First Report of Royal Sanitary Commission,* evidence of Robert Rawlinson, Q. 514 and Dr. Trench, Q. 7801.

52 Correspondence between Lambert, Taylor and Stansfeld, April-May 1872, PRO MH 19/85; 235 H. C. Deb. 3s. 29 June 1877, col. 484; Circular from Sclater Booth to Medical and Engineering Inspectors, 24 May 1876, PRO MH 78/135.

53 Report from Edmund Wodehouse on the establishment of local sanitary authorities, 16 May 1874, PRO MH 32/91.

54 Smith to Lambert, 18 February 1873, PRO MH 32/67.

55 Baldwyn Fleming to L.G.B., 23 February 1881, PRO MH 32/99.

56 Henry Fleming to Lambert, 13 May 1873, PRO MH 78/44.

57 Sclater Booth to Simon, 13 December 1875, PRO MH 78/87.

58 Treasury to LGB, 24 August 1872; Treasury to LGB, 7 January 1873, and Minute of Lambert, 11 January 1873; LGB to Treasury, 6 January 1874. *Review of the History of the Board,* prepared for Treasury Committee, 1884, PRO MH 78/44.

59 *Observations of the Report of the Civil Service Inquiry Commission,* Lambert to Sclater Booth and Fleming, 26 May 1875, MH 19/210; *Review of the History of the Board.*

60 *The Imperial Calendar,* 1874 and 1875. The organisation of the Sanitary

Department between 1874 and 1876 can also be inferred from Sclater Booth's Minute on the sanitary work, 24 May 1876, PRO MH 78/44. Correspondence between Haile, Lambert and Sutton, 17 March 1874 and Haile and Lambert, 20 January 1875, PRO MH 19/87.

61 Under 35 & 36 Vict. c. 79 s. 38, Simon had a salary of £2000. Lambert drew a salary of £1500 under the Treasury Minute of 4 December 1871, PRO MH 19/207.

62 Brand, *Doctors and the State;* Lambert, *John Simon. The Times,* leaders 4 April 1874, p. 6; 12 August, 1874, p. 7; 21 April 1875 p. 9; 5 April 1876, p. 6.

63 Seaton to Lambert, 5 September 1871, PRO MH 19/184; Minute of Lambert, 19 September 1871, *ibid.;* Minute of Stansfeld, 26 September 1871.

64 Minute of Sclater Booth on the sanitary work, PRO MH 78/44.

65 Minute of Sclater Booth on office organisation, 24 May 1876, Ibid.

66 Lambert to Gladstone, 17 April 1880.

67 *Report of the Treasury Committee on the Reorganisation of the Clerical Staff of the Local Government Board,* 8 April 1884, PRO MH 78/44. The members of the Committee were Lambert, J. T. Hibbert and G. L. Ryder.

68 'Statements by Principal Clerks of Departments as to Duties and Establishments', *Minutes of Evidence taken before the Departmental Committee to Inquire into the Sufficiency of the Clerical Staff and Secretariat,* Appendix, statement by W. Wellington Connolly on the Audit Department. (The Evidence taken for the First Report was not published: a printed copy is in PRO MH 78/44.).

69 *Minutes of Evidence taken before the Inquiry Committee,* Q. 2030.

70 *Report of the Civil Service Inquiry Commission,* 1875 (C. 1113) XXIII I, evidence of Lambert, Q. 5568.
This statement has also been inferred from analysing patterns of promotion in the LGB, 1871-1919.

71 Correspondence of November-December 1882, Monk Bretton Papers, Box 52.

72 *First Report of the Local Government Board Inquiry Committee,* 1898 (C. 8731) XL 429, pp. 5-6; Minute of Chaplin, 1 November 1898, PRO MH 78/42. The organisation established in 1898 was not precisely what the Committee had recommended: the Committee suggested that Audits should be in the Public Health Division, and Local Loans in the Statistical Division. They were exchanged by the Chaplin minute, for reasons that appear to be to do with the experience of the available Assistant Secretaries.

73 51 of the 78 entrants by open competition into the LGB between 1884-5 and 1814, have been identfied as graduates of Oxford and Cambridge Universities; J. A. Venn, *Alumni Cantabrigiensis 1752-1900,* II, Cambridge University Press, 1953; C. W. Previté Orton, *Index to Tripos Lists 1748-1910,* Cambridge University Press, 1923; Joseph Foster, *Alumni Oxonienses 1715-1886,* Oxford, Parker & Co., 1888; *The Oxford Historical Register 1220-1900,*

160 Local possessive pluralism

Oxford, Clarendon Press, 1900, and supplement, 1901-1930.

74 *Minutes of Evidence to Inquiry Committee,* evidence of Knollys, Q. 7185. The practice ceased because the combination of roles was thought to be too heavy for one man; Monro to Treasury, 12 August, 1913. PRO MH 107/33.

75 J. Redlich and F. W. Hirst, *Local Government in England,* Macmillan, 1903.

76 4 & 5 Wm IV c. 76 s. 46 and 48; 35 & 36 Vict. c. 79 s. 10; 21 & 22 Vict. c. 90 s. 33.

77 23 & 24 Vict. c. 51.

78 *Minutes of Evidence to Inquiry Committee,* evidence of Hugh Owen, Q. 637; evidence of H. Thomas, Q. 2077; evidence of Alfred Adrian, 6784. Sir Arthur Newsholme, *The Last Thirty Years in Public Health.*

79 The Local Government Board published *Model Byelaws for the Use of Sanitary Authorities* from 1877 onwards. From 1883 they were published as *Knight's Annotated Model Byelaws of the Local Government Board,* Knight & Co., 1883 with further editions in 1885, 1890, 1897, 1899 and 1905.

80 The guides and texts prepared by W. C. Glen and W. G. Lumley on the poor laws, laws of public health and law of local government elections and meetings are too prolific to list here. They date originally from the 1850s, and were subsequently revised by their authors and by other hands. Glen was Legal Assistant to the Board from 1872, having worked previously in the Poor Law Board, and subsequently rose to Principal Clerk in the Legal Department. He retired in 1878. Lumley was Assistant Secretary, then Counsel to the Board in the 1870s.

81 The exceptions are Robert Rawlinson, *Lectures, Reports, Letters and Papers on Sanitary Questions,* London, 1876 and *Suggestions as to the Preparation of District maps and of Plans for Main Sewerage,* LGB, 1978. Most of his technical guides were written before 1871, and the series was not carried on by his successors as Chief Engineering Inspector.

82 At least three Medical Inspectors employed by the Board were active in the Society of Medical Officers of Health. They were Doctors Seaton, Buchanan, and Ballard. Reginald Duffield, 'History of the Society of Medical Officers of Health', *Public Health,* special Jubilee number, 1906; Dorothy E. Watkins, *The English Revolution in Social Medicine 1889-1911,* University of London, unpublished PhD thesis, 1984, pp. 160-243.

83 Robert Rawlinson did not attend the meetings of the Association of Municipal and Sanitary Engineers, but he kept them informed and sought their co-operation in developing and disseminating models of good practice. e.g. *Proceedings of the Society of Municipal and Sanitary Engineers and Surveyors, 1 IV, 1877-8, p. 209.* He also gave papers at the SSA Congresses, and at the early Congresses of the Sanitary Institute, two of the major fora for the discussion of sanitary reform in the 1870s.

84 Throughout this period, it was usual to have at least one official to represent the departmental view on Royal Commissions and Committees of Inquiry. The same official would usually lead for the department in presenting evidence.

85 Patronage facilitated the apppointment of men with special interests in sanitary reform, for example, Lambert, in workhouse reform (for example J. H. Bridges, Poor Law Medical Inspector in the metropolis 1871-93), in pauper education reform (for example, E. C. Tuffnell, who retired in 1874), and in public health (for example Simon and his successors Edward Seaton and George Buchanan).

86 MacLeod, *Treasury Control and Social Administration.*

87 'Statements by Principal Clerks', *Minutes of Evidence,* 1898.

88 *Minutes of Evidence,* 1898, evidence of Hugh Owen, Q. 598.

89 *Ibid.*, Q. 809.

90 The Association of Municipal Corporations dates from 1871-2; the County Councils Association from 1889-90; the Urban District Councils Association from 1895-6 and the Rural District Councils Association from 1896-7. The Poor Law Unions Association was recognised by the LGB in 1898 and the Metropolitan Boroughs were organised through the AMC, and then separately, in the early 1900s. The crucial factor in the formation of the association was the sponsorship of the LGB, for legislation permitting the attendance at meetings to be charged to ratefunds.

91 The main organs were; *The Local Government Chronicle* which began life as *Knight's Official Advertiser,* in November 1855 and changed its title in June 1872, and *The Poor Law Unions' Gazette,* 1857-1903. Some of the professional bodies also maintained journals or bulletins, for example the IMTA's *Financial Circular,* 1896- ; the Society of MOH's Public Health, 1886- ; and the British Institute of Public Health's *Journal of State Medicine.* Towards the end of the period, trade unions and associations began to publish journals, notably the *The Poor Law Officers' Journal,* in 1892, and NALGO's *The Municipal Officer,* in 1911.

92 e.g. in 1975, Sclater Booth took 42 PQs; in 1881 (a year of a cholera scare) Dodson took 96; Ritchie took 95 in 1890, and Chaplin 88 in 1900.

93 *Minutes of Evidence to Inquiry Committee,* Q. 6994.

94 *Report of the Committee on the Status and Duties of the Board of Trade and Local Government Board,* 1904 (Cd. 2121) lxxviii 439. LGB papers generated by the committee are in PRO MH 78/46.

95 Gerald Rhodes, *Inspectorates in British Government; Law Enforcement and Standards of Efficiency,* Allen and Unwin for RIPA, 1981, p. 19. and Appendix I. There is a discussion of the Poor Law/General Inspectorate in J. S. Harris, *British Government Inspection: the Local Services and the Central Departments,* Stevens & Son, 1955.

96 *Reports of Committees of Inquiry into Public Offices,* p. 208. It was usual to appoint men, and later women, in their forties or fifties. *Return of all Inspectors and Auditors . . . of the Local Government Board,* 1906 (350) cii 401.

97 *Statement of President to Joint Deputation of SSS and BMA,* 21 February 1872, PRO MH 19/86.
98 Bernard and A. P. Burke, *Genealogy and Heraldic History of the Peerage and Baronetage, and Genealogy and Heraldic History of the Landed Gentry,* Harrison, successive editions, 1882-1906.
99 Herbert Jenner Fust of Hill Court, Falfield, Gloucester, was a leading figure in the Poor Law Conferences movement before he became a General Inspector. He was General Inspector in the Lancashire District from 1892-1906. H. G. Kennedy was Inspector in Yorkshire from 1886-1900: he had previously been Consul in Sumatra. Kennedy's predecessor was James Davy who held the Lancashire/Yorkshire district till 1882, when the district was divided. Fust was succeeded in Lancashire by A. B. Lowry, a graduate entrant by open competition to the Board, who had been promoted from the administrative grades and who went on, in 1913, to succeed Davy as Chief Inspector. These details from personal files of Inspectors in PRO MH 32.
100 Correspondence between James Davy and LGB, 27 December 1898, PRO MH 32/98.
101 Beatrice Webb, *Our Partnership,* London School of Economics and Cambridge University Press, 1975 edition by B. Drake and M. Cole, p 317 and p. 322.
102 *Report of the Royal Commission on the Poor Laws,* II, Q. 2679.
103 Replies from Inspectors on pauper classification, 1878-1880, PRO MH 32/93.
104 Replies from Inspectors' reports on the treatment of the 'deserving poor', PRO MH 32/93.
105 Based on the published reports of Inspectors in LGB annual reports, unpublished reports and memoranda in PRO MH 32, and evidence of General Inspectors to the various committees of inquiry into aspects of the Poor Law from 1888 to 1900.
106 Lambert to Treasury, 2 February 1872; Treasury to LGB, 8 August 1872, PRO 78/133.
107 LGB to Treasury, 30 October, 1875; Treasury to LGB, 17 November 1875, PRO MH 78/133.
108 LGB to Treasury 25 February 1892; Treasury to LGB, 15 March 1892. PRO 78/133.
109 *Second Report of Royal Sanitary Commission,* evidence of Robert Weale, III, *passim.*
110 *Duties of General Inspectors,* January 1904, PRO MH 78/135.
111 Murray-Browne to LGB, 18 December 1895 and 18 August 1896, PRO MH 32/97.
112 Jenner Fust to LGB, 12 December 1895 and his Annual Report for 1895, PRO MH 32/101.

113 Knollys to Jenner Fust, 30 December 30 December, 1895.

114 *Duties of General Inspectors.*

115 At the end of the 1860s and 1870s, there was a potent case made for dispauperisation, that is the abolition of the statutory right to relief put forward by, for example, Henry Fawcett, *Pauperism; its Causes and Remedies,* Macmillan, 1871; Baron Lyttelton, 'The Poor Laws', *The Contemporary Review,* XXVI, 1875, pp. 169-192 ; W. Walter Edwards, 'The poor law; a proposal for its abolition', *The Contemporary Review,* XXVI, 1875, pp. 639-649. It is reviewed and developed in the classical history of the Poor Law, T. Mackay, *A History of the English Poor Law,* III, P. S. King & Son, 1899.

116 The early history of the Poor Law Conferences is in the 'Introduction' to the *Reports of the Poor Law Conferences,* 1875. Their main political achievements were the LGB Circulars of May 1877 and February 1878 (Nos 11 and 34, 1877-8), *LGB Annual Report for 1878,* 1878 (2130) XXXVII I-1, on the restriction of outdoor relief, and the 1882 Pauper Inmates Discharge and Regulation Act Amendment Act of 1882, which was an attempt to clamp down on vagrancy by detaining vagrants for longer periods in workhouses.

117 For a very partial discussion of this movement and its relation to the lobby for dispauperisation and charity organisation, Mackay, *History of the English Poor Law,* III pp. 517- 579.

118 The Committee for Promoting Boarding-out, chaired by Francis Peeke, was formed in 1871-2 and and was patronised by Lord Shaftesbury, Charles Kingsley and Charles Trevelyan amongst others. It secured prominence in the 1870s partly as the result of a very public controversy generated by Mrs Jane Senior, who was appointed by Stansfeld in 1873 to report on the education of pauper girls, and brought in a report highly critical of poor law schools on educational, social and health grounds; Mrs Nassau Senior, 'The education of girls in pauper schools', 1 January 1874, *LGB Annual Report for 1873-4,* 1874 (C. 1071) XXV I, App. B. No 24. Boarding-out was promoted subsequently by the Association for the Advancement of Boarding-out, whose President in the 1880s was Lord Cranbrook. The LGB did consult the Assocation on its revised Boarding-out Order in 1888, Boarding out Association to LGB, 29 October 1888, MH 20/46. Francis Duke, 'Pauper Education', in Derek Fraser (ed.), *The New Poor Law in the Nineteenth Century,* Macmillan, 1976.

119 Louisa Twining, *Recollections of Workhouse Visiting and Management during Twenty-five Years,* Kegan Paul, 1880; Susan Liveing, *John Henry Bridges.* Modern studies of the issue are James E. O'Neill, 'Finding a policy for the sick poor', *Victorian Studies,* VII, 1964, pp. 266-284 and M. W. Flinn 'Medical services under the Poor Law', in Fraser, *The New Poor Law in the Nineteenth Century.*

120 See statements by LGB officials, for example at: *Minutes of Evidence to Local Government Board Inquiry Committee,* evidence of Hugh Owen, Q. 600; *Report of the Select Committee of the House of Lords on Poor Relief,* 1888 (363) XV, 23, evidence of Davy, Q. 863 and evidence of Henley, Qs. 390 and 456.

121 Knollys to Ritchie, 8 April 1892, PRO MH 32/98.

122 *Annual Report for 1890,* from Inspector Bircham, PRO MH 32/96.

123 Preston Thomas, *Work and Play of a Government Inspector,* p. 246.

124 *Annual Report for 1897,* from Inspector Kennedy, PRO MH 32/102.

125 *Report of the Royal Commission on the Poor Laws,* II, Q. 2027.

126 For example, responses of Inspectors prior to issue of 1877 circular on outdoor relief in their personal files at PRO MH 32; responses on the treatment of vagrants, winter 1886-7 at PRO MH 19/97; responses to the recommendations of the Royal Commission on the Blind, Deaf and Dumb, 1889 (C. 5781) XIX 1, attached to correspondence from Royal Commission to LGB, 17 August, 1889, PRO MH 19/105, and responses on nursing for the outdoor poor attached to East Preston Union to LGB, 17 July 1890, PRO MH 19/111.

127 I have found no digest of inspectors' opinions on this subject. This statement is based on an analysis of the contents of the General Inspectors' Annual Reports to the Board in their personal files in PRO MH 32.

128 The discussion at the Board resulting from Mrs Senior's Report is in Mrs Senior's file, PRO MH 32/91; Report to LGB from Dr Mouat, May 1873, PRO MH 25/24 and 15 April 1875 in PRO MH 32/51; and correspondence with Inspectors Bridges and Henley, April-June 1875, PRO 25/26. See also, Inspector Long at Midland Poor Law Conference, *Reports,* 1875; Inspectors Tristram and Culley at Northern Conference. *ibid.;* Inspector Hedley at Metropolitan Conference, *Reports,* 1877; Inspector Davy at North Western Conference, *Reports,* 1878; Inspector Cane at North Western Conference, *ibid.*, and *Report of Select Committee on Poor Relief,* 1888, evidence of Owen and Henley, Qs. 182 and 710.

129 The LGB supported the introduction of cottage homes in Birmingham at the end of the 1870s; *Annual Report of LGB for 1879-80,* 1880 (C. 2681) XXVI I p. xli and Appendix B, No. 40. Its unease surfaces in *Report of the Chief General Inspector, the Medical Inspector land the Architect of the Local Government Board on the Sheffield Cottage Homes for Children,* and accompanying copies of correspondence, 1897 (C. 113) LXXVI Pt I 689; see also *Report of Departmental Committee on Existing Systems for the Maintenance and Education of Children in the Metropolis,* 1896 (C. 8027 and C. 8032) XLIII 1, especially the evidence of Knollys and Inspector Holgate.

130 Annual Reports and memoranda of Miss Mason 1886-1897, PRO MH 32/92. The Annual Reports are published in the successive Annual Reports of

the Local Government Board.
131 *Report of the Royal Commission on the Poor Laws,* II. Q. 1607. See on this point also, Preston Thomas, *Work and Play of a Government Inspector,* p. 241-6.
132 *Report of Royal Commission on Aged Poor,* 1895 (C. 7684) XIV. 1, evidence of Knoilys, Q. 827.
133 *Minutes of Evidence to Inquiry Committee,* evidence of Inspector Bircham, Q. 3563ff.
134 *Ibid.,* evidence of Jenner Fust and Fleming.
135 *Report of the Royal Commission on the Poor Laws,* Majority Report, 1909 (Cd. 4499) xxxvii I. The discussion of the inspectorate is in Pt. IV, Chapter 1.
136 *Ibid.,* Minority Report, Ch IX.
137 LGB to Treasury, November 1914; Treasury to LGB, 22 January 1915; LGB to Treasury, 26 January 1915; Treasury to LGB, 29 January 1915, PRO MH 78/133.
138 *Report of the Committee on the Organisation, Scales and Duties of the General Inspectors,* 1924, PRO MH 78/134.

Chapter Five
Enforcing local stewardship: the district audit

The audit of local authority accounts by agents of central government was designed to fulfill a number of functions, which were largely a response to the national politics of local government finance. The purpose of the audit of the poor law accounts was envisaged by the 1834 Report to be the enforcement of 'the negative duty not to apply a tax for an unauthorised purpose', and the audit of accounts, the disallowance of illegal spending, and the recovery of deficiencies by surcharging Members and officers were accordingly developed, after 1834, as 'the most simple, ready and self-acting of all expedients for the security of public property'. Effective audit was, therefore, the essential technique for the control and restraint of local public expenditure, and it is not surprising, in the fiscal context of late nineteenth century local government, that, apart from the visits of the General Inspectors to poor law authorities, this negative and detailed control was the most systematic at the Board's disposal.

The audit had a second function in promoting public accountability and in the generation of reliable local financial information: consequently, it had an important political significance for the national politics of local taxation. That is, the political pressure for its extension came from ratepayer lobbies which pressed for more reliable accounts and more robust statistical returns to support their arguments and to mobilise support. Hence, the administration of the district audit was always located with the statistical work in the Local Government Board's departmental structure.

At the end of our period, the audit became the object of attention from the national organisations of local commercial interests, and of propagandists for *laissez-faire* dogmas, who sought to develop a third function, the control and restraint of local authority capital development, especially in relation to municipal trading. This extension of the audit was not achieved, because of the countervailing power of the municipal corporations. What the failure of this movement also meant, however, was that the district audit did not develop an influence over the management of local authority capital expenditure, and, even in revenue expenditure, it was restricted by a narrow conception of financial stewardship. The extension of the district audit was not unhelpful to the development of local government: at the least it promoted financial probity; and accurate accounts and a solid financial reputation were important conditions of borrowing on the open money market and therefore of local capital accumulation. But the rigidities and over-elaboration of the audit proved unsustainable in the face of local custom, and incompatible with the Board's pragmatic approach to central-local relations. And as a technique for the central influence of local administration, it was seriously deficient: for it was not only negative, but it was also unstrategic: it addressed the details of local administration, but failed to reach the patterns behind them. And it created much work in the Board: the period is marked by the development of a burdensome, quasi-judicial business arising from the need to mitigate the worst inflexibilities of an audit that was over rigid especially for the underdeveloped condition of late nineteenth century local government.

In deference to local feeling and to the political opposition to a central audit, the 1834 Poor Law Act prescribed that auditors were to be appointed not by the central authority, but by the local authority.[1] The shift to a central audit can be detected first in the 1844 Poor Law Amendment Act, which was passed in response to complaints from the Poor Law Commission, and by members of the House of Commons, about the quality and efficacy of local auditors.[2] This Act[3] introduced the power of disallowance and surcharge, and provided for appeal to Queen's Bench (or, alternatively to the Poor Law Commission) on points of law.[4] The Bill originally proposed to remove the appointment of auditors from the Guardians to the Poor Law Board, but this was rejected by Parliament: instead, to reduce the patronage of authorities over auditors, authorities were grouped into districts, and district auditors were appointed by the

Chairmen and Vice Chairmen of Guardians in the district.[5] In 1848, the central authority was empowered to remit disallowances and surcharges on grounds of equity.[6] The Poor Law Board exercised a jurisdiction that was cheaper and quicker: it was also more flexible and sympathetic, since it could go beyond the law to the merits of the case. The central bureaucracy therefore became the normal recourse for appeals.

The wedge which eventually levered the audit from local control was the concession of 1846, by which the Exchequer contributed to the salaries of poor law officials, including the auditors:[7] henceforth the Treasury had a direct interest in the audit. In 1853, the Treasury Committee on the Poor Law Board[8] recommended that the audit become a full time service and that the appointment of auditors be transferred to the Poor Law Board: it also recommended a reduction in the number of auditors and larger audit districts. In 1868 the appointment of auditors became a PLB duty.[9]

In 1858, the district audit was extended to local health boards[10] – except those formed by municipal corporations – and, throughout the 70s, it acquired further accounts: the school boards in 1870;[11] the sanitary authorities in 1872;[12] parish accounts (overseers', lighting and watching, and burial accounts)[13] and school attendance committees in 1876;[14] and in 1878 the accounts of highway authorities.[15] The consequence was to make obvious the need for the consolidation of the audit.

The Parliamentary vote taken under the 1846 arrangements paid only for the audit of poor law authorities and rural sanitary authorities (which were, in effect, committees of the Guardians). Auditors were paid directly by the local authority for school board accounts, according to terms imposed by the 1870 Act, and they made their own arrangements with authorities for their other accounts.[16] The auditors disliked these arrangements because their remuneration bore no relation either to their relative experience or to the volume of work, and they received least payment from the most troublesome authorities, the relatively poor, small, often financially incompetent authorities located in inconvenient places.[17] They also offended against the Treasury's convention, that public officials did not take private work but were wholly under the control and at the disposal of the state.[18] In 1879, therefore, the district audit became a fully salaried service under the Local Government Board.[19] A single parliamentary vote was taken for the audit, and the cost was transferred to the local authorities by way of a stamp duty in lieu of fees.[20] Only the reporting arrangements and the frequency of audit now varied from authority to authority: the poor law (including the rural sanitary authorities) continued to be audited half yearly and the auditors reported direct to the Local Government Board not to the Guardians: the other accounts were audited yearly and report made to the authority, with a copy to the Board.

The 1879 District Audit Act also rationalised arrangements for local authority statistical returns. In order to make more complete the annual statistics of national taxation and expenditure, the Home Office had, in 1860, promoted an Act to obtain annual returns of local taxation and expenditure.[21] The Local Taxation Returns were, however, a mess: authorities for different local government purposes had different statutory accounting periods, and the muddle was compounded by the corporations' private acts. And the returns were often incomplete or inaccurate, a situation that, to the central government's severe embarrassment, was publicly revealed by a series of parliamentary returns moved in the late 60s and 70s by the local taxation lobby.[22] A Bill promoted by Pell in 1873,[23] to impose on the Board the duty of checking the corporations' returns, was blocked by the muncipal corporations but in 1877 the Board successfully took powers to rationalise the local authorities' financial year, and to fine clerks who defaulted in making returns.[24]

The 1879 Act provided that for all accounts under the district audit, the authority must submit to the Board a copy of a certified financial statement in place of the Local Taxation Returns.[25] This failed to solve the problem of the corporations, but it provided a much needed injection of confidence in the annual Local Taxation Statement prepared by the Local Government Board. But the unintended consequence was to tie the form of local accounts to the needs of the local taxation statistical returns. The object of the 1860 Act was not to show the financial position of the local authorities, but annual taxation and expenditure: the authorities were required to submit, therefore, a statement of cash payments and receipts, not a balance sheet. And this is what the auditors continued to demand from local authorities. Checking and collating local statistical returns placed a large clerical burden on the Board: in the 1890s a staff of twenty-three clerks of various grades worked in the Statistics Department, yet the publication of the local taxation statements were chronically two or three years in arrears.[26] The Head of S Department told the 1898 Committee that the statistical work of the Board was 'a public disgrace'.[27]

Like the inspectors, the auditors were appointed by patronage, but apppointment to the district audit was less prestigious and financially rewarding.[28] Appointment to the inspectorate was a promotion from principal clerk or district auditor: appointment as auditor was a promotion from second class clerk. Auditors were required to be 'persons of experience and judgement'.[29] Aschrott, who compiled his account of the English poor law system in the 1880s from information given by officials of the Board,[30] reports that posts were often given to Guardian's clerks or solicitors. Until 1914, there were no formal qualifications. Nevertheless, the conventions governing appointment were gradually defined, and it was accepted that auditors must have prior experience in the LGB or in the district audit (by serving unpaid as an auditor's clerk), or be professionally qualified in law or accounting.[31] The Secretary's evidence to the 1903 Parliamentary Committee on Municipal Trading, states that of an establishment of fifty, ten had formal training in accounting, and none were Chartered Accountants.[32] In 1906, the Inspector of Audits and seventeen auditors were solicitors or barristers: with one exception, the others had been appointed from within the LGB, or had served as assistant auditors.[33] That is, as with the indoor work of the Board, the dominant culture was a legal one, tempered heavily by experience. In 1914, the Board gave formal recognition to these conventions: and the Institute of Municipal Accountants secured recognition of its membership for appointment.[34]

Auditors received no training: they were given a copy of the Acts and Orders of the Board, and a list of sanctions and orders issued to their authorities, and put to work.[35] Indeed, the quasi-judicial nature of the audit implied the independence of the auditors from supervision: but it also meant that the district audit was weakly co-ordinated. The danger to local self-government was not that audit would be used by central government to control local authorities, but rather that they would be exposed to an inconsistent and unpredictable jurisdiction.

The guidance offered to the auditors by the Board was largely written and formal: it regularly issued circulars of instruction on audit procedures and in 1879 advised the auditors that its staff was available 'to express their views generally as to any points which arise in reference to the performance of your duties'.[36] In 1877 it had also begun to publish, for its headquarters and field staff, selections from its decisions, the largest group of which were audit appeals.[37] The most important precedents were thus systematically recorded. (It was not till 1904 that the publishers of the *Local Government Chronicle* made them externally available).[38] There was no handbook in which the accumulating guidelines were collected, but in 1899, the Board compiled copies of the main Circulars to auditors, for the information of new appointees.[39] The evidence of Carson Roberts to the Departmental Committee on Local Authority Accounts in 1907 suggests that the auditors were in the habit of meeting six monthly on their own initiative to discuss problems and to agree common techniques.[40]

Co-ordination of the audit was also promoted by the Inspector of Audits, who visited auditors and advised on methods. But the Inspector had his own duties too; under the General Order on Accounts of 1867, he undertook occasional – but often protracted – local inquiries on sensitive appeals raising issues of political sensitivity or criminal liability, and, until 1901, he worked a district of his own. Lloyd Roberts, who became Inspector of Audits in 1892, audited the Metropolitan authorities.[41] This arrangement safeguarded his salary but left him little time for a co-ordinating role. In 1902, therefore, the Inspectorship became a whole-time appointment.[42] Audit appeals were dealt with by the Audit Department of the Board, and the decision was signed by the Assistant Secretary: the Inspector of Audits had only an advisory role in the appellate work.[43]

The audit generated a growing burden of work, both in the districts and in the office of the Board. In 1879, the district audit was responsible for some 18,000[44] sets of accounts. In 1888 the new county councils and the LCC came under the district audit[45] and,

in 1894, the parish councils.[46] In 1902, the new local education
authorities replaced the school boards, so that for the first time
the district auditors dealt with accounts prepared by boroughs.[47]
By 1910, some 25,000 accounts were audited yearly, of which 15,000
(the same figure as in 1879) were parish overseers' (or rate collec-
tors') accounts. This increment is due not only to the formation of
new types of local authority, but also to an increase in *ad hoc* local
bodies, particularly joint committees and public utilities. These
figures hide, however, some changes in the work: the many small
sets of accounts prepared by financially illiterate unpaid overseers
or highway surveyors were gradually replaced by accounts drawn
to standard forms laid down by the new professional bodies. But
this process was by no means complete before the First World
War: overseers continued to collect rates, and the IMTA failed to
penetrate far beyond the municipal corporations, whose accounts
were, in the main, not under the district audit.[48] And the accounts
contained many more transactions, authorised by statutes and
orders growing ever more complex, and by the 1890s some of the
urban authorities' possessed substantial trading enterprises.

In 1879, the Treasury sanctioned an establishment of thirty-
four full time district auditors, plus one assistant auditor who was
endowed with all their powers but surcharge.[49] The districts, which
were drawn to take account of county boundaries, were unequal
in size so that promotion was possible within the service.[50] One
consequence was that there was much more mobility between
districts in the audit than in the general inspectorate. But from the
beginning, many districts were too large. By November 1880, the
Local Government Board was already applying for temporary help
to meet the accumulating arrears in the populous counties of the
Midlands and North, where School Board formation and municipal
enterprise led to a rapid increase in the volume and value of
accounts, and in certain rural districts, particularly Norfolk, where
there were a large number of undistricted highway authorities.[51]
In the autumn of 1881-1882, the LGB persuaded the Treasury that
the problems were permanent and three extra posts were
sanctioned to form three more districts.[52] Thereafter, this pattern
repeats: there is a chronic history of arrears, temporary assistance
and reorganisation. For in contrast to the general inspectorate,

pressure for increases in establishments was irresistible: arrears in the audit delayed the issue of the local taxation returns,[53] and delays in closing their accounts irritated the local authorities. Moreover, the cost was more than met by the stamps paid by local authorities.

In 1894, pressure from the County Councils Association resulted in the permanent constitution of a separate six-district county audit.[54] But despite additions to the permanent and temporary staff, evidence to the 1898 Departmental Committee revealed the district audit to be in a very low state of morale.[55] Auditors complained of overlarge districts, missed holidays, inadequate clerical support, and a complete absence of personal office accommodation. Lloyd Roberts warned the committee bluntly that the pressure was affecting the quality of the work.[56] In 1901, the district audit was consequently expanded to a complement of fifty auditors and seven full time assistants, and completely reorganised into smaller districts, mostly comprising a county.[57] But temporary assistance had continually to be employed on a significant scale.

The audit casework at headquarters consisted in the large, and growing, number of appeals against disallowance and surcharge. The need for central intervention arose from the very trivia of many disallowances: the Board was obliged to operate a safety valve to mitigate the worst absurdities of a rigid audit. Under s. 32 of the 1844 Poor Law Act Amendment Act, auditors disallowed expenditure which was illegal, unreasonable or extravagant. Surcharges were imposed on disallowed expenditure or in respect of other deficiencies in the accounts, where the deficiency arose from the negligence or misconduct of officers or Members. Disallowances in all other accounts were made only in respect of illegal expenditure. The Instructional Circular to Auditors of 31 December 1879 specifically asked auditors to treat the authorities gently: the following quote indicates the routine nature of many surcharges at this date.

> The character of the audit entrusted to you may often oblige you to disallow charges incurred without any intention to violate the law, and in ignorance of the necessity which exists for legal authority of some kind to support all expenditure from the rate or fund in question. The Board are anxious that, so far as is compatible with the discharge of

your duty, your powers should be exercised with all possible consideration for the officers who may submit their acounts to you, and that care should taken by you to avoid all expressions of severity, and to soften by your manner any impression of harshness which the exercise of functions of this nature must occasionally carry with it.[58]

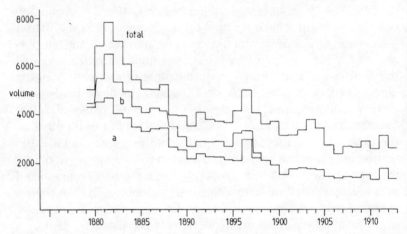

Fig. 6 Volume of Disallowances and Surcharges made by District Auditors in the accounts of local authorities, 1883-1913, showing volume in parish and Poor Law accounts (a); highway accounts (b); and others to make aggregate

Note: The vast majority of (a) is composed of disallowances and surcharges in overseers' accounts and (b) is mostly composed of undistricted parish and surveyors' accounts.

The peaks coincide with the 1888, 1894 and 1902 reorganisations of local government.

Source: Local Government Board Annual Reports

Auditors were responsible for enforcing their own surcharges and the number of disallowances and surcharges was large. In the early 1880s, they ran at 7,500 a year. By 1914, they had steadied at around 2,500-3,000 a year.[59] This still substantial number was, of course, levied on accounts of considerably greater range, volume and value. Figure 6 shows that a significant proportion of disallowances were in the accounts of poor law authorities – mainly overseers' accounts – and, in the early years, in the accounts of surveyors of highways. These officers were often not professional or educated men, and their work was by its nature largely unsupervised. But several hundred disallowances were made every year throughout this period in the accounts of district councils, school boards and town and county councils.[60] In general, the persistence of a high level of more-or-less routine disallowances indicates the slow administrative development of the smaller local authorities, and the peaks reflect disruptions to local administration caused by the Local Government Acts of 1888 and 1894, and the Education Act of 1902. Nevertheless, this pattern must also indicate the slow and uncertain integration, even as late as 1914, of many local authorities into the national, statutory and professional framework of the modern local government system, as well as the effects of the absence of a discretionary local spending power.

Under s. 4 of the 1848 Poor Law Audit Act, the Board exercised an equitable jurisdiction, that is it took account of considerations of justice and policy. It dealt with an appeal in one of three ways: it reversed a surcharge, it confirmed it, or it confirmed and remitted it. Each year the vast majority of surcharges that were appealed were confirmed and remitted: the officials of the Board calculated in 1907 that in the three previous years the ratio had been twelve-to-one,[61] and this was not untypical of the whole period since 1879. Remission recognised the trivial, unwilful nature of most disallowed expenditure, but the Board also used surcharge and remission to administer a warning against expenditures of a more objectionable kind. This is its officials' position in 1907:

> The mere act of confirmation possesses a distinctly educative value. In many instances it is accompanied by a caution. In all, it partakes of the nature of a warning. At the same time, it has no penal force. In itself, it is not a deterrent. Refusal of remission, on the other hand is a deterrent, and a really effective drag upon the tendency towards inexcusable illegalities.[62]

What the Board absolutely refused was to remit the same disallowances or losses recurring in the same authority.[63]

In the early 1880s, about one in seven surcharges were appealed, and despite the fall in the numbers of surcharges, the number of appeals rose steadily from around 1,000 a year in 1882 to 2,700 in 1886. The Board first tried to control the growing correspondence by issuing standard forms for appeals.[64] But the work was immense, and the trivial nature of many surcharges ridiculous. On 13 March, 1883, the Member for Cambridgeshire drew attention to the disallowance of 3s. 3d. for toys in the Wisbech Union Workhouse,[65] a case which received local publicity and, subsequently, embarrassing attention in the national press.[66]

The problem for the Board, however, was that it was just such details which had escaped the statutes and Orders. Its published decisions are full of appeals against disallowances of expenses for hospitality, deputations, purchases of law reports and local government journals, prizes and trophies in board schools, equipment for workhouses, and so on. But the provision of comforts in workhouses also touched a sensitive issue within the Board concerning the implictions of less eligibility,[67] and the reversal of the Wisbech case was followed by the issue of a Circular on the subject of children's play equipment.[68] At the time, however, there was no doubt that such cases did little to enamour the Board to the local authorities.

The Board's response was to take powers under the Local Authority (Expenses) Act of 1887[69] to sanction illegal expenditure. This Act created a large, discretionary power, which received no attention in its passage through Parliament.[70] But authorities were straightway given notice that it would be used only for isolated cases of *bona fide* ignorance of the letter of the law.

> We may add that we do not regard the Act as intended to supply the want of legislation or other authority for particular expenditure or classes of expenditure, and as justifying us in giving prospective sanction to recurring expenses.[71]

The administrative consequences of the 1887 Act were to reinforce the downward curve of appeals and remissions (though there was in 1888 a short sharp peak in this business caused by hosts of small expenditures for the Queen's Jubilee, which was the ostensible reason for the Act). But, of course, 1887 sanctions generated a supplementary business (Figure 7), though it was a business which the Board despatched, it claimed, quickly and easily.[72] The number of 1887 sanctions grew steadily for ten years reaching a peak in 1897 of nearly 3,000 applications. In 1914 the Board dealt with some 2,300 applications.

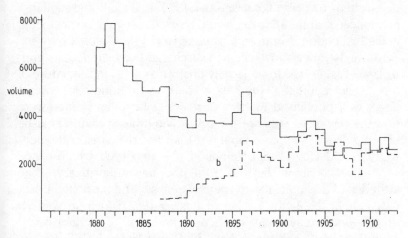

Fig. 7 Volume of applications under the 1887 Local Authority (Expenses) Act
(b) compared to volume of disallowances and surcharges (a)
Source: Local Government Board Annual Reports

1887 sanctions were used in three ways. The Board used its
power to smooth over the irritations provoked by an over strict
audit, especially when new authorities were first trying out their
powers. It used 1887 sanctions to avoid technical disallowances
and purely formal appeals. And it used them 'to prevent or remove
difficulty arising at the audit through doubt as to the legality of
expenditure which appeared to us to be unobjectionable in itself'.[73]
Auditors were under instructions to suspend audits while persons
potentially liable for surcharge were referred to the Board under
the 1887 Act.[74]

Most sanctions under 1887 therefore dealt with minor administrative matters. But it was an instrument which was also available
for the modification of policy. In 1887, the Board determined that
the power covered prospective as well as retrospective expenditure, a power which the Majority Report in 1909 castigated as wrong
in principle if not in law, because it allowed the Board to encourage
local authorities to break the law.[75] In practice the Board rarely
used the Act to sanction a concerted evasion of the restrictions of
statute: though Burns sanctioned attendance at conferences to promote his new Housing and Town Planning Act in 1910[76] and the

much cited Long circular of October, 1904[77] unusually and explicitly announced that the 1887 Act would be used to regularise payments made by London Boroughs for public works for the unemployed.

The use of disallowance and surcharge as a technique of control was recognised to be largely unstrategic. It is in the nature of the district audit that the cases where the routine audit raised large, well publicised matters of major policy significance were few: the obvious cases are those involving the contentious issue of compulsory vaccination in the 1870s,[78] and the cases of the Bedwelty and Merthyr Tydfil Unions in 1898 and 1900, which raised serious issues about the role of the poor law authorities, and the attitudes of the judiciary, to trade disputes.[79] The most significant cases are probably the Cockerton case of 1902, which provoked a major controversy about the scope and future of school board administration,[80] and the case of the Poplar Union in 1906, where claims substantiated by the auditor about extravagant outdoor relief and the general laxity of financial administration led to the highly publicised special inquiry by James Davy. Other less well-publicised disallowances had more limited strategic value to the Board, in long-drawn out struggles with individual authorities.[81]

The overall effect of the district audit was inevitably to promote a narrower rather than a wider interpretation of acceptable practice. We find, for example, disallowances of expenditure on Christmas bonuses for the outdoor poor (1879); bats and balls in board school playgrounds (1879); seaside outings for children and old people (1885); and outrelief to widows with illegitimate children (1904).[82] But the appeals sustained by the Board show that its appellate powers were used to protect local discretion and minor liberalities in the administration of the law. For example, it reversed or remitted disallowances of payments made to a specialist to examine a child in danger of going blind (1878); for the employment of teachers of handicrafts for the blind (1884); for newspapers in the workhouse (1983), for a piano in imbecile wards (1897); for the provision of snuff and tobacco in the workhouse on Christmas Day (1898); for a Christmas bonus for the outdoor poor (1898); for outdoor relief for a deserted married woman (1901), for outrelief to the family of a non-settled man (1904); and expenditure of a school board on prizes for sports (1883); and circulated these decisions for the notice of the auditors.[83]

Many disallowances arose from deficient accounting or administrative arrangements, and one commonly agreed effect of the audit was to exert a steady influence in the direction of better management of business and finance. Interest payments on overdrafts (which were illegal); loans diverted to unsanctioned projects; charges for bank accounts and payments by cheques (which were not approved till 1886);[84] outdoor relief payments unsupported by warrants; rates which overseers had neglected to collect; and minor irregularities in payroll administration[85] form the matter of many surcharges. That is, in so far as the auditors picked up the revenue effects of maladministration, they often reinforced other central measures towards better local stewardship.

The auditors were under instructions to promote sound practice by drawing attention to undesirable procedures,[86] and offering suggestions for improvement. From the 1880s, the Board's Audit Department also offered personal interviews to local officers seeking advice, and local authorities who regularly caused the auditors problems were referred to the general inspector.[87] That is, the Board recognised the distinction made in the Minority Poor Law Report in 1909[88] beween matters of law and matters of policy. However, the distinction was less clear cut in practice: the obligation to surcharge for losses to the accounts, and the discretionary power bestowed on auditors under the poor laws to disallow 'unreasonable' as well as illegal expenditure, inevitably brought the auditors formally into matters beyond the strict application of law. For example, the surcharge which led to the notorious case of Rex v Carson Roberts, 1908, was in respect of loss to the accounts arising from failure by councillors to take the lowest tender for workhouse supplies.[89] The auditor was much criticised by the court and by the Minority Report of 1909[90] for trespassing into matters of local discretion: the historical context of this case, however, was a series of – not unfounded – allegations of corruption in the procurement of supplies and the management of outdoor relief in certain London unions, which led to a review of poor law accounts as well as a number of special inquiries.[91]

The practices which the audit could most easily address, then, were administrative or they were symptomatic and indicative of the approach or policy of the local authority, rather than central to it. In particular, the poor law audit was acknowledged to have largely failed in its original primary purpose,[92] to curb outdoor relief. Danby Fry, then Inspector of Audits, told the 1874 Select Committee on Borough Auditors that the poor law audit's essential function was not the protection of ratepayers, but the promotion of an efficient and uniform administration.[93] But in the poor law, these were often taken to be the same thing. For it was widely believed that low expenditure and a low proportion of outdoor relief, particularly, was indicative of its effectiveness in keeping the working classes independent of the state. 'The Local Government Board', conceded an editorial in the *Poor Law Officers' Journal* in 1906, 'exists largely through the recognition of the fact that it is the business of the state to hold pauperism with as tight a rein as possible'.[94] But Davy told the Royal Commission on the Poor Laws[95] that local circumstances, and the difficulty of sustaining allegations of extravagance in the courts, made it impossible to police outdoor relief effectively through the audit. An exceptional amount of outdoor relief in the accounts of a Union should therefore prompt reference to the general inspector, rather than surcharging.

Davy's view coincided with that of many general inspectors who believed that a negative and rigid audit damaged their relations with local authorities, rather than supported them,[96] and the Assistant Secretary from the Audit Division openly confessed to the Royal Commission in 1909 that the Board would prefer auditors to be less strenuous in disallowing and surcharging small sums.[97] The political difficulties in sustaining a strict audit also emerge in the brief prepared in the department for Runciman who, as Parliamentary Secretary, chaired the 1907 Committee on local authority accounts:

> It is no doubt contended that at the present time the somewhat narrow and unsympathetic attitude which the Commissioners adopted sixty years ago, is no longer tenable, and that the extensive and complicated machinery of local government, based upon a system of unpaid representation, cannot be worked upon precisely the same principles as were appropriate to Boards of Guardians in an age when precision in Poor Law administration was urgently required. If therefore the Board were called upon to defend the existing method of surcharge, they would

probably not employ quite such uncompromising language as was used
by the Commissioners.[98]

For the routine surcharge of all disallowances was known to
be unacceptable to local authorities. The County Councils Association had lobbied against the practice in the 1890s,[99] and in 1894
and 1896 had promoted a bill[100] to limit surcharges to cases of
personal defalcation, by interposing a routine reference to the
Board before a surcharge was made. The bill also proposed to
make the local authorities, rather than auditors, responsible for
recouping deficiencies in their accounts. The bill was, however,
unacceptable to the Local Government Board because of the volume of correspondence which such a discretion would generate,[101]
and the matter was not pursued. The Poor Law Officers Association
also opposed surcharging, and the 'over-elaboration' of central
control[102] and, as we will see, the refusal of the Board to dispense
with surcharging was a major ground upon which the Association
of Municipal Corporations was able to withstand pressure for the
extension of the district audit to the corporations. Yet, despite the
irritation provoked by surcharging, the Board consistently upheld
its importance. And, in this, its instincts coincided with the
pressures arising from the fiscal problems of local government.

The Board clung to surcharging simply because it was its only
effective weapon to constrain local administration, and, by the turn
of the century, central government was in no mood to forego any
curb on local expenditure. Surcharge was justified on the grounds
that the primary client interest of the Board and the local
authorities was the ratepayers. This was the paramount reason,
explained Burns in 1906, why he could not allow the local
authorities more flexibility to respond to unemployment '... he
was bound to subordinate his personal views on many subjects to
his official responsibility as guardian of the ratepayers' purse'.[103]
'The interests of the ratepayers are paramount', explained Auditor
Cockerton to the 1903 Joint Parliamentary Committee on Municipal
Trading, 'It is the interests of the ratepayer that the auditors have
specially to protect'.[104]

This line reflects the political pressures which led to extension
of what was originally the poor law audit to other aspects of local
government administration, where there was less obvious need for

consistency, and where the association of high revenue expenditure and slack administration did not hold. As originally drafted, the Education Acts of 1870 and 1902 made no provision for disallowance and surcharge in boroughs:[105] in each case, they were inserted as a result of pressure from the local taxation lobby. However, the ratepayers never achieved the extension of the district audit to the accounts of municipal corporations.

The 1835 Municipal Corporations Act provided for audit by elected auditors and by a nominee of the Mayor.[106] These arrangements were confirmed by the 1882 Municipal Corporations Act,[107] but they were patently difficult to defend. By common consent, there was little interest in being nominated or in voting for elected auditors. The auditors were reluctant draftees or political jobbers and the audit often incompetent and scrimped. But the local taxation lobby pressed not only for a professional audit, which the corporations would have found difficult to resist, but also for disallowance and surcharge: by holding out for a repressive audit, they destroyed the chances of reform.

The local taxation lobby wanted to bring the corporations under the district audit to obtain certified information about their expenditures, to mobilise urban ratepayers. Their chance to prosecute the issue came in 1874 when the corporations promoted a bill[108] to remove the election of municipal auditors from the scope of the 1872 Ballot Act, on grounds of cost and convenience. Faced with opposition from the Local Taxation Committee and from the Government, who were worried about the integrity of the Ballot Act and who believed that no system of audit would be effective without disallowance and surcharge,[109] the promoters of the Bill agreed to the establishment of a Select Committee.[110] A Committee was accordingly nominated with Pell as Chairman, and with an equal balance of county and municipal members. Pell's draft Report dwelt not only on the costs of election and the problems of a non-professional audit, but also recommended that the elective audit be strengthened by the power of surcharge. But the municipal members forced the removal of all references to surcharging.[111]

The grounds upon which the corporations defended their arrangements were partly positive and partly negative. We find in their evidence some classic early statements of municipal collectivism: as locally-elected bodies, corporations should have the unfettered right, it was claimed, to determine the local interest.[112] The corporations also argued, however, from the deficiencies of the district audit. Their representatives were easily able to demonstrate the Local Government Board's ignorance of municipal affairs, and its weak control over the practice of the auditors.[113] In contrast to the negative impact of the district audit, the corporations' witnesses lauded the innovations made possible by their greater freedom, particularly in health where many were far ahead of the Public Health Act.[114] The Committee could hardly approve the implications of this position, that corporations should be allowed to exceed their legal powers, but commented 'that any audit of ... accounts under the control of the Government is undesirable, and would occasion an unnecessary interference with independent self-government in boroughs'.[115] Thwarted by the Select Committee, the Local Taxation Committee continued its pressure for improved local taxation returns. In 1877, the Government introduced (rather late in the session) a Local Taxation Returns Bill, which proposed an optional power for municipalities to take the district audit.[116] Sclater-Booth believed that small towns would take up this offer, to save expense. But the AMC perceived it to be a thin edge of a wedge and mobilised the borough Members to oppose the bill.[117] Aware that the bill could not be passed if there were sustained opposition, Sclater-Booth agreed to remove all mention of disallowance and surcharge.[118]

The political power of the municipalities to block audit reform stemmed from the nature of the parliamentary politics of local government. Like the Local Taxation Committee, the AMC could organise a cross-party coalition which had not sufficient numerical strength to pass its own bills, but possessed power enough to obstruct bills which were not so strategically important that the Government was prepared to invest vast resources of parliamentary time. That is, on contentious but politically marginal matters like the audit, the AMC in effect possessed a veto.

After 1877, the Local Taxation Committee made little serious effort to reform the municipal audit, contenting itself with token comments and questions in Parliament. Nor did the AMC take the threat to the corporations very seriously. In 1888, for example, it took the greatest exception to the extension of the district audit to the new County Councils[119] but, compared to the much more pressing issue raised by the local government bill, the financial relations of counties and boroughs, the audit question received little of the Association's attention.

In the 1890s, the political salience of the district audit began, however, to increase under the pressure of unease about the growth in urban expenditure. There were intermittent comments in Parliament[120] about the quality and composition of the district audit, and in the Report of the Comptroller and Auditor General on the financial appropriations of 1891-2.[121] Their significance was, however, that they left the district audit tarnished and weakened in resisting the much greater onslaught on its reputation, arising from the municipal trading issue at the end of the 1890s.

The immediate catalysts of the agitation which led to the appointment of the Joint Parliamentary Committee on Municipal Trading in 1900 and 1903, were the very sharp increase in urban debt at the turn of the century, and a spate of private and public bills which threatened to extend the trading rights of town authorities.[122] The campaign united anti-collectivist ideologues with the self interest of commercial and domestic ratepayers. It was, however, an uncomfortable issue for the Conservative Government. For while the cry of socialism on the rates stirred the unease of many a Tory (and was taken up by London Moderates),[123] the Liberal and Lib/Lab defenders of municipal enterprise found fellow feeling with urban Unionists and Conservative borough Members anxious to trumpet the benefits of active municipal government to their towns. The (largely) Conservative leadership of the AMC saw the issue as a direct threat to the independence and aspirations of the corporations: we find, in many of their speeches at this time some of the clearest statements of the collectivist aspirations of organised municipalism.[124] Balfour's strategy was therefore to contain the discontent and to reduce the noise.

The prime movers of the campaign against municipal trading were the dogmatic, anti-collectivist pressure group, the Liberty and Property Defence League[125] and the Central Chamber of Commerce: and its major instrument was the ratepayer organisation, the Industrial Freedom League, which was created under the Presidency of Lord Avebury in 1902. These groups mobilised, between 1899 and 1902, a large number of local chambers, trade and employers' associations, and local ratepayer associations, and rallies were held and petitions drawn up in large quantity.[126] *The Times* carried wide coverage of the campaign, published many letters, and fuelled agitation with a series of leaders in 1902,[127] and the subject received much polemical attention in the learned journals.[128] The major grievance of organised business was that it was compelled to pay heavy rates to provide investment in enterprises which competed on unfair terms. Whereas the muncipalities claimed – and a Return to Parliament moved in 1899 by H. H. Fowler showed[129] – that the growing urban debt was largely remunerative, the anti-trading lobby claimed that the real costs were hidden by inadequate methods of municipal accounting. In particular, it was argued, the rates of depreciation were too small, the administrative costs were pooled with other costs of corporations, and insufficient account was taken of the enterprises' monopolistic position in calculating their comparative returns. The audit thus became a crucial issue in the battle.

Avebury wanted a suspension of new trading powers pending an inquiry into municipal trading. Balfour granted in 1900 a Joint Parliamentary Committee, which, he emphasised, was not intended to be hostile to the corporations, but would consider the principles by which municipal trading should be regulated by Parliament:[130] its purpose was to secure greater consistency in Private Bills, and the AMC did not feel able overtly to oppose a committee with such reasonable terms of reference.[131] The Joint Committee failed, however, to make a substantive report in 1900, and faced with difficult parliamentary programmes dominated by the Education Bills, Balfour fended off proposals for its reappointment in 1901 and 1902.

However, local authority auditing had been kept in the forefront of the politics of municipal government by the Cockerton Judgement of 1902. And in 1902 the AMC suffered a set back when the Government guillotined its amendment to the Education Act opposing the application of the district audit to education accounts:[132] henceforth the largest slice of county borough acccounts and the education accounts of some non county and urban districts came under the district audit. A deputation to Walter Long in November 1902 extracted the less than satisfactory statement that, though the Government had no plans to extend the audit to other corporation accounts, it would not withdraw on education because of the high proportion of expenditure borne by the Exchequer.[133] It was in this context that in 1903 the Joint Committee resumed its work, and started to take a close look at municipal accounts and audit.

The evidence to the Committee was heavily in favour of substituting a professional audit for the corporations' elective audit.[134] The representatives of town councils did not bother to defend their existing arrangements, and the professional accountancy bodies pressed strongly for qualified auditors.[135] Both agreed that the inexperience of district auditors in commercial accounting prohibited them from undertaking municipal accounts, though they favoured the central sanction of appointment and dismissal of auditors, to ensure impartiality. But the representatives of the District Audit, the LCC and the Local Government Board, all emphasised that only a government audit could guarantee independence,[136] and the Board's Permanent Secretary, Samuel Provis, pressed its view that to be effective, the audit must be supported by surcharge.[137]

The 1903 Report of the Joint Committee endorsed the arguments of the corporations, and was strongly critical of the district audit. It recommended that the accounts of all local authorities should be audited by professional accountants to be appointed for five year periods by the local authorities under central sanction. The new auditors should extend their role, beyond the mere certification of figures and facts, to monitor local debt management: and local authorities should establish income and expenditure accounts. It also noted the burden on the Local Government Board of audit-generated casework which, it argued rightly, was disproportionate to the issues involved and inappropriate for a central department. The Committee recommended, therefore, the establishment of an *ad hoc* Commission, to which the Board's powers should be devolved. The composition and status of the central audit agency was, however, a non-issue and received no notice at all when the report was published.

The Report was, of course, immediately endorsed by the

AMC,[138] who were prepared to accept a professional audit to stave off the 'Cockertonisation' of their accounts.[139] However, in December 1903, Long told the Association that the Government would support a bill only if it introduced surcharge and provided for permanent appointments: the Local Government Board was prepared to accept the principle of a professional audit only if its independence from local pressure could be guaranteed.[140] At this point, the AMC ceased to press the matter actively, but in order to head off further pressure from the municipal trading lobby, Long promised a departmental inquiry into local authority accounts[141] This Departmental Committee was eventually set up by John Burns under renewed parliamentary pressure in 1906.[142] It reported in 1907,[143] endorsing the call from the district auditors, the professional bodies, and the major local authority associations for more uniformity of principle and more expertise in local government accounting. The committee was, however, ambivalent about reforms in the direction of income and expenditure accounting and trading accounts, arguing that the local financial returns forced authorities to produce cash accounts, and the unpredictability of grants rendered income too uncertain to be authoritatively estimated.

The Departmental Committee therefore resisted pressure for the district audit to become the instrument of restricting the trading actitivities and capital accumulation of local authorities. And proposals for a more positive role for the audit in the development of local financial administration were not taken up. The audit remained, therefore, a technique for the monitoring and restraint of the details of local authorities' revenue expenditure. Nevertheless, the municipal trading lobby was reflecting and exploiting a general unease about the extension of local debt that went wider than the commercial interests whose markets were spoiled by municipal enterprise. Just as in revenue finance, the centre played an ambiguous role, caught between the needs of consumers and the political power of the ratepayers and property holders, and mediating the demands on the one made by the other. This conflict of roles is most formally developed in the control of capital spending, particularly in the 'local' functions of environmental development. It is to these arrangements that we now turn.

NOTES TO CHAPTER FIVE

1 4 & 5 Wm. IV c. 76 s. 15; On the history of the District Audit, L. M. Helmore, *The District Auditor,* Macdonald and Evans, 1961; and R. Jones, *Local Government Audit Law,* (H.M.S.O., 1981).

2 *Report of House of Commons Select Committee on the Poor Law Amendment Act,* 1837-8 (681) XVIII I p. 36, endorsed by the *Report of the Poor Law Commissioners on the Continuance of the Poor Law Commission and the Amendment of the Poor Law Amendment Act,* 1840 (C. 226) XVII 167 p. 49-50.

3 7 & 8 Vict. c. 101 s. 32.

4 *Ibid.* s. 36.

5 *Ibid.* s. 32.

6 Parochial Debt and Audit Act, 1848, 11 & 12 Vict. c. 91 s. 4.

7 First paid for half year ending 31 March 1847.

8 *Report of Committees of Inquiry into the Public Offices,* 'Report on the Poor Law Board', pp. 210-214.

9 Poor Law Act Amendment Act 1868, 31 & 32 Vict. c. 122 s. 24.

10 Local Government Act 1858, 21 & 22 Vict. c. 98 s. 60.

11 Elementary Education Act, 1870, 33 & 34 Vict. c. 75. ss.59-62.

12 Public Health Act 1872, 35 & 36 Vict. s. 79 ss. 49-50.

13 Divided Parishes Act 1876, 39 & 40 Vict. c. 61 s. 37.

14 Elementary Education Act Amendment Act 1876, 39 & 40 Vict. ss. 30-32.

15 Highways and Locomotives Act Amendment Act 1878 c. 77.

16 *Memorandum on Proposed Legislation on District Auditors,* n.d. enclosed with LGB to Treasury, 22 August 1879, MH 19/213.

17 *Memorandum on Appointment, Salaries and Additional Duties of Auditors,* 7 November 1876, PRO MH 19/86.

18 *Memorandum on Proposed Legislation,* and 239 H. C. Deb. 3s. 15 April 1878 col. 1639.

19 1879 District Auditors Act 1879, 42 & 43 Vict. c. 6.

20 LGB to Treasury, 22 August 1879.

21 Local Government Taxation Returns Act, 1860 22 & 23 Vict. c. 51.

22 *Return of Local Taxation and Expenditure in Each County and Union in England for 1866,* 1867-8 (53) LVIII 707; *Return of Estimates of Rental and Rateable Value of the Several Parishes and Townships of England and Wales, and Amounts Levied in Respect of Rates,* 1867-8 (497) LIX I 679. For the corporations and local commissions, there is a series beginning at 1870 (416) LV 575. An amendment to Return 497 had to be published as 1870 (430) LV 411 to correct the many omissions and mistakes.
210 H. C. Deb. 3s. 16 April 1872 col. 1331; 212 H. L. Deb. 3s. 2 June 1872 cols. 18-19; 219 H. C. Deb. 3s. 19 May 1874 col. 479; 229 H. C. Deb. 3s. 29

May 1879 cols. 1353-4.

On the problems of the returns, see P. G. Craigie, 'The cost of Local Government', Pt. II.

23 Local Taxation (Accounts) Bill, 1872 (220) II 785; and 1873 (16) III 25; *Annual Report of Local Taxation Committee for 1873.*

24 Local Taxation Returns Act 1877. 40 & 41 Vict. c. 66.

25 42 & 43 Vict. c. 6 s. 3.

26 'Statement of Principal Clerks', *Evidence Taken before the Local Government Board Inquiry Committee,* statement of Head of Statistical Department.

27 *Ibid.* Evidence of F. Stevens, Q. 2715.

28 The remuneration set in 1879 was for salaries in a range between £510-£700 a year, from which the auditors paid their clerks. General Inspectors were paid £800-£1000. *The Re-organisation of the Audit Consequent on the District Auditors Act 1879,* 1879, PRO MH 19/90, and *Return to House of Commons on Inspectors and Auditors of Local Government Board,* 1906.

29 *The Re-organisation of the Audit,* 1879.

30 P. F. Aschrott, *The English Poor Law System,* translated by Herbert Preston Thomas, Knight & Co., 1888, p. 186. A footnote on the same page indicated its sources, and Preston Thomas was, of course, a General Inspector at the Board.

31 52 H. C. Deb. 4s. 2 August 1897 col. 116.

32 *Report of the Joint Committee on Municipal Trading,* 1903, evidence of Provis, Q. 130. The membership lists in the Annual Reports of their Council indicate that there were no Members of the IMTA amongst the auditors before the first World War.

33 *Return of Inspectors and Auditors of the LGB*

34 Annual Presidential Address, 1913, *Proceedings of the IMTA,* 1913.

35 *Report of Royal Commission on the Poor Laws,* evidence of E. P. Burd, II Q. 760.

36 *Instructional Circular to District Auditors from LGB,* 31 December 1879, PRO MH 78/132 p. 18.

37 *Selections from the Correspondence of the LGB* (printed for the use of the officers of the Department only), I-IX, 1877-1912, PRO HLG 46/127-135.

38 W. A. Casson, *Decisions of the Local Government Board,* Knight & Co., 1904-; Casson was Editor of the *Local Government Chronicle,* and had been a second class clerk and then auditor at the Board.

39 *Circulars and Memoranda of the LGB Relating to the Duties of District Auditors,* 1899, PRO MH 78/132.

40 *Report of Departmental Committee on the Accounts of Local Authorities,* 1907 (Cd. 3615) xxxvii 711, evidence of Carson Roberts, II. Qs. 1923-4.

41 LGB to Treasury, 30 December 1904, PRO MH 32/104.

42 *Evidence Taken Before the Local Government Board Inquiry Committee,*

evidence of Loyd Roberts Qs. 5533-9; evidence of Knollys Q. 7185. LGB to Treasury, 30 December 1904.

43 *Report of Royal Commission on the Poor Laws,* II, evidence of Pitts, Q. 4181.

44 The statistics relating to the numbers of accounts, disallowances and appeals in the following paragraphs are taken from the Annual Reports of the Local Government Board.

45 51 & 52 Vict. c. 41 s. 71.

46 56 & 57 Vict. c. 73 s. 58.

47 2 Edw VII c. 42 s. 19(3).

48 In 1898-9, the IMTA had 414 members of which 16 worked for administrative counties, 62 for non county boroughs, 5 for Metropolitan vestries and boards, and 7 for UDCs. That is, about a third of local authorities were represented in the Institute. There were no RDC members till 1926. *Proceedings,* 1899, and IMTA, *IMTA: a Short History,* chapter 1.

49 Treasury to LGB, 29 September 1879, PRO MH 16/213. The draft standard letter of appointment as an assistant auditor is in PRO MH 19/90, 5 May 1879.

50 'Increased duties of the District Audit from 1871-1903', *Resume of Establishments of LGB, 1871-1903,* 1903, PRO MH 78/45.

51 LGB to Treasury, 19 November 1880, PRO MH 19/213.

52 LGB to Treasury, 11 September 1881, PRO MH 19/214; LGB to Treasury, 19 December 1881, *ibid.*

53 *Ibid.* Also pressure in 1887 about delays to poor law returns; departmental correspondence 15 November 1887, PRO MH 20/46.

54 Minutes of Executive Council of CCA, 9 March 1892; Minutes of Annual Meeting, 20 March 1892; report of deputation to Ritchie, 27 April 1892; Minutes of Executive Council of CCA, 9 November 1892; *Annual Report of Executive Council of CCA for 1893-4.*

55 *Evidence taken before Local Government Board Inquiry Committee,* evidence of Adams, Jerrold and Lloyd Roberts.

56 *Ibid.* Q. 5703.

57 'The re-organisation of the audit staff 1901', *Resumé of Establishments of the LGB, 1871-1903.*

58 *Instructional Circular,* 1879, p. 17.

59 The annual number of disallowances, appeals and remissions is stated in the Annual Report of the LGB

60 The highest number of school board disallowances and surcharges is 602 in 1881-2; thereafter it declined to around 300, till 1902. The disallowances and surcharges in rural district authorities was highest in the same year at 152 but they were often under 100 in subsequent years. The highest number of urban district disallowances and surcharges was in 1890-1 at 713; they ran between 400 and 600 a year till 1914. Disallowances and surcharges in county council accounts were generally under 100 till 1902; thereafter the transfer of education accounts significantly increased the disallowances and surcharges in both county council and town council accounts.

61 *Methods of Making Surcharges on Members of Local Authorities,* Memorandum to Parliamentary Secretary, 1907, PRO HLG 46/124.

62 *Ibid.*

63 Routine statement accompanying audit statistics in LGB Annual Reports. Also, *Report of Royal Commission on the Poor Laws,* 1909, II, evidence of Pitts, Q. 4240.

64 LGB Circular to Auditors, 15 May 1885, *Annual Report of Local Government Board for 1885-6,* 1886 (C. 4844) XXXI I, Appendix B.

65 277 H. C. Deb. 3s. 13 March 1883 col 365.

66 As usual when the Board was the centre of unwelcome publicity, the officials filed the press cuttings. The file of the case is PRO MH 12/757.

67 Rotten, Owen and Dilke favoured a more liberal attitude than that set by their immediate predecessors, Lambert and Dodson, and were not unhappy to change the policy of the Board. Rotten to Owen, 12 March 1883; Owen to Dilke 22 May 1883, *ibid.*

68 Preston Thomas, *Work and Play of a Government Inspector,* p. 209.

69 50 & 51 Vict. c. 72.

70 321 H. C. Deb. 3s. 10 September 1887 col. 215 and 13 September col. 539, 1887.

71 *Annual Report of LGB for 1887-8,* 1888 (C. 5526) XLIX I p. lxix.

72 *Report of Joint Committee on Municipal Trading,* 1903, evidence of Provis, Qs. 150-158.

73 *Annual Report of LGB for 1908-1909,* 1909 (Cd. 4786) xxvii 499, p. lvii.

74 Minute of LGB to auditors, 30 August 1889, PRO MH 78/132.

75 *Report of the Royal Commission on the Poor Laws,* 1909, 'Majority Report', I, p. 124.

76 Circular no 7, 31 December 1909, *Annual Report of LGB for 1909-10,* 1910 (Cd. 5275) xxxviii Pt. II Appendix II.

77 Circular 37 of 1904-5, 29 October 1904 para. 8, enclosed in Circulars 35 and 36 of 1904-5 to Metropolitan Guardians and Metropolitan Boroughs, 31 October 1904, *Annual Report of L.G.B. for 1904-5,* 1905 (Cd. 2655 xxxi I, Appendix A.

78 e.g the failure to pursue penalties for non vaccination; the case of the Keighley Guardians, *Selections from the Correspondence of the LGB.,* I. 1877; also, *Papers on the Keighley Guardians,* 1876 (436) LXI 305.

79 In the Bedwelty case, the auditor allowed the use of the ratefund to pay for labour yards, opened with LGB sanction, to employ men thrown out of work by an industrial dispute. The ratepayers appealed to the court, and the allowance was overturned. A G v Bedwelty Union, J. P. 792 11 November 1898, and *Selections,* VI. p. 105; in the Methyr Tydfill case, the auditor allowed relief for striking workmen in danger of starving, as well as for their wives and children. This was overturned by the Court of Appeal. A G v Merthyr Tydfill Union 1901 Ch. 516; 69 L. J. Ch. 299; 82 L. T. 662; 48 W.R. 403; 16 T. L. R. 251, and 6 March 1900, C. A.

80 In 1899, the district auditor for the Metropolis, T. B. Cockerton, upheld a complaint from the North London School of Art and disallowed the London School Board's expenditure for teaching adults and aspects of science, that is teaching outside the Education Department's Code. The auditor's decision was upheld by the Court of Queen's Bench in late 1900, and on appeal in 1901; Reg. v. Cockerton 1 Q. B. 1901 322. The Education Bill, 1901, was withdrawn to allow a bill to be passed regularising the illegal expenditure, but the judgement pointed up very sharply the issue of the future of school boards and their powers.

81 e.g. the case of the Bramley Union where the disallowance of excessive outdoor relief in 1895 focussed the issue of the inadequacy of the union's workhouse. Cited in *Methods of Making Surcharges, 1907.*

82 *Selections from the Correspondence of the LGB, passim; Knight's Decisions of the Local Government Board, passim.*

83 *Ibid.*

84 Minute of LGB, 8 June 1886, PRO MH 78/132.

85 *Selections,* and *Decisions, passim.*

86 *Instructional Circular,* 1879.

87 'The Audit Department', *Statement of the Several Duties of the Local Government Board,* October 1883, PRO MH 78/51.

88 *Royal Commission on the Poor Laws,* 1909, p. 983.

89 1 K.B. 407.

90 *Royal Commission on the Poor Laws,* 1909, 'Minority Report', p. 982-3.

91 *Report of the Departmental Committee on Workhouse Accounts,* 1903, (Cd. 1440) xxvi 567; *Report on Poplar Union* by J. S. Davy, 1906 (Cd. 3240) civ 1. There was at this time also a special inquiry by the Inspector of Audits into the West Ham Union in 1908, and a special inquiry into the Mile End Union. The latter is referred to in the *Annual Report of the LGB for 1908-9,* 1909 (Cd. 4786) xxviii 499 p. lvii, and was published as 1909 (Cd. 4011) xcii 541. The former inquiries were the subject of some comment in Parliament: 154 H. C. Deb. 4s. March 26 1906; 156 H. C. Deb. 4s. 4 May 1906 col. 829; 165 H. C. Deb. 4s. 15 November 1906 col. 127; 167 H. C. Deb. 4s. col. 337.

92 *Report of Royal Commission on the Poor Laws,* 1909, evidence of E. P. Burd, II. Q. 4633.

93 *Report of Select Committee of House of Commons on Borough Auditors and Assessors,* 1874 (321) VII I, evidence Q. 1586.

94 *Poor Law Officers' Journal,* XV, February 23 1906, p. 177.

95 *Report of Royal Commission on the Poor Laws,* II, Qs. 2120-1.

96 'One of the most constant sources of annoyances to Boards of Guardians

are the disallowances by the Auditors for trivial expenditures', Inspector Peel to LGB, 10 November 1873, PRO MH 32/104.

97 *Report of Royal Commission on the Poor Laws,* evidence of Pitts, II, Qs. 4226-7.

98 *Methods of Making Surcharges,* 1907.

99 Minutes of CCA Executive Council, 9 March 1892; Minutes of Annual meeting of CCA, 30 March 1892; Minutes of Executive Council, 9 November 1892.

100 1894 (299) III 71; 1896 (152) I. 427.

101 *Report on County Auditors Bill,* July 1894, PRO 19/134.

102 *Poor Law Officers' Journal,* XV January 26th 1906, pp. 81-3.

103 H. C. Deb. 4s. 26 February 1906 col. 891.

104 *Report of Joint Committee on Municipal Trading,* Q. 2748.

105 The issue of the audit arising from the 1902 Act is discussed below, note. 141.

106 7 William IV & I Vict. c. 78 s. 6.

107 45 & 46 Vict. c. 50 ss. 25-28.

108 Municipal Boroughs (Auditors and Assessors) Bill, 1874 (54) III 465.

109 H. C. Deb. 3s. 20 May 1874 col. 592.

110 219 H. C. Deb. 3s. 2 June 1874 col. 918.

111 *Report of Select Committee on Borough Auditors,* pp. x-xvii.

112 *Ibid.* Evidence of Town Clerks of Nottingham, Stockton-on-Tees, Manchester, Cambridge, Sunderland and Hull.

113 *Ibid.* Evidence of Danby Fry, Qs 1637 and 1689.

114 *Ibid.* Qs 1651-6, 1693-1717.

115 *Ibid.* v.

116 Local Taxation Returns Bill, 1877 (220) III 443.

117 Minutes of sub committee of AMC Council, 9 August 1877; Circular to Town Clerks, 23 July 1877, PRO 30/72.9.

118 236 H. C. Deb. 3s. 9 August 1877 col. 680.

119 Minutes of meeting of AMC Council, 5 April 1888, PRO 30/72.18.

120 21 H. C. Deb. 4s. 20 February 1894, col. 903; 36 H. C. Deb. 4s. 26 August 1895 col. 819; 52 H. C. Deb. 4s. 2 August 1897 col. 116; 68 H. C. Deb. 4s. 7 March 1899 col. 32; 75 H. C. Deb. 4s. 25 July 1899 col. 237.

121 12 H. C. Deb. 4s. 19 May 1893 col. 1368.

122 The bills that caused most trouble were, the Light Railways Bill 1896 (94) IV 63 and the Telegraph Bill 1899 (123) VII 243, and the following private bills: Huntingdon Corporation Bill, Manchester Tramways Bill 1899 and the Huddersfield Electric Tramways Bill, 1900. The debate on the latter is at 82 H. C. Deb. 8 May 1900, col. 1041.

123 Ken Young, *Local Politics and the Rise of Party,* Chapters 2 and 3.

124 Speech of Rollit, President of AMC, 81 H. C. Deb. 4s. 5 April 1900 col. 1341; speech of Rollit, 118 H. C. Deb. 4s. 4 March 1903 col. 1430; speech of Burns *ibid.* col. 1436. Also, Rollit's speeches to AMC Annual Meetings 26

March 1898, PRO 30/72.27; 31 March 1900, PRO 30/72.29; 22 March 1901, PRO 30/72.30; 27 October 1902, PRO 30/72.32; and 21 March 1903, PRO 30/72.33.

125 Herman Finer, *Municipal Trading,* Allen & Unwin, 1941, pp. 58-67. N. Seldon 'Laissez-faire as dogma; the Liberty and Property Defence League' in Kenneth D. Brown, *Essays in Anti-Labour History,* Macmillan, 1974; and Edward Bristow 'The Liberty and Property Defence League', *The Historical Journal,* XVIII, 1875, 761-789.

126 *Ibid.*

127 *The Times,* 19 August, p. 7; 2 September p. 7; 8 September p. 7; 16 September p. 7; 22 September p. 7; 11 November p. 9; 8 December 1902, p. 9.

128 D. H. Davies, 'The cost of municipal enterprise', *Journal of the Society of Arts,* XVLII, 1898-9, pp. 224-240 and 265-275; Edwin Cannan, 'Ought municipal enterprises to be allowed to yield a profit?' *The Economics Journal,* IX, 1899, pp. 1-9; H. H. Fowler 'Municipal finance and municipal enterprise', *Journal of the Statistical Society,* LXIII, 1900, pp. 383-407; Lord Avebury, 'The growth of municipal and national expenditure', *Journal of the Royal Statistical Society,* LXIV, 1901, pp. 73-86; R. J. Thompson, 'Local expenditure and local indebtedness in England and Wales', *Journal of the Royal Statistical Society,* LXVII, 1904, 337-367.

Avebury's argument against municipal trading is set out at length in Avebury, *On Municipal Trading,* Macmillan & Co., 1906; and the case for municipal collectivism through private acts in Frederick Clifford, *Local and Private Bills: some Remarks on Pending Legislation,* Eyre & Spottiswoode, 1904.

129 *Return of . . . Reproductive Undertakings Carried on by Municipal Boroughs for the Five Years ending 31 March 1898,* 1899 (88) LXXXIII I 205.

130 81 H. C. Deb. 4s. 29 March 1900 col. 769.

131 *Ibid.* col. 759.

132 *Annual Report of Council of AMC for 1901-1902,* PRO 30/772.33.

133 Report of the deputation to Walter Long, 25 November 1902, Minutes of Council of AMC, 27 November 1902, *ibid.*

134 *Report of Joint Committee on Municipal Trading,* evidence of Edward Offord Smith, W. J. Jeeves, R. Barrow and William Bateson.

135 *Ibid.* Evidence of W. S. Corner, J. M. Fells, C. H. Wilson, William Bateson and Thomas Abercrombie.

136 *Ibid.* Evidence of Sir Samuel Provis, T. B. Cockerton and H. E. Haward.

137 *Ibid.*, Qs. 179 and 238.

138 Minutes of the Council of AMC 10 December 1903, PRO 30/72.33.

139 The phrase in Rollit's; speech to AMC Autumn Meeting, 22 October 1902, PRO 30/72.33; Minutes of Autumn Meeting of AMC, 21 October 1903, PRO 30/72.33.

140 Report of deputation of AMC Council to Walter Long, 10 December 1903,

minutes of AMC Council Meeting, 10 December 1903, PRO 30/72.33.

141 136 H. C. Deb. 4s. 23 June 1904 col. 997; *ibid.* 27 June 1904 col. 1232; 139 H. C. Deb. 4s. 9 August 1904 col. 1549; 142 H. C. Deb. 7 March 1905 col. 575.

142 154 H. C. Deb. 4s. 26 March 1906 col. 731 and 868; 155 H. C. Deb. 5 April 1906 col. 730.

143 *Report of Departmental Committee on Accounts of Local Authorities.*

Chapter Six
The central management of local capital development

The development of local administration in the late nineteenth century was closely tied to local capital accumulation: the implementation of less eligibility depended upon the construction of adequate workhouse accommodation, for example, and public health measures upon works of sewerage and water supply. However, the conventions of local possessive pluralism acted throughout the period to restrict the positive influence of the central bureaucracy on local capital formation. Not only was the intervention of the central authority largely confined to the mediation of public investment requirements with private possessive interests, but these interests also retained a constitutional right of access to Parliament where their conflicts with local authorities were only insecurely moderated by considerations of public policy as represented by the central administrative authority.

Local authorities acquired and exercised powers for capital development either under private bills or under the sanction of the central bureaucracy. Private bill procedures were postulated on local possessive pluralism, in two ways. Firstly, local authorities seeking private powers were treated as private corporations; there was no special recognition of their status as representative public bodies, and they were subjected to the same adversarial conflicts with opposing interests as any other promoter. Secondly, under the Borough Funds Act of 1872, the special consent of ratepayers and owners of rate property was necessary before a bill could be promoted. Departmental loan sanctions were issued under general public statutes which consolidated and extended powers and procedures commonly inserted into private acts. Although the important difference was that administrative sanctions were issued under the authority of a minister charged with public policy, these statutes incorporated the conventions of local possessive pluralism which had gradually emerged in private bill legislation. These conventions therefore assured the influence of interests over local capital accumulation, hindering the assertion of coherent central bureaucratic control.

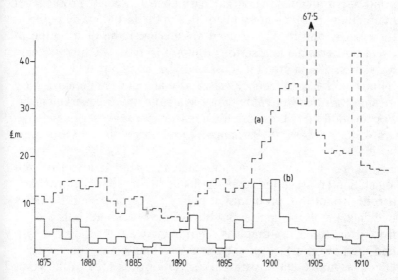

Fig. 8 Value of borrowing authorised by private act of Parliament (b), 1875-1913, compared to local authority income from loans (a)
Sources: Local Government Board Annual Reports and Local Taxation Returns

A significant proportion of the capital development undertaken by local authorities until the first World War was sanctioned by private Act of Parliament (Figure 8). Private bill legislation is therefore very important in the study of central-local relations in this period, not only because of its volume but also because those authorities who took the most advantage of this procedure included the biggest, most prestigious, most innovative authorities, that is the corporations who, through this medium, continued to enjoy a certain detachment from the influence of the central administrative authority.

There are three major reasons why local authorities continued to use a procedure which was notoriously expensive and arbitrary. The first is that they escaped administrative control over projects: and chronic delays in business at the Local Government Board provided a rationale for remaining outside its sphere of influence. The second reason lies in the nature of national parliamentary politics. For much of the period, Irish obstruction, the problems of maintaining parliamentary majorities in the face of party political turbulence, and the unresolved conflict over the distribution of fiscal burdens, made a serious attempt to pass any but strategic legislation frequently too costly to be contemplated by most Cabinets. The consequence was that many powers demanded by local authorities were simply not available under general legislation. In addition to these practical reasons for seeking private powers, direct access to Parliament symbolised the corporations' special status.

There is a sense, then, in which the persistence of private legislation enlarged the scope for local development by providing a route round the problems of policy aggregation and business management at the centre. But the scrutiny of private bills was far from exact; their drafting was often inadequate for their purpose and the powers which they created less than comprehensive and effective. Above all, private bill legislation was prey to the compromises involved in the adversarial process by which it was passed, and as a method of service development it relied entirely on the initiative and foresight of localities and upon the experience and judgement of their professional agents. That is, it was a system for the development of public powers that not only gave maximum scope for the promotion of private interest, but confined the central authority to a largely reactive and marginal role.

The procedures by which local bills passed through Parliament were complex and possessed three features which together explain the power relations involved in private legislation.[1] Firstly, they gave much influence to two parliamentary officers, the Chairman of Ways and Means in the Commons and the Lord Chairman of Committees in the Lords. Secondly, they offered multiple opportunities to opponents to obstruct. They therefore placed a premium on wheeler-dealing to prevent bills being opposed and on expensive professional advocacy by the parliamentary agents. Thirdly, the parliamentary committees which took opposed bills received no direct, independent expert guidance on the financial or technical aspects of bills, and the complex, detailed scrutiny of bills bored MPs. Private Bill Committees met for a few hours only at a time, because of the constraints of other parliamentary business, and bills tended to bunch in the parliamentary year towards the end of the session. It is not surprising, then, that the committees notoriously skimped their work and failed to take strong, consistent lines in the face of powerful interests. Private bill procedures were, it was agreed, prohibitively expensive to all but well resourced promoters and opponents, arbitrary in their outcomes and inconsistent in the powers which they created.

The Chairman of Ways and Means and the Lord Chairman of Committee had much influence over the early progress of bills. Only they could sanction non compliance with the standing orders, they allocated bills to the two Houses and to the committees, and they were the only real co-ordinators of policy as to the content of the bills. They examined bills before they went to committees and, in the case of unopposed bills, virtually constituted the committees. But in the case of opposed bills, they could only report their criticisms to the committee's chairman and hope that he had the inclination and strength to comply.

There were many opportunities for obstruction and amendment. Opponents might petition against bills at the stage of Examination, or move damaging instructions to committees on Second Reading. Their main opportunity of course, was before the committee, which could reject the bill's preamble or any of its clauses. A bill was also liable to be opposed on Third Reading, a procedure which agents thought unfair since MPs had not heard the evidence in committee, or in the other House where it began the procedure anew. As in any other expensive adversarial legal process, there was much pressure to secure agreement out of committee.

The rules on *locus standi* to oppose local bills were strict, and required a direct material interest in the subject of the bill. Ratepayers and electors had no *locus* on any bills promoted by their own authority: they were assumed to be represented by the council. Owners of property however had a *locus,* if they could show that their rates or charges would increase, or that they would become liable to fresh sanitary regulations or other new burdens. All local authorities, except parish councils, enjoyed a *locus* on bills injurious to their locality promoted by other local authorities or by companies. In addition, the interests of owners (and ratepayers) in relation to private legislation were protected by the Borough Funds Act.

Until 1872, municipal boroughs enjoyed a privileged status in relation to the taking of powers: they were exempted from s. 4 of the 1858 Local Government Act which required the consent of owners and occupiers to the adoption of powers, and were able to proceed on the simple resolution of the council. Corporations used the same procedure to apply for private acts.

In 1871, however, the legal right of the Sheffield Corporation to oppose a Water Company Bill in Parliament was challenged before Queen's Bench.[2] The judgement was sympathetic to the Corporation, recognising that the Corporation were acting in the best sanitary interest of the town, but was also clear that they had no legal right to charge the cost to the Borough Fund. The judgement confirmed what the Board's lawyers already understood,[3] that corporations acted under the general law of trusts, that trustees had no right to use trust funds to attempt to extend their powers or to oppose bills in Parliament, and it was due only to the laxity of the municipal audit that the habitual promotion of private bills by corporations had been tolerated. The decision caused dismay and outrage in town councils, and led directly to the formation of the Association of Municipal Corporations[4] 'to watch over and protect the interests, rights and privileges of Municipal Corporations, as they may be affected by Public Bill Legislation or by Private Bill Legislation'.[5]

The corporations immediately introduced a bill to reverse the judgement. The bill was strongly opposed by the public utility companies who forced into the bill the proviso that the promotion or opposition to a bill could be charged to the borough funds only if the consent of owners and occupiers was obtained by means of a s. 4 meeting. The Act, which was passed in 1872, also stipulated that a single ratepayer could requisition a poll of ratepayers to veto the bill.[6]

The Borough Funds Act was extremely inconvenient and

expensive for corporations to implement. The borough franchise was a burgher (or ratepayer) franchise, so they had no register of owners. (But this meant that the Borough Funds Meeting was the only representation for owners in Borough Affairs.) Borough funds meetings were difficult to organise, and apt to be hijacked by vociferous minorities and special interests. Polls were costly and unpredictable, and a single contentious clause could put a whole bill at risk.[7] But the Act also symbolised a view of the corporations to which the AMC objected in principle. '. . . the special appeal to the ratepayers is inconsistent with the principle of local representative government established by the Municipal Corporations Act'.[8] Successive Home Secretaries sympathised with this view but were not prepared to abolish the participation of owners and occupiers under the Act,[9] and so the amending bills promoted in the 1870s and early 80s by the AMC did not reach second reading.[10]

The Local Government Board was also cautious about amending the Act. In 1884, Owen drafted a memo which defined its attitude.[11] He believed that the requisition of a poll by one ratepayer was indefensible, and argued that a clause providing for appeal by owners and ratepayers to the Board should be preferred. But he held that it was necessary to keep the Borough Funds Meeting: 'in many districts the ratepayers attach much importance to retaining the power which they now possess of regulating the proposal of the Local Authority to promote or oppose a bill'.[12] Owen's willingness to amend the poll clause, however, opened the way for negotiation with the AMC: in 1887 its Conservative leadership attempted a deal with Ritchie and Henry Matthews, the Home Secretary. But the Government refused to move on the issue of the borough meeting,[13] and no bill was passed. The LGB's position was breached in 1888 by the Local Government Act, however. A s. 4 meeting was clearly impossible at county level: county councils were therefore empowered to oppose, but not promote bills, subject only to the sanction of the Board.[14]

During the 1890s, the County Councils Association pressed for the power to promote bills in Parliament,[15] and unsuccessfully introduced a bill in 1895.[16] Indeed, some county councils were already using private bill procedure to take powers unavailable in public legislation, at considerable personal risk to their members.[17]

In 1894, the AMC resurrected its own campaign, and introduced a series of bills which were blocked on the advice of the LGB.[18] However, the Borough Funds Act was raised by the AMC deputation to Long in November 1901[19] and in the spirit of this *entente* it was mutually agreed after some negotiation[20] to maintain the rights of owners, and a government bill was introduced, drawn on the lines of Owen's memorandum of 1884. This bill also extended the power to promote bills to county councils.

The general history of private bill legislation in the 1870s and early 1880s is one of collaboration between the officers of Parliament in charge of private bills and the officials of the Board, to achieve greater standardisation and conformity to government policy, especially in relation to loans. This was most successful in the 1880s, after which the growing volume and complexity of bills, as general legislation slipped further and further behind the needs of the larger local authorities, the failure of Parliament to reform its procedures and the increasing burden of business in the Local Government Board, rendered the policing of bills less thorough and penetrative.

In 1872, the Local Government Board was brought within the scope of S.O. 43 which compelled authorities to deposit bills for departmental report. Under Standing Order 173A, 1882, committees were required to confirm that they had received the report, and they were obliged under S.O. 149 to justify any departures from the Board's recommendations. Standing Order 172 of 1871 required local authorities who proposed to borrow money without Local Government Board sanction to provide and prove estimates in their bills.[21] These Orders were, however, less significant than they might appear for reasons to do with the pressure of work, the under resourcing of administrative support and the lack of control over private bill committees in Parliament. The Board never enjoyed the capacity to read all bills relevant to its sphere of interest,[22] and bills frequently arrived at the Board with only hours to spare before they came into committee. The Board's officials had no right to be heard before a committee but were obliged to brief counsel to represent the Board, an action often prohibited by the short notice.[23] The Board's reports were frequently disregarded: John Lithiby, the Board's Assistant Secretary, told the House of Commons Select Committee on the Repayment of Loans in 1902 that the Board had given up drawing attention to the clauses which breached Standing Order 172A, since committees never refused clauses on that ground.[24]

The substantial change in these years was the establishment of some control over the length of local authority loans. In 1882, a new Standing Order, No. 173A, was passed limiting periods to sixty years, and there were subsequently only a handful of cases where it was breached.[25] Nevertheless, it continued to be financially beneficial, despite the costs of promotion, for many local authorities to come to Parliament. In the first place, sixty years became a norm, not a maximum, whereas government departments gave sixty years only for land. And the maximum borrowing period allowed to municipal corporations under the Municipal Corporations Acts was thirty years. Loan sanctions by departments rigidly restricted the period within the repayment should begin: local authorities often successfully took powers from Parliament to defer the first payment for some years until their works were commissioned.[26] Stock facilities and the power to consolidate loans were not available to urban authorities under public legislation until 1891, and private bill powers allowed local authorities to borrow even when they had exceeded the limits of borrowing powers specified in the Municipal Corporations Act and in the Public Health Act of 1875 (which controlled the general borrowing powers of urban authorities). Then again, the Board scrutinised estimates thoroughly, and frequently held an inquiry: authorities had therefore to be able to prove their estimates to the Board's engineering and architectural staff. On the other hand, an authoritative view expressed to the Select Committee of 1902 was that Standing Order 172 had become something of a formality before private bill committees.[27]

The sixty year limit on local loans was passed in August 1882, as a result of a special report of the Police and Sanitary Regulations Committee.[28] This Committee was first nominated in 1882 in response to strong opposition to a number of corporation improvement bills from a small but vocal group of members in the House led by the Liberal backbencher, C. T. Hopwood. Hopwood took particular exception to the extension of powers beyond those found in general legislation, including clauses for the control of child labour by local authorities, the compulsory notification of infectious disease and the regulation of dairies. His argument was that this very common practice was objectionable because it subjected citizens in some towns only to powers which had not been endorsed by Parliament, undermining the constitutional doctrine of equality before the law.[29] The Committee's terms of reference, therefore, were to consider all clauses which went beyond the public statutes.

On the advice of the Local Government Board, the Committee held that private legislation was a useful way to monitor new powers before they were embodied in general legislation. The Committee proposed, indeed, the drafting of model clauses for the notification and prevention of infectious disease and for the regulation of child labour. But it also argued that Parliament should exercise more stringent supervision over unopposed clauses, that borrowing periods should be limited to sixty years, and that parliamentary committees should subject borrowing to departmental sanction. The report severely displeased Hopwood who continued to oppose the bills.[30] It also offended the AMC who took exception to the Local Government Board's meddling intervention in the relations of authorities and Parliament.[31]

The annual reappointment from 1884 of the Police and Sanitary Regulations Committee made possible more thorough Parliamentary scrutiny of clauses by a committee with greater continuity of membership than under ordinary private bill procedure. And, at least in its early years, the Committee operated in collusion with the Local Government Board. Most of its chairmen were Opposition members with ministerial experience at the Board, the Board reported routinely on all clauses which came to the Committee, and its junior legal assistant, H. E. Boyce, attended all its sittings. In contrast, the Home Office was more reluctant to send reports, and refused till 1888 to send an official of its own. In the 1880s, the Committee generally assimilated private bill powers to administrative policy: it regularly reduced loan periods (sometimes to 50 years), and refined and extended its model clauses in line with the Board's recommendations. But it was unable to force into bills the requirement that borrowing must be sanctioned by the Board.[32]

Williams has seen the Police and Sanitary Regulations Committee as manifesting a new principle in the relations of Parliament and local interests; that is, the intervention of a central department in the relations of Parliament and adversarial interests, to represent the public interest.[33] And it was in this belief that the AMC continued to oppose the Committee, which it believed to be biased against municipal collectivism.[34] Dilke told the Association in 1894 that the Government were using the Committee to force corporations to switch to the provisional order system,[35] and the files confirm that the Board's reluctance to amend the Borough Funds Act stemmed partly from this hope.[36]

In practice, however, the Committee was flexible and encouraging of municipal innovation. Certainly, both the Committee and the Board were warmer to the local authorities than the Home Office, whose sporadic interventions in the 1880s were to oppose the extension of local authority powers by private bills.[37] Unlike many private bill committees, however, the Committee required rigorous proof that new powers were needed and could not be obtained in other ways. Its guidelines specified that promoters must demonstrate the existence of strong local opinion for the proposed powers, and real problems that existing powers failed to meet.[38]

Given satisfactory evidence, the Committee allowed authorities to continue, on grounds of local custom and practice, to operate powers which had been superceded by general law, or to experiment with powers which had not yet received Parliamentary approval, subject sometimes, however, to a time limit. Indeed, it was impossible to refuse powers simply on the grounds they exceeded public statutes, because so many had been granted before 1882. What the Committee absolutely refused to do, however, was to allow new powers against an explicit instruction at second reading, or to grant powers which had been proposed in a public bill and rejected by Parliament. This rule rendered even the slow accretion of public powers in the 1890s and early 1900s a two-edged instrument, since when Parliament formally refused to accept in a public bill powers which had routinely been taken in private bills, the Committee felt obliged to cease to grant them.[39] The underlying problem was that there was no statutory 'municipal code' adequate to the needs of nineteenth century urban government. Private bill legislation was, therefore, a safety valve in the face of legislative stagnation.

The infectious disease clauses granted in 1882 included enlarged powers for sanitary authorities to disinfect premises, to compel dairies to furnish lists of customers, and to regulate the disposal of bodies. The child labour clauses provided better means of controlling the casual labour of school age children.[40] In 1886, the Committee agreed a further model clause for the sanitary inspection of dairies.[41] The annual reports of the Committee in the 1880s carry pleas for these powers, which were widely used by corporations, to be embodied in a public statute, and in 1888 the Committee caused an adoptive public bill to be introduced into the Commons.[42] In 1889 and 1890, three separate bills – the Notification of Diseases Act, the Infectious Diseases Prevention Act and the Public Health Act Amendment Act – were eventually passed.[43]

The bills of 1890 did not, of course, relieve the Committee's work for long. By 1895, the Committee was again calling for statutory recognition of routine clauses,[44] including superannuation for municipal officers, the regulation of street trading and embryonic town planning and building development control powers. In the early 1900s, private bill legislation allowed corporations to press ahead with many matters prominent on the agenda of public health reform, including the compulsory notification of TB, the compulsory slaughter of tubercular cows, the medical inspection of dairies located outside a town's boundaries, the compulsory notification of births, and the medical inspection of common lodging houses. In 1906, the House of Lords rejected a clause in a bill approved by the Committee to provide a municipal ambulance service,[45] but in 1908 the Committee was able to report that clauses providing for the appointment of health visitors by the LCC had been successfully taken by private bill.[46] During these years, the Committee also supervised the insertion of a clause for the first permanent local authority motorbus service.[47] And after several attempts at public legislation, a Public Health Bill was eventually passed in 1907.[48]

Although it played a useful role in scrutinising and legitimising innovative clauses, the Police and Sanitary Regulations Committee did not altogether satisfy those who sought more orderliness and control in the extension of local authority powers. Its limitations can be traced to three chronic problems: firstly, an overload of work, secondly, the overloading of the Local Government Board and, thirdly, its failure to secure the collaboration of the corporations and their agents.

The Committee normally dealt only with some dozen or so bills a year, but in the late 80s and early 90s, its scrutiny of clauses typically occupied some thirty or forty sittings. In 1890, the Committee sat fifty times.[49] In 1892, therefore, the Committee was instructed to divide itself to cope with its work.[50] In 1901 and 1902, difficulties in finding members and a Chairman meant that the Committee could not be appointed[51] but it was successfully reappointed in 1903 and again given powers to divide.[52] But the view of the civil servants was that by the 1900s the difficulties of its composition, and the fragmentation of its work, had injured both the consistency of its decisions and the cohesiveness of its membership.[53]

The ratio of bills to sittings indicates that the work was detailed: the Committee reports that members found its business laborious and we may presume they found much of it tedious. It was also technical, dealing with points of legal precedent, accounting practice and civil engineering. In 1893, therefore, the annual report recommended the appointment of an Official Advisor to act as an independent counterweight to the representations made by the parliamentary agents.[54] In 1894, H. E. Boyce was appointed as the Board's Parliamentary Agent.[55] But in general, the servicing which the Board could offer the Committee deteriorated rather than improved, for the increase of the Committee's business in the early 1900s, and the duplication of sittings, was not matched by increased administrative capacity, and an official no longer attended all its sittings.[56]

There was in consequence of these difficulties a patent weakening of the collaboration of the Committee and the LGB, and a growing tendency to mutual recrimination. As the views of the Board's officials on the subject of municipal debt moved closer to that of the Treasury, they expressed frustration with the Committee for not standing up to the local authorities.[57] On the other side, the Committee complained about the Board's tardiness in delivering reports,[58] and in 1903 reported that the Board was refusing to prepare digests of Police and Sanitary clauses, on grounds of pressure of work.[59]

The Committee also complained that its work was unnecessarily increased by the way in which bills were prepared by agents. Some of its criticisms amount to allegations of professional incompetence – sloppy drafting, failure to follow the required procedure, inadequate or misleading citation of precedents, innacurate or unsustainable estimates, for example – and point to the misuse of an expensive procedure for trivial and inconsequential powers. But some – failures to use model clauses and to observe limits on borrowing, and attempts to obtain powers beyond general legislation, for example – demonstrate, rather, that corporations and agents perceived it was worth taking their chances with the Committee, despite the trouble and cost of promoting bills. That is, despite the P. and S. Committee, Parliament continued to be seen as an altogether less rigorous arena, in which the balance of initiative and control over local powers lay more positively with the local authority than if the authorities had gone to the central administration.

Local authorities acquired powers under public acts by one of three means, all of which were predicated on possessive local pluralism in varying degrees. Firstly, in order to save Parliamentary time and to standardise local powers, certain clauses routinely granted to local authorities were consolidated into public Acts, so that they could be inserted into private bills by reference. The most important of these for local development purposes were the Lands Clauses Acts of 1845 and 1869,[60] by which local authorities acquired land. These Acts provided for valuations by surveyors appointed by the local justices (who were assumed to represent local landowning), and for arbitration by local juries where there was a dispute over compensation, or where land was taken other than by consent.

Secondly, powers were taken by voluntary adoption of permissive clauses in public statutes, for which the 1848 Public Health and 1858 Local Government Acts were the models. These Acts also consolidated powers in private acts. The 1848 Act required that, except where the death rate exceeded 23:1000, the initiative for adoption lay with ratepayers, one tenth of whom were necessary to petition for adoption.[61] The innovation in this Act was the devolution of power to sanction adoption to an administrative department, which was required to conduct a local inquiry.[62] Local inquiry performed two useful functions: it brought central technical expertise into localities, and it provided an independent agency to conciliate local conflicts. The Act permitted the central authority to make an absolute Order or, where conflict remained unresolved, a Provisional Order, and it *required* the Order to be Provisional where a proposal to extend urban boundaries was opposed by rural ratepayers who would become liable to the town rate.[63] The significance of an opposed Provisional Order was that it became subject to the opposed private bill procedure in Parliament. The 1858 Act allowed boroughs to adopt powers by simple resolution,[64] but in other urban places the consent of a meeting of owners and occupiers, or a resolution by an improvement commission elected by owners and occupiers, was necessary.[65] A smaller proportion of owners and occupiers could appeal against adoption.[66] Both Acts gave special representation (by plural voting) on local boards[67] to owners as well as ratepayers, and bestowed a power of veto on water companies affected by their adoption.[68] In both cases, the sanction of the central authority was required, after local inquiry, to loans[69] and to the the making of by-laws,[70] and a statutory limit (fixed as a ratio of the assessable value) was placed on the authority's accumulating debt.[71]

These Acts display certain features which continued to be conventional in all adoptive public acts, including the housing, allotments, small holdings, infectious diseases and planning acts of the late nineteenth century. Firstly, except in the boroughs, the initiative lay with ratepayers and owners, rather than the authority. Secondly, owners and corporate interests were given special rights of representation and appeal. Thirdly, where conflict remained unresolved, or where the rating liability of possessive interests was specially involved – as in the disturbance of boundaries – or where property was taken by compulsion, these Acts usually preserved the right of appeal to Parliament. And fourthly, they severely limited and controlled the rights of local authorities to enter into competitition with private utility companies, and this was reinforced by the amendment inserted by commercial interests into the Borough

Funds Act, which expressly prohibited competition with existing companies.[72]

The third way in which local authorities became active under public statutes was by using non adoptive general powers. The Public Health Act of 1875,[73] which consolidated clauses in previous public health, sanitary and nuisance legislation, is the model of such legislation in relation to environmental functions, where local possessive interests were considered to be specially involved. The main development was that individual localities did not have to go through special procedures to create the local machinery to work the Act, and so this stage was no longer dependent on the conciliation of local interests. But in most other respects, the principles governing the use of powers remained unchanged. The 1875 Act adopted the lands clauses for the taking of land by consent,[74] and provided for compulsory purchase by Provisional Order.[75] Water companies maintained their veto on public waterworks.[76] Most of the Act dealt with the exercise of local authority powers against householders and landlords and much of it, consequently, defines their rights of notice, appeal and compensation.

Many of the Board's Provisional and Departmental Orders were made only after local inquiry, especially where they involved boundary changes, arbitration of compensation, and default complaints, or where the authority proposed to exceed its borrowing limit. The vast majority of local inquiries were taken by the engineering inspectors, though a smaller number were taken by the general inspectors, or by general inspectors sitting with an engineering inspector,[77] or by the Inspector of Local Loans and Acts.[78] The engineering inspectors formed a non resident inspectorate, working from the offices in London. They were recruited by patronage either from private civil practice or from the engineering branches of the armed services.

The Board inherited a staff of four inspectors from the Local Government Act Office.[79] In 1874, the establishment was increased to five, and Robert Rawlinson was designated Chief Engineering Inspector, to co-ordinate their work and act as the Board's technical adviser. In 1876, the establishment was increased to six, and increased again in 1879 by the addition of an assistant to the Chief.[80] The establishment remained at this level until 1888 when, following an inquiry into the technical departments,[81] two extra posts were created.[82] Further posts, including a second deputy, were sanctioned after the 1898 Committee. As with the other field services of the Board, this increase was too slow and too small: there is constant evidence in the files of mounting arrears, chronic stress on the staff, lost holidays and disruptive bouts of illness, brought on by overwork.[83] The administrative staff of the Board complained that files were lost in the engineers' growing piles of paperwork:[84] but most significantly, the arrears delayed the Board's responses to formal applications,[85] provoking the resentment of the local authorities.[86]

As we have already noted, the quasi-judicial nature of this business restrained inspectors from a proactive role in local capital development. It also discouraged the public explication of consistent technical principles. For example, the reports made by the engineering inspectors remained the property of, and were exclusive to, the Board. This attitude reflects some of the technical and political realities of the Board's situation. Local authorities often commented on the Board's failure to give a strong lead, yet complained bitterly if their own pet schemes were rejected.[87] The Board's insistence that authorities take local professional advice saved recriminations, and made better allowance for local capacities and traditions. 'Plans and details may be the best possible', Rawlinson told the Municipal Engineers in 1878, 'but the ultimate result depends on daily local supervision, and this the Board does not give; neither local action nor local responsibility is superceded. Each engineer and each locality must devise and execute the local works, and the district must alone be responsible for local expenditure'.[88]

However, tired of the trouble of looking over 'defective, crude, ill-understood and ill-digested schemes',[89] Rawlinson continued in the 1870s his LGAO practice of preparing model plans for sewers, house drains and water supply, to be made available for authorities to adapt to their own needs, and he associated himself with studies on the controversial question of sewage disposal methods, which were disseminated through the professional associations and through the Sanitary Congress of 1876.[90] However, the Treasury baulked at the cost of duplicating his plans, and this developmental thrust petered after Rawlinson's retirement.

The use of Provisional Orders in England was limited to a few powers in Acts relating mostly to sensitive aspects of urban development. The common feature of Provisional, as opposed to Departmental, Orders was that they involved the disposition of land, property rights and boundaries. Most Provisional Orders made by the Board were for the compulsory purchase of land under the Public Health Act of 1875. A second significant category of Provisional Orders were made under general statutes which allowed the Board to sanction the amendment or repeal of local acts: most of these Orders extended the borrowing limits of authorities and, particularly around the turn of the century, a significant expansion of local authority borrowing powers was created in this fashion. A handful of Provisional Orders were taken out each year under the Gas and Water Facilities Bill of 1870, the Contagious Diseases (Animals) Act 1878, the Highways Act of 1878, the Brine Pumping (Compensation) Act of 1889, the Housing of the Working Class Act of 1890 and the London Government Act of 1899. Figure 9 shows that the pattern of growth and decline in Provisional Orders was similar to that of private Bills, with a noticeable acceleration in volume and value at the end of the 1890s and a subsequent sharp decline. That is, there was no significant transfer of business from Parliament to administrative authority, rather each reflects changes in the underlying determinants of local capital accumulation, particularly changes in the price and supply of funds, and changes in the political attitudes to municipal action.

There were significant limits to the usefulness of Provisional Orders. Although the Borough Funds Act prohibited the use of private Acts to take powers available by Provisional Order,[91] many private Acts contained powers which could have been taken by Order, because the authority also needed powers which were not thus available, or because they wished to exceed the limits of borrowing laid down in their constitutive Acts. Moreover, the Board refused to make a Provisional Order where it perceived that significant opposition persisted after local inquiry, because opposition to one Order in a confirmation bill endangered all Orders in that bill. The Board's statistics show that at the most one or two Orders a year were opposed or withdrawn after being submitted to Parliament.[92] A common argument for the extension of the Provisional Order system was that a local inquiry conducted by the agents of the central authority was a far more effective method than parliamentary private bill procedure for reconciling conflicting interests. What this rate of success more likely shows is that controversial matters were successfully filtered out before being submitted to Parliament.

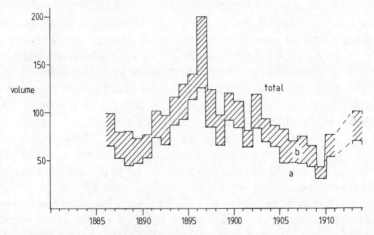

Fig. 9 Volume of Provisional Orders sanctioned by the Local Government Board, 1887-1914. The aggregate is composed of Provisional Orders not repealing or amending local acts (a) and those repealing or amending local acts (b). The latter usually involved the extension of borrowing power originally granted under a private act.
Source: Local Government Board Annual Reports

Nevertheless, the LGB's officials believed that the development of both provisional and departmental powers was a necessary condition of asserting more control over local authority capital accumulation, and that more systematic access to local decisonmaking through local inquiries would enable them to moderate the influence of possessive interests and thus facilitate the acquisition by local authorities of finance and land. Here, the interests of the Board coincided with more general problems of nineteenth century government, namely the problems of securing greater control over both public and private parliamentary business, in the face of an overcrowded legislative agenda and insurgent nationalism.

In 1872, J. G. Dodson, then Chairman of Ways and Means, moved a seminal resolution in the House calling for the extension of the Provisional Order system as a method of reforming private bill procedure.[93] His reasoning was that the public interests in private bills should be formally acknowledged by the intervention of a responsible minister.[94] The debates revealed some general sympathy with private bill reform, but active hostility from commercial interests, and no great support for the use of Provisional Orders.

In the early 1880s, Dodson worked with Gladstone on possible schemes for devolving Parliamentary business in response to Irish obstruction,[95] and officials in the LGB (over which he now presided) pressed for the extension of departmental powers for the regulation of local stock and for borough boundary extensions, the maining of roads, and the control of infectious diseases.[96] However, Dodson's view was that these powers were too controversial to remove from Parliament. In the mid 1880s, the issue of private bill reform was taken over by a group of Scottish Unionists MPs led by Craig Sellar, who perceived the devolution of private business from London to be a promising expedient to head off demands for more radical constitutional change, as well as a relief to Scottish commercial and municipal interests. Sellar provoked a major debate in 1883,[97] and promoted legislation in 1884, 1886 and 1887.[98] But he favoured an independent Commission of judges and other notables for local inquiries, not a government department. And a joint committee of both Houses of Parliament nominated in 1888, under the chairmanship of Dodson, endorsed Sellars' scheme.[99]

Though, as Salisbury recognised,[100] the balance of interests in this issue made significant reform politically remote, the structure of Unionist politics made it expedient to bring in a bill for Scotland.[101] But it was not till 1899, after much haggling with commercial, professional and local interests over the control and composition of a local inquiry commission, that a scheme was passed. The scheme provided for the extension of the Provisional Order system by the appointment of an independent tribunal to scrutinise unopposed Orders, and a joint parliamentary committee for opposed Orders.[102]

The evidence given for the Board to the 1888 Committee by its legal adviser, J. F. Rotton,[103] strongly favoured greater administrative intervention, but he was pessimistic that Parliament would cede controversial matters to officials. Rotton's view was that the Board needed extended powers to authorise the compulsory purchase of land for gasworks and of water rights, and again mentioned stock, boundaries and infectious diseases. And Boyce asked to submit a scheme to counter the view that the Provisional Order system was incapable of dealing with controversial matters.[104] Provisional Orders, he argued, would not only relieve Parliament, but promote greater uniformity and control and enable all points of view to be carefully considered by an unbiased and responsible minister.[105] And in 1902, he pressed the Select Committee on Private Business for Provisional Order powers for gas, water and the acquisition of land, arguing strongly that much more business should be settled without recourse to Parliament at all.[106]

During the 1890s and early 1900s the AMC pressed for reform of private bill procedure and for cheaper, easier ways to take land.[107] They particularly objected to the Lands Clauses Acts, because the arbitration arrangements involved expensive professional charges, and because they believed that the justices and local juries were often prejudiced towards landowners. Along with commercial interests, the AMC unsuccessfully promoted bills to transfer the sanction of compulsory purchase to the central authority, and to substitute bureaucratic arbitration of compensation.[108] And in the 1890s, sanitary and agricultural reformers, also unsuccessfully, promoted bills to ease the acquisition of land by local authorities for improvements and allotments.[109] The 1902 Committee was pressed to endorse these reforms,[110] but while there was a consensus in principle for such changes, other important witnesses recoiled from their implications. The Urban Districts and County Councils would not accept restriction of their access to Parliament, on the grounds that private bill procedures were more flexible and sensitive.[111] But the most persuasive argument used by the local authority witnesses against the transfer of business to the Board was endorsed by Boyce.[112] And this was the chronic overload of its staff, and the notorious delays in the exercise of its powers.

In contrast to the development of public health and improvements (which were 'local' functions), the Poor Law Amendment Act of 1834 is the model for public legislation controlling a more 'national' function. Loans could not be raised and parish property alienated, without the sanction of the central authority,[113] and the Act placed a limit on the debt accumulated by the authority.[114] Under this Act, the central authority was given very intrusive powers over day to day administration – the appointment and dismissal of officers, the regulation of relief, the conduct of workhouses and so on – but the two powers which would have given it positive access to the local capital structure of the poor law are missing: the central authority had no power to compel the building or modification of institutions, without the consent of ratepayers and owners, and it had no right to modify the areas of Unions. The latter is significant since it prevented the central authority universally enforcing the administration of the workhouse test by forcing parishes into Unions with adequate workhouses, and the Assistant Commissioners were obliged to negotiate rather than impose unionisation on reluctant parishes.[115] The result was that the formation of Unions was slow, and in some places negotiations produced strange and inconvenient boundaries. The 1844 Poor Law Act plugged an important loophole, whereby parishes were divided by the Justices to block the creation of settlements:[116] it also allowed the central authority to attach or detach parishes from Unions without the Union's consent.[117] It was the threat of this power which eventually persuaded the last English Union to acquire a workhouse in the 1870s.[118] The lateness of this date, however, indicates the extreme reluctance with which the Board entered on this strategy. It was only in the metropolis, and only after the workhouse scandals of the early 1860s, that the Poor Law Board acquired the power to dissolve a recalcitrant Union altogether.[119] But it was a power which the LGB officials would have liked for the provinces.[120]

The 1870 Education Act gave the Education Department power to appoint members of the local school board, where the board was refusing to build adequate schools.[121] But, of course, the ratepayers were compensated, to an extent, by grants in aid of the education rate. Within the Local Government Board's remit, the only default power of this kind was that under s. 299 of the 1875 Public Health Act, and the experience of working it did not persuade the Board's officials that it should be extended.

S. 299 powers were an extension of powers originally acquired under s. 49 of the 1866 Sanitary Act. The introduction of s. 49 powers have been hailed as a very significant accretion of central power over local government:[122] but by intention, if not by outcome, this section was much less radical a departure than might first appear, and it did not set a precedent for such powers to be developed widely by central government.

Under common law, those who controlled property were held to possess a duty to prevent nuisance to other property holders. The nuisance legislation of the 1860s built on this traditional obligation by giving holders of property the right to complain to the local justices to secure the removal of nuisances, and it imposed a duty on the local authority to inspect nuisances, scavenge, and so on.[123] The proposal in 1866 was to extend the rights of inhabitants of property by a power to apply to the justices to compel the local authority perform its duty in respect of water supply and sewerage. However, a number of large town councils, organised by Joseph Heron, Town Clerk of Manchester (who was in 1870 to be instrumental in the establishment of the AMC), reacted strongly to the indignity of elected corporations being placed under the supervision of magistrates.[124] The Government therefore substituted a complaint to the Local Government Act Office, and the Home Secretary was empowered, after local inquiry, to appoint commissioners to undertake the work in default of the local authority. S. 29 was, however, far from satisfactory, both in its drafting and in principle. In 1868, an amending bill had to be passed to confirm that the works could be charged to the ratefund and that loans could be raised,[125] but the few cases – seven in all[126] – where the power was used caused totally disproportionate trouble: there were problems guaranteeing the quality of work undertaken by local commisioners, problems forcing local authorities to take possession of the completed works, and problems getting incompetent authorities to operate them properly.[127] The experience confirmed the officials' view that constitutional principle and expediency coincided: the role of the central authority was to motivate the local authority to undertake their duty, not to relieve them of it.[128] In 1874, the Local Government Board therefore took an alternative power to make an Order, enforceable by application to Queen's Bench for a *mandamus*, to compel the authority to do its duty.[129]

There is now no way of counting how many complaints under this section were received by the Board, but the number of cases where a formal local inquiry was instituted were few –around a dozen in an average year – and the vast majority of these did not result in a formal Order. Between 1875 and 1885, 114 inquiries were undertaken and five Orders made; between 1895 and 1905, fifty-nine inquiries were made and eleven Orders made.[130] A survey of the Board's case papers confirms their official statements, that only where a local authority showed wilful intransigence was the Board prepared to enter into formal default proceedings:[131] its reluctance to do so stemmed partly from the administrative and legal difficulties of successfully prosecuting a default case, and partly from a strongly articulated view that formal intervention by the central authority in more than a very few exceptional cases was both impracticable and inappropriate.

For dealing with default cases was a sensitive, time and labour consuming business, the outcome of which was often barely worth the trouble it caused. Much of the difficulty lay in the narrow construction which the lawyers placed on 'default'. There was a view among the less legally-minded of the Board's staff that a default should be inferred from the very lack of provision, or from the unsatisfactory sanitary condition of a locality. However, in a series of cases, notably the case of Bolton Local Board in 1877-8, it was decided that the local authority must be culpable and wilful in default,[132] that the condition of the locality must be dangerous, and that the necessary works must be able to be carried out at reasonable cost. These conditions created much opportunity for the spirit of the law to be evaded by a determined local authority,[133] and obliged the Board to exercise a high degree of discretion in deciding whether to pursue defaulting authorities, which its critics argued negated the whole point of the section.

Even if an interventionist judiciary had been waiting at the end of the line ready to support the central authority, the default procedure was hardly short and sharp. There were endless opportunities for delay by local authorities. Firstly, in line with the conventions of public health legislation, only a local resident could initiate a complaint, not a local MOH and not a Local Government Board inspector. In practice, this meant that most default cases were set in motion by local pressure groups, or by neighbouring public authorities offended by a persistent nuisance, and this section usually involved the Board in messy local conflicts. The Board was required to hold a local inquiry; reasonable time had then to elapse for the authority to respond; and a further local inquiry had to be arranged if the authority submitted plans for loan sanction, however inadequate and obviously diversionary. If no plans were forthcoming a formal Order could be made imposing a time limit for action, and only when this lapsed without a genuine attempt by the authority to comply, could the case realistically come to court. It is not surprising that a high proportion of default cases were spun out over several years. And at any stage, a move by the local authority, however ineffective, could negate the grounds for default.[134]

Moreover, the local inquiry often uncovered difficulties which could plausibly be used to counter allegations of culpability. A local authority might receive conflicting professional advice; issues of water supply were complicated by local water rights and by the statutory privileges of water companies; and local conflicts could hinder the establishment of an effective scheme, where, for example, the politics of a borough extension led a suburban authority to refuse to be connected to a town scheme, or a rural authority to refuse an outfall to an urban sewer. If land had to be compulsorily purchased, the Board's Provisional Order sanctioning the application might be overthrown by opposition in Parliament. Default cases often reflected bitter local political divisions, and the Board was diffident about pressing a default against a recent local electoral mandate, except where there were clear overriding circumstances, such as an acute epidemic. And, in the rural districts which were the most frequent subject of default allegations, it could not be denied that the cost of sewering or supplying water often bore a disproportionate relation to the local rateable value.

The files show that in such circumstances, the Board frequently accepted schemes which it knew to be cheap palliatives rather than long term solutions to the sanitary problems of a locality. The administration of default powers was essentially the administration of compromise: what looked like a coercive, mechanistic, straightforward power involved in practice discretion at its most messy and flawed. Taken at face value only, the statement of a contemporary American commentator on English central-local relations that 'the power of the Board over defaulting authorities is far reaching and effective'[135] is too simplistic: any value that these powers had lay primarily in their deterrent effect, but his view that 'the few cases in which it is exercised are sufficient to convince all that it is not a mere form but a genuine reality, and that in cases of negligence, it will be exercised'[136] is weakened by the inescapable impression that the authorities against whom complaints were made simply did not believe that such powers would actually be used.[137] And in the absence of conditional grants, the existence of default powers gave the Board little positive leverage on the quality of local authority capital development.

Default powers appeared, however, to offer the centre clear and direct control over local authorities, and this is what made them an attractive proposition to social reformers frustrated by the slow responses of the Board and of localities to social and environmental problems. The call for default powers in slum clearance, house construction and other public health functions was a consistent aspect of the health reformers campaign throughout the whole life of the Local Government Board, and the question of how to stimulate more institutional provision in the poor law an equally pressing issue in its modernisation, culminating in the recommendation of the Majority Report on the Poor Laws in 1909, that the Local Government Board should be given powers to compel the building of satisfactory accommodation for the indoor poor.

In general, however, the Board did not wish for default powers, for a number of reasons. Although a minority of general inspectors of the Local Government Board hankered after default powers as a response to the chronic problem of workhouse accommodation,[138] the more orthodox view of the senior inspectors was that compulsion would irritate the guardians and succour agitation against the poor law.[139] If the workhouse test were always to be enforced, Hugh Owen stated in 1898, regardless of local circumstances and attitudes 'we should not be able to maintain the Order . . . a safety-valve is required'.[140]

It was also the consistent view of those with influence in the Board that, like conditional grants, the administration of default powers was too detailed and too labour intensive to be undertaken on a wide scale by a central authority. There is also the impression that some officials thought that sanitary work, particularly, was below the dignity of a central department. '... their nature is only such, for the most part, as is fitting for the action of Local Inspectors of Nuisances, such as perambulating close streets and alleys and ascertaining that petties strink or pigsties are disagreeable to the nose; and the Inspectors finding that there is no general distribution of water or any sewage system in a village, recommend that the defect be removed'.[141] The same point was made more objectively by Owen in his evidence to the Royal Commission on Working Class Housing in 1884-5, on the enforcement of the Torrens and Cross Acts to deal with urban slums. The Central Authority, Owen said, could involve itself only in strategic matters; the detailed inspection of individual nuisances and slum houses, which would be necessary to sustain a default complaint in a court of law, were beyond a central authority on grounds of capacity, cost and constitutional convention: they '... would place the Department in an entirely different position from what it fills now'.[142] Similarly, ten years later, President Shaw-Lefevre, rejected pressure from London MPs to make the payments to London vestries under the London Rates Equalisation Act of 1894 conditional upon the performance of their public health powers, on the grounds that the Board had not the capacity to undertake the necessary local inquiries.[143]

As a result of its experiences of s. 49 powers before 1874, the Board was especially anxious not to get involved again in the appointment of Commissioners in default of local authorities, and we will observe in the next chapter that this was a central issue in the conflict in 1917 over the post war housing programme between the Board and Minister of Reconstruction.

Contemporary discussions of default powers therefore focus a number of issues between the Board and its critics about its management of the local authorities. At a stage in the development of local government when substantive defaults in both poor law and public health administration could doubtless have been found in many localities, the Board continued to exercise a wide tolerance in its dealings with local authorities. The officials of the Board held to a clear conceptual distinction, based on the limits of central administrative capacity and the distinctive nature of local interests, between the proper responsibilities of central and of local authorities. This concept was based on several, mutually reinforcing features of their situation; the resource costs of harrassing individual local authorities, their dependence on the administrative systems of local government, and the normative deference accorded to local possessive rights by constitutional and statutory convention. The price of this approach, however, was the acceptance that even minimum standards could not be enforced. It is not surprising if its costs were unacceptable to those who wished to press ahead more vigorously with social reform and capital development.

NOTES TO CHAPTER SIX

1 The major authority on the history of private bill procedure is O. C. Williams, *The Historical Development of Private Bill Procedure and Standing Orders in the House of Commons,* I HMSO, 1948, and I have relied on this source for much technical information in the following paragraphs. Also, C Dodd and H. W. W. Wilberforce, *Private Bill Procedure: a Guide to the Procedure upon Private Bills,* Eyre and Spottiswoode, 1898; J. Redlich, *The Procedure of the House of Commons: a Study of its Historical and Present Form,* Constable Co., 1908 and D. L. Rydz, *The Parliamentary Agents,* Royal Historical Society, 1979.
2 A G v. Corporation of Sheffield, 6 L. R. Eq. 653.
3 *Statement of Existing Law as to Application of Funds of Local Authorities,* n.d. 1873, PRO HLG 29/80.
4 *The Times,* 27 March 1873, p. 10.
5 AMC Constitution, Article II.
6 35 & 36 Vict, c. 91 s. 4.
7 Memorandum by Hugh Owen on Borough Funds Act Amendment Bill, 1884, 22 April 1884, PRO HLG 29/80, and Report of the Law Committee of the AMC to Council on 28 April 1887, PRO 30/72.17.
8 Report of AMC Law Committee, 28 April 1887.
9 Statements of Cross and Harcourt to deputations of the AMC March 1875 and May 1881 in AMC memorandum in support of the 1884 Bill, PRO HLG 29/80. Reports of the deputations are in *The Times,* 12 March 1875, p. 12 and Annual Report of Council of AMC for 1882, PRO 30/72.11.
10 Bills were promoted in 1876, and in every year from 1882 to 1889.

11 Memorandum by Hugh Owen, 22 April 1884.
12 *Ibid.*
13 Report of the Law Committee. 28 April, 1887.
14 51 & 52 Vict. c. 41 s. 15.
15 Deputation to Ritchie from CCA, 27 April 1892 reported in Annual Report of Executive Council of CCA for 1892-3; Minutes of the Annual Meeting of the CCA, 22 May 1895; Resolution of the Executive Council of CCA, in Minutes of 27 October 1897; Circular to County Councils, reported in Annual Report of Executive Council of CCA for 1897-8.
16 LG Act Amendment Bill 1895 (38-Sess. I) IV 1.
17 i.e., Lancashire, West Riding and Middlesex County Councils; Minutes of the Annual Meeting of the CCA, 22 May 1895 and Provis to Long, 11 March 1901, PRO HLG 29/80.
18 Bills were promoted from 1894 to 1900. The Local Government Board's reports on them are in PRO HLG 29/80. Also, report of Law Committee to AMC Council, 18 October 1895; report of interview with Home Secretary, in Council Minutes, 16 April 1896; and Report of Deputation to Home Secretary and Parliamentary Secretary to Local Government Board, 14 January 1897, PRO HLG 29/80.
19 Report of deputation to Long, 29 November, 1901, in PRO 30/72.30 and in PRO HLG 29/80.
20 Papers on negotiations in 1901-3 are in PRO HLG 29/80.
21 The numbers of the standing orders varies from year to year as amendments were made. I have used the numbers in the contemporary editions at the date referred to. Also, Williams, *Private Bill Procedure,* I, chapters 6 and 7.
22 *Report of the Select Committee of the House of Commons on Private Business,* 1902 (378) vii 321, evidence of H. E. Boyce, Q. 1522.
23 These difficulties are apparent in handling the contentious case of the Sheffield Corporation Waterworks Bill of 1887, which was a test case for the policy laid down in 1882 on length of loans, and where the Corporation was awarded ninety years on a technicality. Correspondence and reports, 1 July 1887, PRO MH 12/15494.
24 *Report of the Select Committee on the Repayment of Loans,* 1902, evidence Qs. 614-619.
25 *Report of the Select Committee on Repayment of Loans,* para. 9, lists four cases only where sixty years was exceeded. Apart from the Sheffield Bill, they were; the Bury Water Bill, 1889; and the Derwent Valley Joint Water Bills of 1899 and 1901. All were brought to the attention of the House of Commons and proceeded as special cases.
26 *Ibid.* Evidence of Lithiby, Q. 618.
27 *Ibid.* Qs. 633-637.
28 *Special Report of the Select Committee on Police and Sanitary Regulations,*

1882 (226) xii 345 paras. 1-6.

29 266 H. C. Deb. 3s. 21 February 1882 cols. 1223-4; 267 H. C. Deb. 3s. 7 March
    1882 col. 320. The Bills were the Liverpool Accrington, Blackburn, Man-
    chester and Bolton Bills.

30 270 H. C. Deb. 3s. 19 June 1882 col. 1559-80.

31 273 H. C. Deb. 3s. 8 August 1882 col. 1132.

32 The statements in this paragraph are based on the Reports of the Police
    and Sanitary Regulations Committee from 1884 to 1889.

33 Williams, *Private Bill Procedure,* I, pp. 218-9.

34 e.g. Circular letter from Secretary of AMC to Town Councils, 31 March
    1894, PRO 30/72.23.

35 Speech to Annual Dinner of AMC, 9 March 1894, *ibid.*

36 Written note by John Lithiby on Local Government (Bills in Parliament)
    Bill 1903, HLG 29/80.

37 *Special Report of Committee on Police and Sanitary Regulations,* 1886
    (178-I) XI 249, para. iv; *Special Report of Committee on Police and Sanitary
    Regulations,* 1887 (250) xi 225, para. v.

38 *Special Report of Committee on Police and Sanitary Regulations,* 1893-4
    (321) XIII 447, para. iii.

39 *Special Report of Committee on Police and Sanitary Regulations,* 1908
    (257) IX 619, para. 6.

40 *Special Report of Committee on Police and Sanitary Regulations,* 1882,
    Appendices I-III.

41 *Special Report of Committee on Police and Sanitary Regulations,* 1886,
    para. iii.

42 *Special Report of Committee on Police and Sanitary Regulations,* 1888
    (300) XV 1 para. iii; Public Health Amendment Bill, 1888 (184) VI 241.

43 51 & 52 Vict. c. 72; 52 & 53 Vict. c. 64, and c. 59.

44 *Special Report of Committee on Police and Sanitary Regulations,* 1895
    (386) XII 113, para. 7.

45 *Special Report of Committee on Police and Sanitary Regulations,* 1906
    (254) xi 305, para. 10.

46 *Special Report of Committee on Police and Sanitary Regulations,* 1908
    (257) ix 619.

47 *Special Report of Committee on Police and Sanitary Regulations,* 1904
    (254) xi 305, para. 11.

48 7 Edw. VII c. 53.

49 *Special Report of Committee on Police and Sanitary Regulations,* 1890
    (320) XVII 7, para. iii.

50 4 H. C. Deb. 4s. col. 1508.

51 Williams, *Private Bill Procedure,* p. 220. On the problems of Chairmanship
    and membership, *Report of Select Committee of House of Commons on
    Private Bill Procedure (Scotland),* 1898 (307) XI 625 Qs. 1204-5; and *Report*

of Select Committee on Private Business, evidence of C. E. Troup, *passim.*

52 *Special Report of Committee on Police and Sanitary Regulations,* 1903 (314) vii 541, para. V.

53 *Report of Select Committee on Repayment of Loans,* evidence of John Lithiby, Q. 822; *Report of Select Committee on Private Business,* evidence of C. E. Troup, *passim.1*

54 *Special Report of Committee on Police and Sanitary Regulations,* 1893-4, para. iv.

55 *The Imperial Calendar,* 1895.

56 *Report of Select Committee on Repayment of Loans,* evidence of John Lithiby, Qs. 730-1.

57 *ibid.* Qs. 750-1.

58 *Special Report of Committee on Police and Sanitary Regulations,* 1904, para. iii; *Special Report of Committee on Police and Sanitary Regulations,* 1905 (247) vii 77, para. iii.

59 *Special Report of Committee on Police and Sanitary Regulations,* 1903 (314) vii 541, para. iii.

60 8 & 9 Vict. c. 18 and 32 & 33 Vict. c. 18

61 11 & 12 Vict. c. 63 s. 8

62 *Ibid.* s. 8

63 *Ibid.*

64 21 & 22 Vict. c. 98 s. 12

65 *Ibid.*

66 *Ibid.* s. 16

67 11 & 12 Vict. c. 63 s. 20; 21 & 22 Vict. c. 98 s. 24.

68 *Ibid.1 s. 20 and s. 73.*

69 *Ibid.* s. 114 and s. 57.

70 11 & 12 Vict. c. 63 s. 115.

71 *Ibid.* s. 117 and 21 & 22 Vict. c. 98 s. 73(2).

72 *Ibid.* s. 2.

73 38 & 39 Vict. c. 55.

74 *Ibid.* s. 176(1).

75 *Ibid.* s. 176(5).

76 *Ibid.* s. 52.

77 *Opinion from the Law Officers as to Recovery of Costs in Relation to Local Inquiries,* 19 November 1887, PRO MH 19/19.

78 *Minutes taken before the Local Government Board Inquiry Committee,* 1898, Q. 67.

79 The establishments figures in this section are taken from The Imperial Calendar, and from *Resumé of Establishments of LGB from 1871,* 1903, PRO MH 78/45.

80 *Minutes taken before the Local Government Board Inquiry Committee,* Q. 393.

81 *Report on the Engineering and Medical Officers and Inspectors of Audits, Local Acts and Local Loans and Legal Adviser,* 23 March 1887, PRO MH 78/44.

82 Treasury to Local Government Board, 28 April 1887, PRO MH 78/44. The deal was that the increased costs would be passed on to local authorities in the form of increased fees for local inquiries, but Ritchie failed to secure the necessary legislation, *Statement Showing the Average Number of Cases Completed by the Engineering Inspectors,* 1897, PRO MH 32/95.

83 The personal files of the Engineering Inspectors are in PR0 MH 32/95.

84 Correspondence between the Clerical Staff, Secretariat and Engineering Department, April-May 1886, PRO MH 19/98.

85 LGB to Treasury, 26 August, 1882, PRO MH 19/214; Treasury to LGB, 7 February 1884 et. seq., PRO MH 19/215; LGB to Treasury, 9 February 1885 et. seq. *ibid. Statistics of Work in LGB. Collected 1896,* PRO MH 78/44; *Statement Showing the Average Number of Cases, ibid.,* also lists the arrears in the 1890s.

86 Report of deputation of AMC to LGB, Council meeting 26 November 1896, PRO 30/72.25; *Minutes of Evidence taken before the Local Government Board Inquiry Committee,* Qs. 388-434 and Q. 885.

87 16 H. C. Deb. 4s. 25 August 1893 col. 1000; *Second Report of Local Government Board Inquiry Committee,* 1898 (C. 8999) XL 447, evidence of F.C. Hulton and T. C. Edwards, especially Qs. 5318, 5361, 5399, 5324-31

88 Rawlinson speaking to Midlands District of the Association of Municipal and Sanitary Engineers and Surveyors, 16 April 1878, *Proceedings of the Association,* IV, 1877-8.

89 *Ibid.*

90 *The Times,* 15 May 1876, p. 7, and see. e.g. correspondence about the Society of Arts' Exhibition on Sewerage, March 1876, PRO MH 25/27.

91 35 & 36 Vict. c. 91 s. 10

92 The numbers of Provisional Orders taken out each year under the various Acts, and the number withdrawn and opposed, are published each year in the LGB's Annual Reports. They show that in many years, none were opposed; at the most two or three a year were opposed.

93 210 H. C. Deb. 3s. 15 March 1872, col. 17.

94 Ms. notes in Dodson's hand, n. d. but apparently 1872, Monk Bretton papers, Box 40.

95 PRO CAB 37/3.

96 Unsigned official memorandum on Private Bill Legislation prepared for the President, Monk Bretton Papers, Box 51.

97 293 H. C. Deb. 3s. 6 March 1883, col. 1611; 285 H. C. Deb. 3s. 14 March 1884 col. 1554.

98 Bills to amend the system of Private Bill Legislation; 1884-5 (25) IV 645; 1886 (22-I) V 113; 1887 (107) V 381.

99 *Report of the Joint Select Committee of the House of Lords and House of Commons on Private Bill Legislation,* 1888 (276) XVI I.

100 'You will have against you (1) the rich landowners, who will look on a costly private bill system as a protection against a too frequent use of the power of expropriation, (2) the rich companies who look on it as protection against the undue multiplication of competitors, (3) the Parliamentary agents and counsel whose living it will destroy'. Salisbury to Goschen, 16 October 1888. Salisbury Papers.

101 *Memorandum for Cabinet in Regard to Private Bill Legislation Relating to Scotland,* 9 March 1889, PRO CAB 37/23, and *Memorandum for Cabinet on Local Government (Scotland) Bill and Private Bill Procedure,* 6 April 1889, CAB 37/24.

102 Private Bill Procedure (Scotland) Act, 1899, 62 & 63 Vict. c. 47.

103 *Report of Joint Committee on Private Bill Legislation,* Qs. 4777-4814.

104 Boyce to A. J. Balfour, 28 June 1888, Long Papers.

105 *Ibid.*

106 *Report of Committee on Private Business,* 1902, Qs. 1539 and 1556.

107 Reference to Law Committee of Lands Clauses Act and Private Bill procedure, *Annual Report of AMC Council for 1882,* PRO 30/72.11; Memorial to President of Local Government Board on Lands Clauses Acts, *Annual Report of Council,* 1883, PRO 30/72.12.

108 Lands Clauses Consolidation Acts Amendment Bill, 1875 (96) iii 209; 1883 (160) vi 441; 1884 (78) iii 517.

109 County Councils (Valuation and Purchase of Land) Bill, 1890-1 (294) i 461; 1891 Acquisition of Land (Local Authorities) Bill, 1890-1 (268) i 9; Local Authorities (Purchase of Land) Bill, 1892 (244) I 247; Local Authorities (Valuation and Purchase of Land) Bill 1892 (33) iii 593; Local Authorities (Acquisition of Land) Bill, 1893-4 (247) I 63; Acquisition of Land (Local Authorities) Bill, 1896 (25) I 255. These are the bills that were ordered to be printed by the House of Commons. They were not the only bills drafted and introduced.

110 *Report of Select Committee on Private Business,* evidence of Horatio Brevitt, and Appendix 7.

111 *Ibid.* evidence of C. E. Baker, Sir R. Littler, and Appendix 5.

112 *Ibid.* Evidence of H. E. Boyce, *passim.*

113 4 & 5 Wm IV c. 76 s. 21

114 *Ibid.* s. 24.

115 See the reports of the Assistant Commissioners in the Annual Report of the Poor Law Commissioners in the late 1830s.

116 7 & 8 Vict. c. 101 s. 22.

117 *Ibid.* s. 114.

118 The papers on the Todmorden Union 1871-5 are in PRO MH 12/6278 and 6279. The threat was that part of the union would be annexed to the

Rochdale Union and part to Halifax. The workhouse at Todmorden was eventually built in 1875-6. Inspector Smith used this power, for example, to persuade the Radford Guardians in Nottingham to improve a chronically overcrowded workhouse in 1870-1, Report to Board 21 August 1871, PRO 32/67.

119 30 & 31 Vict. c. 6.

120 *Report of Royal Commission on Poor Laws,* II, evidence of Alfred Adrian, Q. 722.

121 33 & 34 Vict. c. 75 ss. 63-66.

122 R. M. Gutchen, 'Local improvements and centralisation in nineteenth century England', *The Historical Journal,* IV, 1961, p. 91. R. J. Lambert, 'Central-local relations in mid-Victorian England: the Local Government Act Office, 1858-71', *Victorian Studies,* VI, 1962-3, p. 139.

123 e.g. 18 & 19 Vict. c. 121 s. 40.

124 *First Report of Royal Sanitary Commission,* evidence of Joseph Heron, Qs. 2340-2358.

125 31 & 32 Vict. c. 115 s. 8.

126 The cases were; Wetheringsett, Southover, Epping, Hillmorton, Sudbury, Barnard Castle and Brentwood. Legal difficulties prevented the pursuit of a Darlington case. *First Annual Report of the LGB,* 1871-2, (C. 156) XXVII I p. xlviii. No further cases were pursued by means of this section till the law was changed in 1874.

127 Especially the cases of Sudbury, PRO MH 12/12028 and 12029; Billericay Guardians (Brentwood), PRO MH 12/3359, and Hillmorton Parish, PRO MH 12/13458 and 3459, where to avoid litigation the Treasury had to be induced to agree to special cheap loan terms to get the local authorities to take possession of the works. In the case of Sudbury, a special drainage district had been illegally constituted on the advice of the engineering inspector, and in Billericay and Hillmorton, the sewer constructed by the Commissioner was defective.

128 'Report of Tom Taylor', *Annual Report of LGB for 1871-2,* p. xlviii, and *First Report of Royal Sanitary Commission,* III, 216-220; *ibid.* evidence of Robert Rawlinson, Qs. 523-522, 575-580; *Report of Select Committee on Public Works Loans,* evidence of John Lambert, Qs. 728-730.

129 37 & 38 Vict. c. 89 s. 20.

130 The numbers of cases are published in the Local Government Board annual reports.

131 *Minutes taken before the Local Government Board Inquiry Committee,* 1898, evidence of Hugh Owen, Q. 442.

132 From shorthand notes of the case of R. and the Local Government Board ex parte the Bolton Poor Law Union, 6 March 1878, PRO MH 12/5623.

133 e.g. cases of Roborough, 1892, PRO MH 12/2843; Sawbridgeworth, 1890, PRO MH 12/4553; Amersham, 1892, PRO MH 12/399, St Helens, 1895, PRO

MH 12/6105, where despite obvious deficiencies, proceedings could not be pursued.

134 These observations based on papers (filed under the relevant Poor Law Union in PRO MH 12) in the following cases: Honiton Town Council, 1878-9, 1287; Panteg Local Board, 1878-9, 8166; Cheshunt Local Board, 1880-3, 7043-7052; Bridge RSA, 1886-8, 4850; Heston & Isleworth LB, 7893; Sawbridgeworth, 1890-1, 4553; Roborough, 1892, 2483; Staines RSA and Sumnbury UDC, 1891-6, 7786; Rochester USA, 1890-2, 5270; Chesham LB, 1893-4, 399, St Helens, 1895, 6105.

135 M. R. Maltbie, *English Local Government of Today; a Study of the Relations of Central and Local Government,* New York, Columbia College, 1897, p. 105.

136 *Ibid.* p. 106.

137 e.g. the newspaper record of comments at meetings of the Cheshunt Local Board in PRO MH 12/7045 and 7051.

138 e.g. report of Inspector Murray Browne to LGB, March 1873 on outdoor relief, PRO MH 32/97; and Baldwyn Fleming to LGB, 7 November 1872, PRO MH 32/99.

139 e.g. Inspector Doyle to LGB, 5 October 1871, PRO MH 32/20.

140 *Minutes of Evidence Taken before the Local Government Board Inquiry Committee,* Q. 600.

141 Dr. Edward Smith to Sutton, 18 February 1873, PRO MH 32/67.

142 *First Report of the Royal Commission on the Housing of the Working Classes,* Q. 248.

143 28 H. C. Deb. 4s. 3 August 1894 col. 377.

Part Three
The challenge to the Local Government Board

Chapter Seven
Towards alternative models of central–local relations

By the early 1900s, then, the conduct of central-local government relations by the Local Government Board was organised by established conventions and routines, reflecting a pluralist understanding of the role of the state in relation to the fiscal and possessive interests which were perceived to be the special constituencies of local government. The paradox of the Board is that its *raison d'être* arose from the reformist consensus of enlightened metropolitan opinion in the 1860s, and especially from the Chadwickian perception of the connection between sickness and poverty, but that it found itself holding the ring between the imperatives of national policy and the interests of ratepayers and of property holders disturbed by the emerging administrative state. So that the Board became not the leading edge of the instrumental state, but a byword for compromise, pragmatism and conservatism induced by its sensitivity to the conventional rights of traditional and partial interests.

What this study shows in part is that attitudes at the Local Government Board noticeably shifted during its lifetime. If the Board occupied a structurally ambiguous position between client interests of service delivery, ratepaying and property holding, then there are many examples to demonstrate that for its first couple of decades, or so, its officials were more vigorous in pursuit of the first than subsequently. Lambert, Dalton and their contemporaries were prepared to take on the Treasury and Ministers, to fight for grants, for easier public works loans, for stronger powers, for more staff. There is therefore the question why, particularly after 1900, the Board became less attuned to local service development, and more oriented to the interests of ratepayers and the Exchequer.

One cause of this shift is obviously the deepening fiscal crisis of the local state, and the chronic inability of national governments to effect a financial settlement. The Board simply became diffident about pressing local authorities to take on more duties and its staff more sensitive to the growing national networks of the local authorities. But this shift also reflects changes in the Board. During the 1880s and 1890s, the founding staff were gradually replaced by a new cadre of officials, most of whom (in the administrative line) came into the Board through open competition rather than patronage. Much has been made elsewhere of the fact that the Local Government Board, which had less glamorous work, a lower status, and lower salaries, than the more traditional offices, had to be content with candidates for entry to the civil service who failed (or who had not the contacts) to gain entrance to the more prestigious departments.[1] Although this undoubtedly had an effect on morale at the Board after the turn of the century, it misses the main effect of the introduction of open competition on a wider scale: the young officials in the Board were still very bright people - they came sixth or tenth out of a list of a hundred or two, rather than first or second, and many of them had Oxbridge firsts and prizes[2] - but they were career bureaucrats who happened from circumstance rather than predilection to find themselves in the Local Government Board. Whatever the morality of patronage, at least Ministers could, if they chose, pick people to run their departments who had a personal commitment and an independent interest or reputation in its field of interest. John Lambert, for example, is a figure that belongs in a type with Chadwick or Trevelyan: he had clear political affiliations with the Liberals, but he had experience and reputation as a public health reformer in his own home town, and an explicitly stated position on the interventionist role to be played by the instrumental state in social progress.[3] Likewise, John Simon, Lambert, J. H. Bridges (the medical inspector of the London poor law), and Robert Rawlinson may not have made comfortable colleagues, but their conflicts arose from autonomous commitments to their special fields.

Of course, the general inspectors and technical staffs of the Board continued to be appointed under patronage (though the former came to be a career outlet for the First Division), and the real tragedy of the Board is not so much that *technical* expertise was marginalised, but that, consequently, the Board failed to exploit those with authentic energy, connection and judgement. In contrast, the administrators were dependent for their interpretation of issues on internal written records and departmental wisdom: the simple point that strikes the researcher who spends much time with files accumulating in a department over some fifty years, is the extent to which bureaucratic conservatism arises from the constant recycling of the same briefs, from want of alternative analyses within the organisation.

General administrators were trained to reflect the dominant political climate, and the underdevelopment of the local government policy community meant that the officials of the Local Government Board continued to be heavily dependent upon formal sources of political analysis. We have seen that the preoccupation with the formal requirements of financial stewardship more than used up its statistical capacity, and the Board never developed a network of local officers to report on local conditions, as Simon had proposed, and it never exploited the networks built up by the local authority associations or the professional bodies. A factor which contributed to the isolation of the Board was that its officials perceived its organised client interests, the ratepayer organisations and the national associations of local government, as lobbyists rather than collaborators, so that their relations were largely formalistic and adversarial rather than mutually influential.

Why the national associations of local government were not drawn into a more corporatist or collaborative relationship with the Local Goverent Board is an therefore an important question. One reason is undoubtedly cultural. The dependence of the Board on quasi-judicial methods and legal training encouraged a detached, bureaucratic relation with pressure groups, and a second reason is the fragmentation of the national local government system: the AMC and CCA, particularly, competed with each other for money and for powers but, as we will see further in this chapter, above all they competed for authority and leadership within the local government system and, even, with the central authority. The Local Goverent Board was obliged therefore to remain detached and neutral in its official dealings with the associations. Moreover, the political necessity of communicating with five local authority associations, together with the national organisation of the poor law authorities, presented some obvious physical and psychological barriers in the way of consulting the local authority associations frequently and routinely.[4] The third and probably overwhelming reason, is the fiscal tension between local government and central government: quite simply, the Local Government Board had little to offer in the way of hard financial concessions in regular consultative machinery, and its development would merely have opened the centre to yet more demands. It served the central government on the whole to keep local authorities at arm's length, and to pursue their functional separation from the national political system rather than their more complete integration.

If relations with the local authority associations were formal, then relations with the other developing national network of local government, the professional bodies, were distant. For the professional bodies lacked the Parliamentary Committees of MPs that could build bridges for the associations into national political arenas, and they lacked social connection and equality of status with Whitehall. And we have already noticed, that, with the exception of the MOHs, the institutes were unable to use the professional officers of the Board as an informal way into its deliberations.

The officers of the Board responded conscientiously and courteously to representations from the professions; functional relations were established and business done, especially on matters relating to the recognition and organisation of the professions.[5] But the Board resisted admitting the institutes to influence on wider issues. And the rationale of this was constitutional: that is, its view was that it could not deal with the professions over the heads of their employers, the local authorities, whose members took the political and, particularly, the financial responsibility for local government.[6] And so, the IMTA for example, channelled its contributions to the local taxation issue through the AMC.

There is in our period, some degree of hierarchical organisation of local government interests: the central bureaucrats did facilitate the formation of the associations,[7] and assumed, in their dealings with them, that they spoke for their class of authority. The apotheosis of this process was reached, for example, in 1917-1919, when the agreement of the local authority associations was, belatedly perhaps, sought, on Prime Ministerial instruction, to the new Ministry of Health. But the use of this emerging policy community was confined to issues of national policy affecting local government structure. The Local Government Board did not perceive the associations or the professions to be a means by which its influence on the practices of local authorities might be extended, and it did not exploit the associations as sources of information about local conditions or opinions. It continued, rather, to rely on the general inspectorate and on direct circulation of authorities.[8] Nor did it ever establish advisory committee machinery as some other departments were beginning to do in the 1890s and 1900s.[9] Indeed its officials resisted such suggestions whenever they were mooted. The contacts of the associations with the Board were, in the period before the First World War frequent, but they were *ad hoc,* and they were not close. The consequence was that there was only a weakly articulated, and divided, policy community of service deliverers to counter, firstly the financial pressures of ratepaying, and secondly, the reform lobbies of the 1900s.[10]

In the absence of positive financial or political strategies to counter the domination of central-local relations by local possessive interests, we find a central-local system displaying many of the features which have been held to characterise it later in the twentieth century: there is the multiplication of procedural checks on local government, the subjection of authorities to increasingly complex quasi-judicial control and to the routines of detailed financial accountability, but there is a noticeable underdevelopment of mechanisms for the assertion of strong incorporating leadership by the centre.

Given the apparent abdication of the Local Government Board from the positive leadership of local government, and the consequent 'frustration of social policy', it is not surprising that, right from the beginning of the life of the Board but increasingly stridently after the turn of the century, there was significant pressure for the development of alternative approaches to central-local relations, generated by positive aspirations to incorporate the localities into a national policy system. Running through discussions of central-local relations we therefore find a preoccupation with the nature of political authority and political leadership within the central-local system.

The common ground between between the staff of the Board and its critics is their perception of the relatively slow cognitive and technical development of local government, compared to national government. There are two rationales which were used legitimise this assumption, and to point the way to alternative strategies for development. The first, which was shared by many of the lay staff of the Board, blames the low quality of local administrators on the withdrawal from local government, and especially from the Poor Law, of those occupying positions of social and economic leadership in boroughs and counties.[11] District and union level government became the arena of small farmers, tradespeople and shopkeepers, who, by virtue of their social class and economic position, were held to be cut off from the most progressive ideas and the wider perspectives available to leisured or national elites. This rationale depended upon the Millite assertion (which as we saw in the opening chapter is in turn heavily dependent on the underlying assumptions of Mixed Government) that the leisured classes were more 'intelligent' than those who earned their living by wage labour or personal enterprise, because of their greater economic – and hence intellectual and moral – independence, and their access to a metropolitan, or cosmopolitan, culture. That is, in mid-late Victorian discourse 'intelligence' relates less to mental or physiological capacity than to concepts of class and associated moral and intellectual development. It is possible, therefore, to see the arguments for intermediary authorities, and the formation of arenas in which they could be pressed – notably the Poor Law Conferences and the CCA – partly as a reaction of nationally articulated traditional elites to the petty embourgeoisification of local government in the mid nineteenth century.

A second rationale was one which led more explicitly to the alternative model of central-local government relations, the technical-bureaucratic model which we have already explored in Chapter Four. This looked to the assertion of technical authority and rational modes of thought, and to the liberation of the central-local system from the influence of possessive interests. Although it was not always pressed, the logic of this model is hostile to local representative institutions, and dismissive of the underlying assumptions of the political diplomatic model of central-local relations adopted by the Local Government Board. Its culmination was the successful conclusion in 1919 of the campaign to establish a Ministry of Health to replace the Local Government Board.

The common feature of both these rationales was that they led to pressure for the establishment of larger-scale, intermediate authorities, hierchically connecting centre to localities, to subject local authorities to closer tutelage than is possible by a central authority. Intermediate authorites would provide a forum through which the property owning interests and 'intelligence', on the one hand, or professional expertise on the other, could exert a counter-vailing influence to that of ratepaying. And this is a reform which, of course, became doubly plausible because of the obvious overload of the Local Government Board.

We can trace proposals for a Ministry of Health and for inter-mediary authorities in the BMA/SSA campaign in 1866-9 for the establishment of the Royal Sanitary Commission. A central thrust of their programme was the grouping of local sanitary authorities, to provide scope and resources for the appointment of full-time Medical Officers of Health (who, they believed, would become an important source of pressure and tutelage on local authorities).[12] Further, larger, grouped authorities would detach sanitary officers from the influence of property holders on local boards. The public health lobby also pressed for the removal of supervisory and appellate powers from the local justices (who were assumed to be compromised by a constituency of landlords) and for the stronger enforcement of local health duties by the central authority, which, they assumed, would be a Health Department dominated by doctors.

The Royal Sanitary Commission heard evidence for intermediate authorities from three sets of witnesses. Firstly, civil engineers – including the LGAO's senior engineering inspector, Robert Rawlinson[13] – pressed for drainage authorities, defined by watersheds. These were favoured partly for topographical convenience, but also to provide a tier of government with knowledge of, but independence from, the local authority for the exercise of default powers in sanitary matters. Watershed authorities would be characterised by strong technical staffs. Rawlinson's argument was endorsed by Tom Taylor, the Secretary to the LGAO,[14] on the grounds that default powers required too particular an administration to be conveniently exercised by the central authority. Secondly, the agents of rural landowners troubled by the pollution of their rivers by neighbouring towns, argued for large scale conservancy or county authorities to arbitrate between local authorities, urban industry and agricultural interests.[15] And Lord Fortescue argued for county boards[16] on the assumption that county government would be dominated by ex officio justices representing landowning interests rather than by ratepayers, and would therefore be more sympathetic to capital investment for drainage and water supply: the interest of landowners, it was asserted, lay in adding capital value to land and, moreover, ex officios would be independent of the votes of ratepayers who had a short term financial interest against accumulating debt. All of these sets of witnesses agreed that intermediate authorities would be blessed with greater 'intelligence'.

The case for intermediate authorities did not, however, enjoy wide official endorsement. John Simon believed that they would weaken the direct reporting relationship with local government he wished the Board's Medical Department to establish;[17] representatives of local authorities of all kinds condemned them as tending to confuse rather than rationalise the structure of local government;[18] and the Earl of Devon, President of the Poor Law Board, stated that he preferred to strengthen pressure on the local authorities by developing the central inspectorate.[19] The Majority reported against intermediate authorities on the fundamental political ground that town councils would not accept subordination to county elites.[20] And after the Commission reported, the new President of the Local Government Board, James Stansfeld, strongly repudiated the suggestion implicit in all this evidence, that public health development depended on large scale capital investment, to reassure the local taxation lobby.[21]

However, faced with the LGB, which was palpably not a Ministry of Health, and Stansfeld's unwillingness to take a tough line on the grouping of local authorities for the appointment of MOHs,[22] the public health lobby began, in the early 1870s, explicitly to campaign for intermediate authorities as a more effective medium to secure sanitary investment.[23] The arguments used were in part the now familiar ones that large authorities brought intelligence and professional expertise to bear on administration, but it was also asserted that the LGB would become overburdened and that a countervailing influence was needed against the inevitable centralisation of power in its bureaucracy. A large deputation from the BMA/SSA to Stansfeld in 1872,[24] however, was met by an unambiguous rebuttal, which was endorsed as departmental policy by his successor Sclater Booth in 1874.[25]

The sanitary reformers' suspicion of local representative authorities is paralleled by attitudes of poor law reformers in the 1870s and 1880s and, in particular, by the leaders of the Poor Law Conference movement, many of whose organisers occupied high status positions in county political life.[26] What united them was the belief that the rigorous implementation of the workhouse test would reduce pauperism and cut the poor rate. But they also believed that in the poor law, authorities needed to spend to save money. Their point of contact with other poor law lobbies and with the officials of the Local Government Board (who were generally contemptuous of what they took to be the politically impracticable centralising tendencies of most of their ideas) was a belief that the key to improved administration was capital development, that is specialist, institutional accommodation, to secure better classification of the poor. The Conferences' leadership emphasised that this would lead to strict administration of the workhouse test for the able-bodied poor; the medical reformers saw classification as a way to improve provision for the sick; the pauper education lobbies assumed it would lead to more cottage homes and specialist accommodation for children. What united all poor law reformers was the belief that the small general mixed workhouse, upon which many Unions relied, was a drag on improved administration.

The consensus was, therefore, that provision for the indoor poor, at least, should be transferred to larger areas, for two reasons.[27] Firstly, guardians elected annually by ratepayers found it expedient to pay cheap outdoor doles rather than court unpopularity by taking out large loans for building, whereas, it was assumed, county authorities would be dominated by *ex officio* guardians who would take a more informed, independent, long-term perspective. The second argument was that specialised institutions required larger catchment areas to be efficient.

In the late 1870s and early 1880s, central government was pressed to extend the area of chargeability for the indoor poor and for reforms designed to reduce the influence of ratepaying electors on poor law administration, including triennial rather than annual elections for guardians,[28] the transfer of the indoor poor to county boards and a capitation grant for the indoor poor to encourage guardians to transfer the outdoor poor to institutions.[29] These aspirations were shared by many, though by no means all, of the general inspectors of the Board, but both inspectors and officials assumed that the reform of Union elections would be politically unacceptable and refused to endorse such proposals.[30] Likewise, Stansfeld advised the Yorkshire Conference in the early 1880s that there was no hope of a subvention for the indoor poor while Gladstone dominated national finance.[31] Nevertheless, the Board accepted the view that the full development of the poor law depended upon the transfer of the indoor poor to county government and, consequently, of the outdoor poor to reformed district government.

The bills prepared for local government reform between 1878 and 1886 accordingly provided for the transfer of the poor law to local government.[32] But this proposal was based on a consensus of the poor law *cognescenti* and was much more contentious in wider arenas. The debates in the regional Poor Law Conference showed that ordinary guardians would strongly resist the dissolution of Unions[33] and, as we have already seen, many central politicians became very nervous when it became clear that the county authorities might be popular bodies. The fate of Goschen's proposal in 1888, to tie the distribution of the probate grant to the rate of indoor pauperism, showed that there was by no means a consensus behind the principles of 1834 in Parliament. Above all, by the 1890s, the poor law was too sensitive a subject to load on already time consuming measures for local government reform. Neither the Local Government Act of 1888 nor the Liberal Parish Councils Act of 1894 provided, therefore, for the transfer of the Poor Law. Nevertheless, as Parliamentary Secretary to the LGB, Walter Long actively worked on a scheme in 1891-2 to follow a Conservative district councils bill,[34] and the Parish Councils Act of 1894, which assimilated poor law electoral arrangements to district council arrangements,[35] was widely seen as paving the way to a future transfer.[36] The LGB continued to assume that this would occur, albeit in the longer rather than the shorter term.

What the 1888 Local Government Act did provide, however, was for the devolution of certain central administrative powers over local authorities to the new county councils. Throughout the 1880s both Gladstone and Salisbury hoped and claimed that their governments were contemplating not just a reform of local government structure but a great measure of decentralisation[37] and Salisbury assumed that the devolution of powers to counties would help reconcile the squirearchy to the new councils.[38] S. 10 of the Local Government Bill of 1888 therefore provided for the transfer to county councils of significant powers to sanction loans, appointments, the adoption of powers and other matters from the Home Office, Local Government Board and Board of Trade.

The difficulties were entirely predictable. There was bitter opposition from the AMC,[39] but Ritchie was subject to counter-pressure for devolution from Conservative and Unionist county representatives and from Liberal public health reformers.[40] He nevertheless compromised by agreeing that the transfer be effected not by the Act but subsequently by Provisional Order, and further undertook that an Order would be brought to Parliament in the next session.[41] A s. 10 Order was duly prepared for 1889, and referred to a Select Committee. The Select Committee recommended against confirmation, in the light of the boroughs' opposition.[42]

Throughout the next decade or so, the more active county councils began to look for a larger role than that provided by the 1888 Act. In the 1890s, the CCA pressed for powers to provide isolation hospitals,[43] for the control of river pollution,[44] for trading standards[45] and, especially, for the transfer of education to county councils.[46] All were eventually achieved, though they were much compromised by struggles with the boroughs over jurisdictions. A difficulty was that the CCA made no secret of its aspirations to develop counties as intermediate authorities within the local government system. This emerged most clearly in the parliamentary debates on the Liberals' Parish and District Councils Bill in

1893-4.[47] In particular, widespread unease about the Bill's financial implications raised major issues about the nature and extent of controls over spending and borrowing powers.[48] H. H. Fowler, the LGB President, successfully resisted many CCA claims for tutelary powers, but was forced to concede a county council veto on parish loan sanction to operate concurrently with the Board's sanction.[49] The often trivial borrowing of parish councils was thus made subject to two separate local inquiries.

In 1897, the CCA was presented with a fresh opportunity to press for the resurrection of s. 10, when the Local Government Board Inquiry Committee was appointed. The Lancashire and the West Riding County Councils obtained the unanimous approval of the Association to propose a scheme which differed only marginally from the 1889 Order.[50] The scheme and their evidence placed special emphasis on the importance of county control of housing and public health functions,[51] an emphasis which reflects the special activity in this field of these two authorities. Their case rested partly on the belief that they should be liberated from the indignities and inefficiencies of supervision by the Local Government Board, and partly on the explicit claim that they should be considered to be 'Provincial Councils' accorded a special status and occupying special relations with the minor authorities.[52]

The strength of their case was that they could relate a wealth of anecdotal evidence to demonstrate the disproportionate effort and time spent by both central and local authorities in the sanctioning of local schemes, the absurd detail of LGB regulations, and the frustrating lacunae in the county councils' environmental powers. They also struck a note which resonates in the Board's own papers when they complained of the backwardness of many district councils, which the central authority was failing to address. But the Board's officials were able to point out that two thirds of county councils had yet to appoint a MOH or establish a public health committee.[53] Hugh Owen argued that devolution would confuse central-local relations and destroy the hope of uniform standards.[54] But, as in 1889, what killed the scheme was the implacable opposition of the town councils.[55] Faced with supervision by county councils or the LGB, the AMC and UDCA unhesitatingly chose the Board. 'The Local Government Board, with all its faults, is at all events a perfectly impartial tribunal to appeal to ... You prefer your grand-mother to live in London'.[56]

The devolution issue was compounded, however, by the nationalist issue. In 1892, a group of Welsh counties exploited powers in the 1888 Act for joint county committees[57] to establish the Joint National Council of Wales and Monmouthshire, and began to press for a s. 10 devolution of loan sanctions, default powers and the audit to this agency, in recognition of the special needs and status of Wales.[58] An unsuccessful bill was promoted in 1893-4,[59] and in 1896 Lloyd George began to raise the issue on an annual basis in the Committee of Supply.[60] The debates he provoked turned on the efficiency of the Local Government Board as much as the needs of Wales, and became the annual occasion for the Board's deficiencies to be publicly rehearsed. In 1902, the Welsh counties promoted a private bill for the transfer of powers to a Welsh National Council.[61] The LGB opposed piecemeal devolution in prin-ciple, on grounds of administrative untidiness, and it opposed devolution to Welsh counties in particular, because it believed them to be amongst the least developed in machinery and exper-tise.[62] Chaplin and Long also argued forcefully in Parliament that the central authority's ultimate duty to protect the ratepayers – present and future – prohibited the devolution of loan sanctions and audit to a subordinate authority.[63] Nevertheless, Long was forced to agree in Parliament in 1902[64] to introduce a government bill for devolution by Provisional Order on the application of indi-vidual county councils. But the Transfer of Powers Act of 1903 also provided, at the insistence of the boroughs, that an Order could not be confirmed if a majority of minor authorities affected by it objected,[65] and this was sufficient to ensure that no Order was ever made.

The case pursued by the county councils against the Local Government Board reflects real problems in the national manage-ment of policy, particularly environmental policy. It was the issue of housing which, as the century turned, particularly epitomised the difficulties created by contemporary conventions of central-local relations for policy development. As we have already seen, housing became a prominent issue in the 1900 general election and in the Parliaments of the 1900s.

The assumptions in the nineteenth century Housing Acts were that the local authority had a duty to prevent the habitation of unfit houses and of nuisances from slums, but that it should provide housing only in default of, and in ways which minimised interference with, the local market. Local authority building was permitted only where costs would be recovered by selling the development for private management, and the authority was not empowered to subsidise rents from the ratefund. The logic of this position was that the centre could take no power to compel local authorities to build at a loss, and this effectively debarred the development of default powers in housing until after the First World War. Rural district authorities had no direct powers to undertake building schemes under Part III of the 1890 Act, but could do so only after satisfying the County Council that the above conditions were satisfied.[66] At the turn of the century, local authorities had no power to establish land banks or to manage housing. Moreover, the powers to close and clear houses and to acquire land were subject to the usual safeguards for property rights under the Public Health Acts: the powers to close and clear houses were exercisable only on application by offended householders, and powers to acquire land other than by agreement could be exercised only under Provisional Order. That is, the intrusion into local property relations was governed strictly by the conventions of local possessive pluralism. In addition, it was still believed that housing was a local matter, governed by the mutual obligations of local possessive interests: the report of the 1901 Royal Commission on Local Taxation excludes housing from the grant system, on such grounds.[67]

One of the most consistent conventions of local possessive pluralism was that the central authority intervened in local property relations only on local application: that is, it had no independent remit to intervene on the application of its own inspectors or on the ground of national policy. It was involved primarily as referee. In housing, this had proved quite insufficient to get local authorities moving, and the LGB officials had therefore shown sympathy to pressure in 1889-90 from the LCC to allow MOHs to apply for closure of slum housing, under county council sanction,[68] and this was written into the 1890 Housing Act.[69] By the turn of the century, however, the view of the CCA and the medical and housing reform lobbies was that a more positive hierarchical system of controls was needed, articulated through the counties, to subordinate the local authorities to professional tutelage and monitoring. That is, the issue of default and the delegation of public health powers to county councils reopened many of the discussions which had surrounded the role of the Board's Medical Department.

In 1903-5, Hay and Macnamara argued in Parliament for a register of house ownership to be kept in every local authority, to control slum landlords, and for professional surveys of the housing stock, to allow the more systematic exercise of the MOH's powers linked to county council default powers.[70] The National Housing Reform Council and the BMA urged the establishment of systematic reporting by district MOHs, through County Councils, to the Medical Department of the Board,[71] and these reforms were endorsed by the official Committee on Physical Deterioration in 1904[72] and proposed in a private members bill in 1905.[73] However, it was recognised that these proposals implied the strengthening of the medical inspectorate. William Power, the Board's Medical Officer, therefore took the opportunity in 1904 and again when the Select Committee on Rural Housing reported in 1906,[74] to press, without success, for the redeployment of his staff from routine vaccination inspection, which he believed was suffering diminishing returns, to undertake systematic inquiries into housing in rural areas.

The argument inevitably turned to the quality and nature of the Local Government Board as the supervisory body for public health. Hay, particularly, took on a role as the scourge of the Board, systematically attacking its credibility whenever its affairs were raised in Parliament,[75] and publishing vitriolic articles on its style and culture.[76] The charge was that the Board lacked specialist machinery: it had no staff specifically entrusted with housing, no routine means of obtaining intelligence on housing conditions, and conducted no systematic field investigation of public health matters. Hay's immediate demand, therefore, was for a specialist housing department within the Board.

There was also a view that the Board's remit had become too wide: in 1901, Sir Walter Foster, a former Parliamentary Secretary to the LGB, and a veteran public health reformer, characterised it as the 'Cinderella of Departments', the depository for all domestic chores which no one else wanted,[77] and this criticism was pressed by housing lobbies when Burns's housing bill was published in 1908.[78] It was argued that a specialist health minister was needed to co-ordinate action on health, on the basis of coherent, professional intelligence and advice.[79] This should be organised either by divorcing health from local government and the poor law, or by reorganising the Board as a federal department, so that health would have its own junior Minister and Permanent Secretary. The county councils, however, took the opportunity to lobby hard for the Board's housing powers to be devolved to them, and for default powers over district authorities:[80] counties should henceforth be considered the 'supervising authority in matters of public health'.[81]

The view of the officials of the Board was that the ideas of the reformers were thoroughly impracticable. They believed that the complexities and shifts of housing tenure in urban areas like London made a housing register of limited value.[82] Even Power assumed that a significant increase of the medical staff was impossible in the financial climate of these years.[83] The conventional wisdom, reinforced by the events of 1889 and 1897, was that the use of county councils as default authorities would not be tolerated by the urban authorities. In any case, county authorities had not proved to be specially motivated or active in the field of public health or sympathetic to the reformers' plans.[84] For example, although the Board had from 1872 held to the policy that MOHs should be full time officers with tenure and a professional salary, the resistance of the major local authority associations[85] had prevented the Board taking legal powers to enforce this, so that many authorities still operated what the Board considered totally unsatisfactory arrangements, or none.[86] In 1900, F. J. Willis of the Board's Sanitary Department had pressed Kershaw instead to consider LGB default powers for housing construction in rural areas, but was warned that it would be impossible to make councils manage houses they had foisted on them.[87]

Kershaw was therefore cool when it was proposed in the early drafts of the 1909 Housing Bill to use county councils as default authorities, since he believed they would cause much friction, especially with the urban districts.[88] He was supported by the

Board's legal advisor, Alfred Adrian,[89] and their views were doubt-less reinforced by strong protests lodged by the RDCA and the UDCA.[90] Adrian, however, sensed a great opportunity to release public health legislation from at least some of the hindrances exerted by possessive interests: and a lifetime of dealing with the complexities of the law of real estate convinced him that housing reformers, especially the NHRC which had drafted the model bill for Burns,[91] underestimated the tangle of common and statutory rights, enshrined in public law and a multifarious set of local acts, into which local authorities would fall in attempting to use planning powers. He believed that it was necessary to establish administrative powers to slash through the tangle by the preremptory repeal of existing rights, but that only a politically responsible central minister would be acceptable for such draconian powers.[92] Adrian therefore argued strongly (but not altogether successfully) against the loading of the bill with a host of detailed provisions designed to unpick earlier law, in favour of the delegation to the Board of extensive powers to make subordinate legislation, including the repeal of private acts.[93] He also pressed on Burns the necessity of specifying departmental rather than provisional orders for sanctioning town planning schemes, to prevent the obstruction by interests in Parliamentary private bill committees.[94] Adrian's reasoning in this coincided with Burns's instincts, but this strategy severely exacerbated the problems of piloting the bill through Parliament, since it allowed all the bill's opponents to unite around the cry of 'centralisation'.[95] The bill was passed only after very protracted debates and after government pressure on the House of Lords.[96]

In delivering it from local interests, the Board's officials had no intention of turning environmental control over to the professionals. They were therefore uneasy about the proposal to give MOHs the right to institute default proceedings against local authorities, and sceptical about their competence and strength of influence over county councils. In particular, they were unclear what would happen if the county councils refused to act on the MOH's recommendation. Who would act in default of the default authority? They preferred therefore that default powers be exercised by the Board, on application of owners and occupiers.[97] Burns was, however, forced to promise to publish a Gazette,[98] on the model of the Board of Trade's Labour Department's Employment Gazette, as an organ of central intelligence in housing, a Housing Inspectorate was set up as a technical department of the Board and a Housing Comptroller appointed to oversee the housing business. But the Comptroller was J. A. E. Dickinson who, in 1909-10, had been 34 years in the Board and whose background was in the administration of loans, orders and local Acts:[99] in other words housing and planning continued to be seen largely in procedural terms.

In the event, of course, local authorities were very slow to use the powers of the 1909 Act. This may have been no surprise to Kershaw and Willis, who had long argued[100] that the key to the development of housing and health was finance rather than powers or machinery. The Report of the 1912 Departmental Committee on Local Taxation is a landmark here in that it argues specifically that housing in particular and environmental health in general had become matters of national importance, and should be supported by block grants based on population. The collapse of the 1914 Budget meant the issue of central finance for housing was not, however, addressed until the reconstruction period.

The response of the LGB to the housing crisis at the end of the war has been well documented elsewhere,[101] and the personnel of the Board much criticised for their 'invertebrate' proposals. The issues raised by the Reconstruction Panel on housing in 1917 can be seen as a continuation of the struggles between the LGB and the housing lobbies before the War. Addison, the Minister of Reconstruction, and Lord Salisbury, the Chairman of the Housing Panel, pressed for regional commissioners to develop a national building programme, acting if necessary in default of local authorities, and above all, for the statutory acknowledgement that housing should be a mandatory duty of local authorities.[102] Kershaw assumed, still, that authorities could not be compelled to build at a loss. He also believed that a building programme undertaken by national government, or by commissioners in default of local government, would encourage localities to abdicate their duty, and that the introduction of default powers would blight local action: the state could not manage local housing schemes, and the local authorities would not manage houses they had not built themselves.[103] Above all, he continued to believe that only the guarantee of capital subsidies and cheap loans would move local authorities.[104] And modern research has confirmed that the failure of housing in the immediate post war years was largely a failure of housing finance.[105]

The immediate case for the Ministry of Health which was established in 1919 was, not, however, the failure of environmental policy, but the failure to address the problems of the poor law after the publication of the 1909 Reports. It has been said that the motivation for poor law reform was lost by 1908-9 because of the diversion of the interest of Lloyd George and Churchill to schemes for unemployment and national insurance, developed through alternative agencies to the local Guardians and the LGB.[106] In the short term, that is, the poor law and, to a large extent, the local authorities were simply by-passed. In the medium term, the significance of this process is that it gave rise to a fragmention of administrative interests, the reintegration of which was the new Ministry's formal *raison d'être:* however, it was this very structure of interests which all but killed Addison's campaign in 1917 and 1918. Moreover, the very difficulties which stood in the way of poor law reconstruction in 1910 did not disperse in the intervening period, and conspired, in 1919, to produce a department which in many ways was merely a renamed Local Government Board.

In 1910, following the report of the Poor Law Commission, the Cabinet received a paper prepared not by the Local Government Board but on Asquith's personal authority.[107] This paper accepted the transfer of the poor law to county councils, in principle, but listed a series of more urgent items that should be dealt with first, including provision for the unemployed, mental defectives, vagrancy, and labour exchanges. Various reasons have been put forward for the failure to reconstruct the Poor Law before the First World War, including the divisions in the reform lobby between the Majority and Minority schemes, and Burns' alleged revulsion from further major legislation after his difficulties in passing the 1909 Housing and Town Planning Act.[108] We know that at least one of the Board's general inspectors believed that county councils would resist the transfer of the poor law, because they considered

themselves too overloaded to take on new duties,[109] and Newsholme, the Board's Medical Officer, gives the problems of overhaul-
ing local government as a reason for the failure to implement the
Majority Report.[110] In the circumstances of 1909-10, finding
parliamentary time for the notoriously contentious issues of local
government structure would have been well nigh impossible. And
it may also be assumed, with Jose Harris, that the most important
barrier was local government finance:[111] a financial settlement was
clearly necessary to secure the agreement of the local authorities
to a major reorganisation of local government.

The formal reason for the Ministry of Health scheme piloted
by Addison in 1917-1919, was the development of personal health
care interests outside the ambit of the Local Government Board.
Personal health administration was undertaken through the
national insurance machinery set up in 1911, and through LEAs
and local councils in consequence of the Board of Education's
growing interest in child and maternal welfare. This prompted an
obvious case for the reintegration of this provision with the poor
law medical services and environmental health administration
supervised by the LGB.[112] But there was also a political background
to the issue, and this lies in the failure to incorporate the stubbornly
independent Burns into a reformist cadre by a faction within the
Liberal Party which became increasingly influential after 1907.
Masterman, Runciman, McKenna, Macnamara and Addison,
(together with the Webbs) possessed both a deep partisan suspicion of the officials of the Local Government Board and low confidence in the capacity and enthusiasm of the local authorities as
the instruments of social change.[113] From their organisational base
in Education and National Insurance, and in collusion with a few
'outsider' officials such as Morant and Newman,[114] they promoted
social programmes which consciously cut across the responsibilities of the Board, inviting the antagonism rather than the collaboration of the Board's officials and, as the latter saw it, wilfully
disrupting their financial control over the local government system,
and undermining the Board's reputation and authority.[115] In 1912-
13, the campaign was taken up by the Unionist Social Reform Committee, led by Viscount Astor, whose interests were focussed particularly on the housing and health issues.[116] A Ministry of Health

therefore had influential support in both political parties.

There is no doubt that the Local Government Board's political standing was low in the period before the First World War, and that this is attributable not only to the assault of the public health and poor law reformers but to its low status within Whitehall. The status of the Board was a live issue in the early 1900s, partly as a by-product of agitation for higher recognition by the national organisations of commerce and trade,[117] the client community of a Whitehall department with similar status, the Board of Trade, and partly as a result of agitation within the ranks of civil servants who were anxious about pay, prospects and morale in departments outside the circle of old, traditional, high status offices of the Secretaries of State.[118] The response was that the LGB called for lower order diplomatic skills than the traditional departments of the Secretaries of State,[119] and, despite the lobbying of the local authority associations,[120] this view was endorsed by the Jersey Committee, which reviewed the status of the BoT and LGB in 1904.[121]

The case in defence of the Local Government Board is that despite its loss of authority, it is nevertheless widely acknowledged to have undertaken in the years before and during the War a useful amount of service development, by administrative means rather than by legislation, in certain specific areas – notably the control of tuberculosis and venereal disease, and maternal health.[122] And it did so despite other obvious handicaps; the isolation and limitations of Burns, the chronic problems over local government finance and the strategic gaps in the armoury of its powers over local government. It also undertook in the period 1910-1914 a considerable amount of work to update the poor law, which, arguably is as much as could have been attempted given the lack of political consensus either for the break up of the poor law or its transfer to county government.[123] Most of the criticisms of the Board by contemporary reformers and, subsequently, by academic historians, amount to statements that its political and permanent heads failed sufficiently to challenge the constraints and value framework of the existing system of central-local relations, and that it allowed other less inhibited agencies to take the initiative in social policy. The case against Christopher Addison and those who helped him construct the Ministry of Health between 1917 and 1919, must be that, while they responded, in the interests of achieving their bill, to the formal demands made by the local authority lobbies and by the Local Government Board, their contempt for the Board and for its management of central-local relations, blinded them to the political logic and persistent values underpinning the system, and that they failed adequately to address them.

In the summer of 1917, Addison was faced by a Prime Minister who insisted that no bill for a Ministry of Health could be presented to Parliament while significant, salient opposition persisted.[124] Addison had therefore to secure the agreement of the President of the Board and the local authorities; he had to reconcile the insurance lobbies – the friendly societies, commercial companies and trade unions – to loss of special representation which they had been granted on the National Insurance Commissions in 1911, and he had to satisfy the medical lobbies, who had always been in the forefront of the pressure for a health department.

The main feature of the scheme that was sold to the medical, labour and insurance lobbies was that the new Ministry would bring health professionals directly into its main organisational structures, and provide for the direct representation of the medical, labour, consumer and national insurance interests by means of advisory committees.[125] The price which these lobbies demanded from Addison was that the new Ministry should not be based on the Local Government Board, which they identified with the stigma of the Poor Law and which had been so discredited by the reformers' campaigns.[126] This Addison found impossible to deliver: partly because Hayes Fisher, the President of the Board, was able to make a successful case that local government and health could not be separated, and partly because Addison was forced to accept that, at least in the short term, health and the Poor Law could not be separated.

If a large part of the Local Government Board's problem was its association with the image of the unreconstructed Poor Law, Addison's problem was that this image turned out to be somewhat dated. He was unable to deny the response of the officials of the Board, that the Poor Law had become so dominated by the care of the sick that it had become impossible to disentangle the law, the institutions and the staffs dealing with personal health from

other aspects of Poor Law administration.[127] And the very creation
of the Board in 1871 rested on a principle they would not now
repudiate, that curative health care could not be divorced from
preventive health administration, including housing.[128] The Board's
other major objections to a narrowly drawn, professionally-based,
Ministry of Health was that the sponsorship of service development
– especially capital development – could not be detached from the
supervision of local government structure, loans, borrowing and
expenditure. A health department, the officials argued, must
necessarily also be a local government department.[129] The issue
was, therefore, whether the new ministry would primarily represent
professional and consumer interests, or ratepaying and local
government interests.

It is often said that the Ministry of Health project was saved
by the publication in January 1918 of the report from the Committee, chaired by Sir Donald Maclean, which Addison asked to consider the transfer of the poor law to local government.[130] The acceptance of this Report by the Government was widely interpreted to
signal the dissolution of the Poor Law.[131] The members of Maclean's
Committee included some of the keenest protagonists of 1909,
including Beatrice Webb and Robert Morant, and the report finally
reconciled the Majority and Minority of 1909. It was drafted by Sir
Samuel Provis, former Permanent Secretary to the Local Government Board, and warmly approved by Sir Aubrey Symonds, Assistant Secretary for the Poor Law Division since 1913 (who was also
a member of the Committee)[132] and was very much to the taste of
the Board's Secretariat. It recommended the abolition of the Guardians, the transfer of their functions to the major local authorities,
the abolition of the mixed workhouse in favour of specialised
institutions, the establishment of specialist local authority committees for the unemployed and home assistance, and the integration
of the provision for the sick and disabled under the poor laws with
that under the law of local government, including the Public Health,
Lunacy and Mental Deficiency Acts.

Symonds and his colleagues believed the report provided the
political mandate for the reintegration and development of a coherent welfare system, based on the local authorities (from which the
government had been distracted before the war by the hiving off

of national insurance, pensions and child health to other agencies), and for a national health service.[133] Symonds envisaged the establishment of a salaried medical service to replace the expensive, inefficient and incomplete national insurance panel system, and the development of a comprehensive hospital and consultancy service. However, the Board's officials assumed that the poor law medical service and the poor law infirmaries would form the foundation of the health service, and Symonds therefore fought hard for the transfer of the Poor Law to the new Ministry. But he was also clear that the transfer of the Poor Law to local government would not be quick or easy. It implied, he argued, the time-consuming, legislative consolidation of the poor laws and a political decision, which Maclean had shelved, about the future of outdoor relief.[134] And – as always in matters of local government reorganisation – reform also involved dealing with a deeply divided local government community.[135] The representatives from the local authority associations on the Maclean Committee all signalled that the division of powers and rates, and especially the future of the Guardians' assessment powers, would be a major source of conflict in the dissolution of the poor law authorities.[136] Above all, Symonds also assumed, the transfer of the poor law could not be effected without a settlement of local finance,[137] an assumption confirmed by the initial reactions of the local authorities. Lancashire County Council, a particularly large and influential county within the CCA, took the view, for example, that the transfer of functions would overload county councils.[138]

The promise which was held out by Maclean, that the poor law would not long survive the peace, was, however, the inducement that Addison was able to use to get the medical and insurance lobbies to accept a Ministry based in effect on the Local Government Board. But he was forced by the Cabinet Committee on Home Affairs (under pressure from the LGB and the local authorities) to withdraw his offer of a formal explicit statement to this effect in the preamble to the Ministry of Health Bill.[139] And despite Addison's own recognition that the Local Government Board's case was effectively won, he had an uphill, and not totally successful struggle, to win the explicit support of the local authorities and of Hayes Fisher.

The local authority associations and the President of the Local

Government Board all stuck on the same two points. The first was the title of the new Ministry. Hayes Fisher and the local authority associations were doubtless prejudiced against the very idea of a Ministry of Health. The Ministry of Health campaign had been conducted over the years in terms highly offensive to the Board and to the authorities, and the very name of the new Ministry now signalled to them that social policy had been captured by the medical interest.[140] Addison was therefore obliged to accept the title 'Health and Local Government'. The second outstanding difficulty was more substantive, and it concerned the co-option of consumers and professionals into local and central government. The Minority Report of 1909 looked to specialist committees of the local authority, with co-opted experts sitting alongside elected members.[141] And this principle seemed to the local authorities to have been officially endorsed by the bill that was to become the Maternal and Child Welfare Act of 1918,[142] and by Maclean. They therefore insisted formally on the freedom to specify their own committee structure and membership.[143] Likewise, they objected to plans being circulated for departmental advisory committees, which they feared would interfere with their client relationship with the new Ministry.

The insurance lobbies pressed for representative advisory councils, to replace the representation which they had enjoyed in the administration of national insurance. The BMA also pressed for advisory councils with representatives of the major professional colleges and associations. The Local Government Board officials disliked the formal, routine institution of interest representation in Whitehall, because they believed it interfered with departmental freedom to manage policy.[144] However, the determination of the BMA to press two procedural issues conveniently gave them a rationale for their objections. For the BMA insisted that the councils should have the statutory right to initiate policy advice, and to publish advice which the Minister chose to ignore.[145] This, the Board claimed, patently challenged the authority of the responsible minister,[146] and Addison recognised that such demands could not be acceded to. The advisory committees which were established in the new Ministry were advisory only.[147]

In its formal, organisational arrangements, the Ministry of Health departed from those of the Local Government Board. In place of the dominance of the generalist Secretariat, Addison organised the medical officers and administrators into two parallel hierarchies, at the top of which the Permanent Secretary and the Chief Medical Officer enjoyed equal status.[148] The staff of medical officers was substantially expanded, and organised into five specialist groups,[149] and in 1919, Addison established a specialist Housing Department.[150] The Ministry also began to acquire a regional organisation, to which supervisory powers of the headquarters were devolved: the post-war housing programme was organised through Regional Housing Commissioners and the medical support organised for national insurance also acquired a regional structure.[151] Addison continued, however, to use a district-based general inspectorate.

However, the title of the Department was somewhat misleading. Significant areas of the state's health interests remained outside its responsibility: the school medical service was not transferred from the Board of Education; lunacy and mental deficiency remained with Commissioners in Lunacy; and the occupational health interests of the factory inspectors remained outside the Ministry. Nor was it the case that the change of machinery signalled a shift to a financially less constrained system of central-local relations. It has been well shown[152] that though the 1919 Housing Act at last established the principle of state subsidies for local authority housing, its implementation was much damaged by rising costs and by the squeeze of public works loans imposed by the Treasury. And no comprehensive settlement of central-local financial relations was achieved until 1929.

Recent research[153] on the early years of the Ministry of Health has shown that, after the departure of Morant and Newman, its first Secretary and Medical Officer, the Ministry reverted, under the new Permanent Secretary, Sir Arthur Robinson, to a diplomatic, consensus seeking style, and to a preoccupation with bureaucratic form, redolent of the Local Government Board. This has been ascribed to the persistence of factors identified in the present work: that is, the political vulnerability of the Ministry to the salience and fragmentation of national local government interests, the legalistic foundation of its powers, and the dominant generalist culture of Whitehall.

The present study of the Local Government Board has revealed, in addition, a structural problem in the situation of the Board which was repeated in the Ministry of Health, and this is the conflict of its roles. I return here to the analogy developed at the end of Chapter Three. Both the Local Government Board and the Ministry of Health combined the role of a spending service department and with that of a 'Treasury' for local government. They were responsible both for service development and for the financial and administrative integrity of the local government system, and they were consequently involved in three systems of pressure and client interest: those who paid for local government; those who represented, through the local authority associations, the managers of local government services; and the professional lobbies who represented a competing claim to dominate service delivery.

In the case of the Local Government Board, the first set of pressures were strengthened by the prevailing conventions of local possessive pluralism, and by the political salience acquired by certain ratepaying interests in consequence of the long-drawn out financial crisis of local government and the problems of parliamentary and political management at the end of the nineteenth century. And in so far as the local authority associations acquired some power at the end of the period, it was largely the negative sanction of less than enthusiastic co-operation with the centre, rather than active collaboration in service development. That is, in the case of the Local Government Board, the interests of service delivery were swamped by financial pressures. How far the conventional, financial, and cultural factors which constrained the Board diminished, and whether the balance of interest shifted in the Ministry of Health, is, however, another question.

NOTES TO CHAPTER SEVEN

1 MacLeod, *Treasury Control and Social Administration, passim.* The contemporary argument was put in D. A. Thomas, 'Anomalies of the Civil Service', *Fortnightly Review,* LXXI, 1903, pp. 874-886 and M. Foster, 'The Growth of the Local Government Board', *The Nineteenth Century,* LIII, 1903, pp. 107-112.

2 A similar point has been made by Ross, 'The Local Government Board and after'; Preston-Thomas, *The Work and Play of a Government Inspector,*

pp. 195-200; and by MacLeod, *Treasury Control and Social Administration,* pp. 22-3. The statistics have been checked in the lists of marks awarded in competitions for First Division clerks in PRO CSC 10, 1882-1914.

3 John Lambert, *Modern Legislation as a Chapter in our History,* Eyre and Spottiswoode, 1865.

4 For example, it was a worry expressed by the local authority associations about the proposed formation of statutory advisory committees in the new Ministry of Health in 1918-1919, that it would be impracticable to allow full representation of the range of local authority interests. Report of Conference with the representatives of the four local authority associations, 31 January 1918, PRO MH 78/81.

5 For example, in 1894, the LGB set up a Joint Board of organisations interested in sanitary affairs (the Royal Institute of British Architects, the Sanitary Institute of Great Britain, the National Health Society, the Worshipful Company of Plumbers, the British Institute of Public Health, the Incorporated Society of Medical Officers of Health, and the Association of Municipal and Sanitary Engineers) to agree syllabuses for the examinations for sanitary inspectors. 'Annual Report', *Proceedings,* of the Association of Municipal and Sanitary Engineers, XX, 1893-4.

6 e.g. Watkins notes that this was the response of the LGB to representations in the 1890s from the Society of MOHs for LGB control over appointment and dismissal of their members. Watkins, *The English Revolution in Social Medicine,* p. 211.

7 With the exception of AMC most of whose members' accounts were not audited by the District Auditor, legislation had to be passed on the formation of each association, to allow local authorities to charge the ratefund with subscriptions and expenses of members. The promotion of such a Bill marks the *de facto* recognition by the Board of the legitimacy of the association.

8 For example, the Board's response to the issue of housing loans in 1901 was to issue a circular inviting opinions of local authorities, *Memorandum on the Housing of the Working Classes,* by W. H. Long, February 1901, PRO HLG 29/83; and its response to the issues of infant mortality and underfed children raised by the medical lobbies and the Physical Deterioration Committee in 1904 and 1905 was in the first case to commission special studies in the metropolis by its Poor Law Medical Officer, and in the second to alert the general inspectors to keep a special watch on the matter. 136 H. C. Deb. 4s. 14 June 1904, col. 13; 143 H. C. Deb. 4s. 20 March 1905, col. 427.

9 Advisory committees were established by the Board of Education Act, 1899, 62 & 63 Vict. c. 33 s. 4; and by the National Insurance Act 1911 1 & 2 Geo V c. 55 s. 58 and in the reorganisation of the Board of Trade, 1918, (Cd. 8912).

10 I am using the term 'policy-community' as in R. A. W. Rhodes *Power-depen-*
dence, Policy Communities and Intergovernmental Networks, University
of Essex, 1985, p. 18. He defines policy-communities as 'networks characterised by stability of relationships, continuity of restricted membership,
vertical interdependence based on shared service delivery responsibilities, and insulation from other networks and invariably, the general
public (including Parliament). They have a high degree of vertical interdependence and limited horizontal articulation. They are highly
integrated'.

11 Changes in patterns of local recruitment and leadership are discussed in
John A. Garrard, 'The history of local political power – some suggestions
for analysis' *Political Studies,* XXV, 1977, pp. 252-269; John A. Garrard,
Leadership and Power in Victorian Industrial Towns, 1830-80, Manchester
University Press, 1983; P. J. Waller, *Town, City and Nation: England, 1850-*
1914, Oxford University Press, 1983. There are interesting explorations of
idioms of leadership and deference in T. J. Nossiter, *Influence, Opinion*
and Political Idiom in Reformed England: Case Studies from the North East,
Hassocks, Harvester Press, 1976. Contemporary perceptions about the
changing composition of the Boards of Guardians are explored in the
evidence published with the *Report of the Select Committee of the House*
of Commons, 1878 (297) XVII 263. I have explored the concept of 'intelligence' utilised in this section more fully in my own unpublished thesis;
Christine Bellamy, *Aspects of Constitutionalism in England in the Nineteenth*
Century, University of Nottingham, unpublished PhD thesis, 1974.

12 The sources for these statements are as in Notes 1-3 to Chapter Four.

13 *First Report of the Royal Sanitary Commission,* evidence of J. B Denton,
Major-General Sir William Dennison, Joseph Chilton and Robert Rawlinson.

14 *Ibid.* Evidence of Tom Taylor.

15 *Ibid.* Evidence of Joseph Snowball, *Second Report of Royal Sanitary Com-*
mission, III, evidence of Thomas Huskisson.

16 *First Report of the Royal Sanitary Commission,* evidence of Lord Fortescue.

17 *Ibid.* Evidence of John Simon.

18 *Ibid.* Evidence of C. W. Johnson, Lord Egerton, Lord Penhryn and Joseph
Heron.

19 *Second Report of Royal Sanitary Commission,* III, evidence of Lord Devon.

20 *Ibid.* p. 54.

21 210 H. C. Deb. 3s. 5 April 1872 col. 1266.

22 We saw in Chapter Two that under pressure from the Local Taxation
Committee in the Spring of 1872, Stansfeld agreed to a grant towards the
salaries of MOHs, the only new expenditure envisaged by the Public Health
Act of 1872. But he also came under pressure from the Poor Law Medical
Officers Association who wished their members to be eligible to be
appointed, and it was in the spirit of the economical case for the LGB to

be based on the machinery of the PLB that local sanitary administration should use local poor law officers. Though the Board favoured large areas and whole time appointments, it did not, therefore, insist upon them and the general inspectors negotiated whatever they believed desirable and acceptable to their authorities. The various schemes they agreed are described in their files in PRO MH 32: also, PLMOA to LGB, 26 November 1872, PRO MH 25/23. On this episode, see Lambert, *John Simon*, p. 536-9.

23 The major statements of the public health lobby's position are: *Memorial of Joint Committee on State Medicine,* 1872, PRO MH 25/22; and Report of Sanitary Conference called by the Joint Committee, *The Times,* 15 May 1876. Also, 'Report of the Joint Committee to the Health Section', *Transactions of the National Association for the Promotion of Social Science,* 1873

24 Report of statement of Stansfeld to deputation from Executive Council of BMA. reported in *The Times,* 22 November 1872, filed as statement of LGB policy in PRO MH 19/86.

25 Lambert to Sclater Booth and Minute of Sclater Booth, 16 February, 1874, *ibid.*

26 Many of the most active members of the Conferences were ex officio Guardians rather than elected Guardians, including Baker, their founder, Layton Lowndes of Shropshire, Baldwyn Leighton of Shropshire, G. W. Hastings of the West Midlands, and Wyndham Portal of the South East district. Pell was an elected Guardian.

27 Statements based on discussions at Poor Law Conferences, 1875-1880, recorded in the annual reports.

28 The argument for triennial elections was to detach elected Guardians from the alleged electoral pressure towards softness in poor law administration arising from annual elections. This case was pressed particularly by the North West District Conference, in which J. T. Hibbert was a prominent figure; e.g. PRO HM 35/25, correspondence of 1 May 1874. In 1878, Hibbert successfully moved for a Select Committee (which he chaired) which endorsed the scheme in principle, In 1880 Hibbert approached Dodson who was sympathetic but non committal. Report of 6th Annual Conference of North West District, 1880, *Poor Law Conference Reports,* 1880.

29 'County Boards' was recommended to be the theme for the 1879 district conferences by the Central Conference in December, 1878, and the arguments can be followed in the 1879 district reports: likewise, 'The extension of chargeability' was recommended for 1881 and again for 1882. *Poor Law Conference Reports,* 1878, 1879, 1881 and 1882. The typical argument is put in Lord Fitzmaurice, 'Areas of rural government' in Probyn, *Cobden Club Essays.*

30 *Report of Select Committee on Poor Law Guardians,* evidence of Danby Fry and J. J. Henley.

31 Response to paper by William Vallance on 'The influence on the poor of

a wise and strict administration of outdoor relief' to Yorkshire Poor Law Conference, 1881. *Reports of Poor Law Conferences,* 1881.

32 For reasons discussed in Chapter Three, most bills prepared in these years were never introduced and published. Those that got as far as Cabinet are in the Monk Bretton Papers, especially Boxes 54 and 66. There is also a set of bills in PRO HLG 29/17.

33 In 1881 there was considerable dissension at the Yorkshire, Northern and West Midlands district conferences, and at the Central Conference. *Poor Law Conference Reports,* 1881.

34 There is an undated memorandum in the Long Papers, filed with papers from 1891-2, setting out proposals to transfer the administration of the indoor poor to county councils. Long Papers, 947/33. The memorandum is accompanied by a copy of a resolution from the Royal Commission on Agriculture, 1882, in favour of the transfer, by copies of resolutions passed in the Poor Law Conferences in the 1880s, a memorandum from Owen, and a supportive report on the subject from Inspector Jenner Fust to Chief Inspector Knollys dated 31 November 1891. Jenner Fust's and Long's papers assume that outdoor relief will eventually be a district or municipal function.

Dr John Brown has suggested that this memorandum is Long's 1904 agenda for the Royal Commission on the Poor Laws and dates from this later period. It is clear, however, both from the documentary context and from internal evidence – it refers for example to the forthcoming reform of district government – that Long was working in 1892 on a scheme for poor law reform to accompany a possible Conservative district councils bill. Aspects of the Majority scheme of 1909 have therefore a much longer ancestry than Dr Brown suggests. John Brown, 'The Appointment of the 1905 Poor Law Commission', *Bulletin of the Institute of Historical Research,* XLII, 1969, pp. 239-42. Ritchie to Salisbury, 21 January 1890, and Ritchie to Salisbury 30 December 1891, Salisbury Papers, make it clear that Ritchie had a district councils bill drafted in the early 1890s.

35 56 & 57 Vict. c. 73 Part II.

36 The clearest statements are Stansfeld's and A. J. Balfour's at 18 H. C. Deb. 4s. 2 November 1893 cols. 140 and 250. Also speeches of Paget and Hobhouse at cols. 279 and 309. Balfour, Hobhouse and Paget spoke for the Conservatives, the CCA and Local Taxation Committee in favour of deferring district government reform for a Royal Commission on the Poor Law.

37 Gladstone's position is discussed above, Chapter Three. Salisbury, Speech to National Union at Newport, *The Times,* 8 October 1885 p. 7.

38 Speech of Salisbury at Caernarvon, *The Times,* 11 April 1888 p. 12.

39 327 H. C. Deb. 3s. 19 June 1888 cols. 623-655; Minutes of the meetings of the AMC Council, 5 April 1888 and 3rd May, 1888, and special meeting of the Association, 4 June 1888, and report of depution to Ritchie, 5 June

1888 in PRO 30/72.18.

40 327 H. C. Deb. 3s. 19 June 1888 cols. 623-655, speeches of Playfair and Powell and of Hobhouse.

41 327 H. C.Deb. 3s. 22 June 1888 col. 996.

42 *Report of Select Committee of House of Commons on the Government Departments (Transfer of Powers) Bill,* 1889 (275) XI 1.

43 Minutes of Annual Meetings of CCA, 30 March 1892 and 1 March 1893. Infectious Hospitals Acts were passed in 1893 and 1901: 56 & 57 Vict. c. 68 and 64 Vict. and 1 Edw VII c. 8.

44 A Bill was first introduced by Powell for the CCA in 1893-4, as (417) 391 and reintroduced annually into the 1900s. A conference was held with AMC in 1898 to attempt to resolve difficulties. Minutes of Executive Council, 26 January 1898.

45 A committee on weights and measures was set up by the CCA following representations from West Riding and conference with AMC on 22 November 1896, *Annual Report of Executive Council,* 1896.

46 The subject of school education is first recorded in 1897, Minutes of the Annual meeting 12 May, 1897. Thereafter education dominates the agendas.

47 See e.g. the discussions about county councillor representation on parishes and Boards of Guardians, 18 H. C. Deb. 4s. 24 November 1893 col. 1742; 20 H. C. Deb. 4s. 21 December 1893 col. 144; 21 H. C. Deb. 4s. 19 February 1894 col. 800: about the role of county councils in the contentious process of the compulsory acquisition of land for allotments, 19 H. C. Deb. 4s. 29 November 1893 col. 307; 20 H. L. Deb. 4s. 2 February 1894 col. 1737; 21 H. C. Deb. 4s. 15 February 1894 col. 476; 21 H. L. Deb. 4s. 23 February 1894 col. 935: and about the powers of county councils over the alienation of parish property, 19 H. C. Deb. 4s. 29 November 1893 col. 151.

48 19 H. C. Deb. 4s. 1 December and 3 December 1893 cols. 329-419.

49 19 H. C. Deb. 4s. 4 December 1893 col. 419.

50 Minutes of Annual Meeting of CCA, 12 May 1897, and Minutes of Executive Council of CCA, 26 January 1898. The scheme approved by the CCA is in the latter.

51 *Second Report of Local Government Board Inquiry Committee,* 1898 ((C. 8999) XL 447, evidence of F. C. Hulton (Clerk to Lancashire County Council) and T. C. Edwards (Solicitor to West Riding County Council).

52 *Ibid.* Q. 7756.

53 *Ibid.* 8341

54 *Ibid.* Q. 8396.

55 *Ibid.* evidence of R. Borroughs, Town Clerk of Morley, and C. Costeker, Town Clerk of Darwen.

56 *Ibid.* Qs. 8082 and 8288.

57 51 & 52 Vict. c. 41 s. 81

58 J. Herbert Lewis, Chairman of Flintshire County Council, and George Evans, Vice Chairman of Carmarthen County Council, to LGB, 12 March 1892, PRO HLG 29/83, Papers on Government Departments (Transfer of Powers) Bill, 1903.

59 1890-1 (411) VII 167; 1892 (115) IV 655.

60 Debates in Committee of Supply, 44 H. C. Deb. 4s. 10 August 1896 col. 400; 48 H. C. Deb. 4s. 2 April 1897 col. 450; 64 H. C. Deb. 4s. 8 August 1898 col. 565; 72 H. C. Deb. 4s. 2 June 1899 col. 265; 97 H. C. Deb. 4s. 16 July 1901 col. 602; and Resolution at 82 H. C. Deb. 4s. 8 May 1900 col. 1127.

61 Local Government (Wales and Monmouth) Bill, 1902 (2) iii 239.

62 Report on the Local Government (Wales and Monmouth) Bill, 1902, in PRO HLG 29/83.

63 101 H. C. Deb. 4s. 17 January 1902 col. 239.

64 114 H. C. Deb. 4s. 6 November 1902 col. 272.

65 3 Edw VII c. 15 s. 1(3).

66 53 & 54 Vict. c. 70 s. 55.

67 *Final report of the Royal Commission on Local Taxation,* pp. 11-12.

68 Memorandum by Dalton 5 December 1889 on letter from Home Secretary to LGB, 2 December 1889, PRO HLG 29/34.

69 53 & 54 Vict. c. 70 s. 30

70 118 H. C. Deb. 4s. 18 February 1903 col. 142; 120 H. C. Deb. 4s. 2 April 1903 col. 924.

71 Hay to Balfour, enclosing Aldridge to Balfour, 11 May, 1905, PRO HLG 29/96; BMA to Balfour, 23 November 1905, Gerald Balfour Papers, PRO 30/60.53; also record of views of Society of Medical Officers of Health in same file; Memoranda from NHRC, 6 October 1906 and report of Deputation, 7 November 1906, PRO HLG 29/96.

72 *Report from the Inter-departmental Committee on Physical Deterioration* 1904 (Cd. 2175) xxii 1; LGB Report on the recommendations of the Committee, Gerald Balfour Papers, PRO 30/60.53.

73 Public Health Bill, 1905 (71) iv 409 (not printed).

74 Memoranda by Power, 19 June 1904 and 30 April 1907, HLG 29/96.

75 120 H. C. Deb. 4s. 2 April 1903 col. 924; 131 H. C. Deb. 4s. 2 June 1904 col. 653; 152 H. C. Deb. 4s. 27 February 1906 col. 653.

76 G. G. Hay, 'Home truths about housing', *The National Review,* XXXIX, 1906, pp. 111-121; 'The Local Government Board', *The Contemporary Review,* XCIX, 1908, pp. 54-63.

77 97 H. C. Deb. 4s. 16 July 1901 col. 634.

78 Housing, Town Planning etc. Bill, 1908 (178) ii 871.

79 Memorandum of NHRC, 5 May 1908, PRO MH 29/97; Memorandum of Garden City Association, 13 May 1908 *ibid.* Letter from Constance Cochrane of the Rural Housing and Sanitary Association, *The Times,* 28 April 1908 p. 15 ; and from RDCA, *The Times,* 9 May, 1908, p. 7.

80 Resolutions of CCA on housing, Minutes of Executive Council of CCA, 29 April, 1908, sent with letter from Lord Belper to LGB 27 May, 1908, PRO HLG 29/97; representations from full time MOHs of County Councils to LGB, 7 May 1908, *ibid.*; Memorandum by Sir John Dickson Poynder on amendments to the Housing and Town Planning Bill, 14 June 1908, *ibid.*

81 Resolutions of CCA Executive Council, 29 April, 1908.

82 Minutes of Adrian and Monro, 25 April and 30 April, 1900, PRO HLG 29/66; Provis to Thring, 28 February 1907, PRO HLG 29/96.

83 Memorandum by Power, 19 June 1904.

84 Memorandum by Alfred Adrian, 19 March 1907, HLG 29/96.

85 The AMC had always resisted proposals by the Society of MOHs and sanitary reformers to make the appointment of MOH compulsory because they objected in principle to being instructed what officers they should employ and on what terms. e.g. Resolution passed at Annual Meeting 21 March, 1903, PRO MH 30/72.33. The CCA agreed in 1905 to approve the appointment of MOHs by counties but only above a certain population.

86 The Board's officials cited Parliamentary Return, 316 of 1904, lxxxii 735, which showed that at that date fifteen county councils had whole time MOHs, twelve part time MOHs, and thirty five had made no appointment. Filed in PRO HLG 29/97. They also calculated that in April 1907, twenty-six county councils had made no appointment; note on correspondence from CCA, 31 March, 1907, *ibid.*

87 Memorandum by Willis on Housing of Working Classes, 8 January 1900, PRO HLG/66, and annotation by Kershaw.

88 Note by Kershaw, 13 May 1907, *ibid.*

89 Memorandum by Adrian, 19 March 1907, *ibid.*

90 RDCA to LGB, 8 March 1907, PRO HLG 29/96; Report of Parliamentary Committee of UDCA, 20 May 1908, PRO HLG 29/97; Report of RDCA Parliamentary Committee, 26 May 1908, *ibid.*; RDCA to LGB, 12 June 1908, *ibid.*; Report of Deputation of RDCA to Burns, 26 May 1908, *ibid*; telegram from RDCA Conference, 9 July 1908, *Ibid.*, UDCA to LGB, 1 February, 1909, PRO HLG 29/99; RDCA to LGB, 8 March 1909, *ibid.*

91 The model bill is in HLG 29/96.

92 Memoranda of 20 April 1907, and 5 December 1907, *ibid.*

93 *Ibid.* The 1909 Act is notoriously complex and obscure. Its drafting by Adrian has been cited as an example of the low quality of the Board's staff; Brown, *John Burns,* p. 141. and 'John Burns at the Local Government Board', p. 163. However, the Legal Adviser was not employed to draft or formulate legislation and, as usual with such a bill, it was drafted by the Parliamentary Counsel to instructions from the Secretariat; e.g. Provis to Parliamentary Counsel, 27 March, 1907. PRO HLG 29/96. Adrian's view of the 1907 and 1908 drafts was that they were overloaded with detail, feeble and convoluted: 'My general conclusion from an examination of the draft

Bill is that the excellent purpose which the Board have in view will not be helped by legislation on the main lines of this collection of clauses', Memorandum of 20 April, *ibid.*

94 *Ibid.*

95 Brown, *John Burns,* pp. 141-145. The override powers inserted on Adrian's recommendation were also objected to by the CCA; CCA to LGB, 18 February 1909, PRO HLG 29/99.

96 Burns, *Diary,* 19 September 1909, October 1909, 12 November 1909, Burns Papers, Add. Mss. 46327.

97 Memoranda of Adrian, 19 March, 1907 PRO HLG 29/96 and 23 December 1908, PRO HLG 29/99. LGB report on Garden City Association representations, 19 May 1907, PRO HLG 29/97.

98 188 H. C. Deb. 4s. 12 May 1908 col. 966.

99 Personal file of J. A. E. Dickinson, Comptroller of Housing and Town Planning, PRO MH 107/30.

100 e.g. 'Mr Hay does not seem to realise that the matter of cost is at the bottom of the difficulties of almost all housing questions', brief for G. Balfour, n.d. 1905, Balfour Papers, PRO 30/60.53. The LGB's view on grants and capital subsidies was discussed above, Chapters Two and Three.

110 The view most in sympathy with my own is Young and Garside, *Metropolitan London,* pp. 143-153. Less sympathetic accounts are in P. B. Johnson, *Land Fit for Heroes; the Planning of British Reconstruction, 1916-19,* University of Chicago Press, 1968; Kenneth and Janet Morgan, *Portrait of a Progressive.*

102 Christopher (Viscount) Addison, *Politics from Within,* Herbert Jenkins, 1924, pp. 217-8; *Final Draft of Summary of the Housing Panal,* PRO RECO 1/469.

103 Johnson, *Land Fit for Heroes, passim.* Local Government Board's Housing Department statement on *Financial Assistance by the State in Relation to Housing of the Working Classes After the War,* PRO RECO 1/466.

104 Kershaw to Vaughn Nash, 24 August 1917, *ibid.*

105 Paul Wilding, 'The administrative aspects of the 1919 Housing Scheme', *Public Administration,* LI, 1973, pp. 307-326.

106 Harris, *Unemployment and Politics,* p. 165; Honigsbaum, *The Struggle for a Ministry of Health,* especially chapters 3 and 4; Bentley B. Gilbert, *The Evolution of National Insurance in Great Britain: the Origins of the Welfare State,* Micheal Joseph, 1966, p. 253.

107 2 March 1910, PRO CAB.98/40. The paper is over the initials of Asquith. Given its content, it is probably the paper prepared for Haldane, referred to by Beatrice Webb, *Our Partnership,* p. 418.

108 Brown, *John Burns,* p. 147-9; The contemporary analysis by Symonds, the Head of the LGB's Poor Law Division is not dissimilar. Memorandum on the medical services of the Poor Law, March 1917, in PRO HLG 29/115.

109 *Report of Royal Commission on the Poor Law,* I, memorandum by Dr. Downes. Brought to Cabinet's attention in PRO CAB 98/40.

110 Sir Arthur Newsholme, *The Last Thirty Years in Public Health,* especially chapter 11.

111 Harris, *Unemployment and Politics,* p. 267; J. R. Hay, *The Origins of Liberal Welfare Reforms; 1906-1914,* Macmillan, 1975, pp. 39-42.

112 Honigsbaum, *The Struggle for the Ministry of Health,* especially chapter 2.

113 e.g., 'The LGB officials are (certainly were) open enemies, which will not lighten your task. You will have to collect assistance from the municipal people, etc.', Hobhouse to Runciman, 21 December 1905, Runciman Papers, WR 12/1; for Masterman's attitude, Masterman, *C. F. G. Masterman,* p. 76; p. 104; and his letter to Asquith, 15 January 1909, quoted pp. 212-222.

114 Honigsbaum, *The Struggle for the Ministry of Health,* especially chapters 3 and 4. For the victories of the Board of Education over the LGB, see Christopher (Viscount) Addison, *Four and a Half Years,* Hutchinson, 1934, I, pp. 14-49; Newsholme, *The Last Thirty Years,* chapter 20. On the influence of 'insiders' and 'outsiders' on bureaucratic innovation and stagnation, J. Caldwell 'The genesis of the Ministry of Labour', *Public Administration,* XXXVII, 1959, pp. 367-391 and R. Davidson and R. Lowe, 'Bureaucracy and innovation in British welfare policy'.

115 See e.g. the memorandum from Kershaw to Burns, 12 March 1912, PRO HLG 29/106, referred to above in Chapter Three.

116 Sir George Newman, *The Building of a Nation's Health,* Macmillan, 1933, p. 118, gives this as a specially important factor and lists the committee's members.

117 MacLeod, *Treasury Control and Social Administration,* pp. 45-49. Sir John Lithiby's views sum up attitudes within the LGB to the campaign, 11 March 1918, PRO MH HLG 29/115.

118 Richard A. Chapman and J. R. Greenaway, *The Dynamics of Administrative Reform,* Croom Helm, 1980, p. 118.

119 15 H. C. Deb. 4s. 25 November 1902, col. 378.

120 Copies of resolutions in support of the change of status from AMC and UDCA Spring 1903, PRO MH 78/47.

121 *Report of the Departmental Committee on the Status of the Board of Trade and the Local Government Board,* 1904 (Cd. 2121) lxxviii 439.

122 Newsholme *The Last Thirty Years* traces the developments in the public health work.

123 *Memorandum Prepared in the LGB Showing Legislative and Administrative Action Taken Since the Report of the Royal Commission,* March 1914, PRO HLG 29/260.

124 Addison, *Politics from Within,* p. 223, and statement of Lloyd George to Deputation of insurance interests, 11 October 1917, PRO MH 78/80.

125 The negotiations between Addison and these lobbies are documented in PRO MH 78/80. The main events are narrated in Addison, *Politics from Within*, chapter 16; Addison, *Four and a Half years*, II, 437-606 and Honigsbaum, pp. 38-52.

126 The medical lobby's position is stated in a series of model schemes published and submitted to Addison between July 1917 and September 1918; especially, BMA to Addison, 29 December 1917, and report of meeting with RCP, RCS and MOHs, 4 September 1918, in PRO MH 78/80. The insurance lobbies submitted a scheme on 17 September 1917, and it was discussed with Lloyd George and other ministers, 11 October 1917, *ibid.*

127 Memorandum by A. V. Symonds, 22 March 1917, enclosed in Monro to Heseltine, 22 November 1917, PRO HLG 29/115.

128 Memorandum by Monro on Public Health, circulated to members of the Cabinet by Hayes Fisher, 7 October, 1918, ibid.

129 'It would be very unwise to set up a Ministry of Health which is to be guided to some extent by medical advisers without the financial responsibility which attaches to the LGB as the department concerned with local finance, rating and audit: a doctor-ridden department would be a misfortune'. LGB memorandum on Ministry of Health Bill, 11 September 1918, *ibid.*

130 *Report of the Committee on the Transfer of Poor Law Functions in England and Wales,* 1917-1918 (Cd. 8917) xviii 529.

131 The report was published for the Labour Party Conference in January 1918, to signal the Government's acceptance of the eventual break-up of the Poor Law to mobilise support for the Ministry of Health Bill. Correspondence between Henderson and Addison, January, 1918, PRO MH 78/82.

132 'Poor Law reform is long overdue. The need for a complete reorganision of the existing system has long been recognised by all but those who for various reasons cling to the traditions of the past . . . Hitherto the driving power necessary to secure the passage of a complete measure of Poor Law reform has been lacking. It may now, however, be looked for in the movement which has led to the demand for the establishment of a Ministry of Health', Memorandum by AVS circulated by Hayes Fisher to Cabinet, 7 October, 1918. PRO HLG 29/115. Also, Heseltine to Symonds, 24 January 1918, PRO MH 78/72.

133 Memorandum by Willis on powers to be transfered to Ministry of Health, November 1917; see also, memorandum by Symonds, 22 March 1917, and memorandum by Monro, circulated 7 October 1918, PRO HLG 29/115.

134 Report by Heseltine to Addison on discussions with Symonds, 7 February 1918, PRO MH 78/72.

135 Memorandum from Symonds, circulated 7 October 1918, Appendix A, on the special problems of the minor local authorities.

136 *Report of Committee of Transfer of Poor Law Functions*, memoranda by

Montagu Harris, H. G. Pritchard, and R. J. Curtis. All are filed also in PRO MH 78/72.

137 Memorandum of Symonds, circulated 7 October 1918, PRO HLG 29/115.

138 Extract from report of Parliamentary Committee of Lancashire County Council, n.d. 1918, in PRO MH 78/72.

139 Minutes of meetings on July 9th and July 18th, 1918, in PRO CAB 26, and Addison to Hayes Fisher, July 19th, 1918, PRO HLG 29/115.

140 Monro to Hayes Fisher, 22 March 1918, says the title is 'symptomatic of the lobbies that will control the new ministry'. *Ibid.*

141 *Report of Royal Commission on the Poor Laws,* I, 'Minority Report'

142 8 & 9 Geo V c. 29 s. 2. See e.g. discussions betweeen Addison and the Local Government Associations, 28 February 1918, PRO MH 78/81

143 This is an issue raised in all the reports cited above, note 136, and in the Report approved by the AMC, 23 January 1918, PRO MH 78/72.

144 For example, their reaction to the report of the Physical Deterioration Committee on this subject, 1905, Gerald Balfour Papers, PRO 30/69.53.

145 Heseltine recognised that the BMA's claim was of the 'highest constitutional importance', 19 January, 1918, PRO MH 78/80; notes of meeting between medical lobby and Addison, 10 October 1918, *ibid.*

146 Hayes Fisher to Addison, 14 March 1918 sums up his objections, PRO HLG 29/115. The negotiations with the local authority associations on the Ministry of Health Bill are in MH 78/81.

147 9 & 10 Geo V c. 21 ss. 4 and 56.

148 *Organisation of the Medical Staff at the Ministry of Health,* precis of meeting of the medical staff, 7 July 1919, PRO MH 107/24; and *Memorandum on the Principles Governing the Relations Between the Medical Staff and the Administration Staff, Ministry of Health,* 23 August, 1919, PRO MH 107/26.

149 *Organisation of the Medical Staff, ibid.*

150 Wilding 'The administrative aspects of the 1919 Housing Scheme'.

151 *Ibid.*

152 *Ibid.*

153 Steven Stacey, *The Ministry of Health 1919-29; Ideas and Practice in a Government Department,* unpublished D. Phil. thesis, University of Oxford, 1984.

Chapter Eight
Conclusion

The central authority for local government in a unitary system such as Britain can have many functions and many client interests, and this study suggests that the emphasis between these functions and clients in any historical context depends upon political context and the administrative culture. The reputation of the Local Government Board was formed by contemporary writers within a social democratic or statist model of central-local relations, and it has been perpetuated by academics within the twentieth century discipline of social policy. One lesson from this book is that the very term 'social policy' – as in the phrase, 'the history of social policy' – may be misleading in studying the development of the domestic functions of the British late nineteenth century state. For it attaches the notion of 'policy' to an implicit collectivism: it begs the very question that services were perceived to be collectively consumed and that their development and administration were (or should have been) designed to achieve wider social purposes beyond the direct benefits accruing to those interests which directly utilised them. There is no doubt that the Victorians had a well developed sense of the public function and the public good. They understood clearly the case for the collective production of many desirable goods and service, and there was no question but that some services and goods were produced for reasons of public policy rather than private consumption. The obvious cases in our study are education and the poor law, in which public provision was readily acknowledged to promote the stability, legitimacy and efficiency of the state. Hence, they were recognised as 'national' functions, that were 'onerous' to the ratepayers in so far as the rates bore their cost. Yet the poor law was placed on the rates for more than administrative convenience: the poor rates were agreed to be a

traditional burden of real property, because the poor law also performed a direct service to local property holders: it pacified the
workmen, secured local property against bread riots, and ensured
a supply of workers for the local farms and mills. Poor rates were,
therefore, a *quid pro quo* for a private share in the consumption
of a public service.

The dichotomy between the public and private consumption
of publicly produced goods is crucial to an understanding of
central-local relations in this period. The distinctive sphere of local
government was private consumption, the distinctively 'local' services those that served immoveable or 'real' property and its
occupiers and owners. Of course, there was also emerging a third
or intermediary view, that a collectivity can be smaller than a state;
and that a local 'community' may be a unit of collective consumption. This was a view put forward by municipal collectivists, who
held that by belonging to and working in a place, the individual
shared in its welfare beyond his direct and private consumption
of municipal services. However, this was a view that was largely
confined to the towns, and it is a view that, paradoxically, justified
their continued detachment from such influences and controls as
the centre asserted over localities. It was a collectivist view, but it
was not in the short term helpful to the assertion of a statist or
integrationist view of local administration in a national policy
system.

As a central authority, the Local Government Board operated
in a political culture that accorded high deference to local posess-
ive pluralism: and its organisation, its style and, especially the roles
it pursued, must be understood in that context. Its problems – and
its reputation – arose from the fact that that culture was not compatible with emerging notions of the instrumental state. The *raison
d'être* of the Local Government Board was collectivist: it would not
have existed but for the developing functions of the administrative
state. Yet the Board operated between the demands of a growing
body of general public law – which imposed more and more duties
on local authorities – and the constraints of procedural rights and
financial doctrines which suggested priority for local interests. For,
before the First World War, the state failed both to assert its right
to control local services by financing them, or to dismantle the

rights and privileges of property holders which constrained local public action. In this context we are obliged to reformulate both the standard critiques of the Board generated by its statist critics and the conventional understandings of the central-local system we noticed in Chapter One.

As a central administrative authority for local government the Board acted as a guarantor, a reporter, a mediator and a tutor: and in these roles it had different and competing clients. It stood guarantor for the statutory rights of individuals and interests with whom the local authorities dealt, and whose taxes and property they appropriated for their public functions. It reported on local government to Parliament and the public, and it enforced the accountability of local government to its electors and ratepayers. It mediated between private interests and public policy, and between the rigidities of law and the demands of internal diplomacy, by deploying its quasi-judicial powers. And through blue books, statistics, and its inspectors, it attempted to tutor the local authorities in the nationally defined principles of sound administration. Only the latter role did not have a statutory base: the aspiration to tutelage arose less from legal duty than from the unquestioned assumption in the central administrative elite that it was intellectually and empirically more developed than those who ran the localities. And it was a role that was crowded out by the pressing demands of the statutory business. The tasks and duties of both headquarters and field staff of the Board were defined by statutes designed to accommodate the interventionism of the administrative state to the structure of individualist and pluralist rights and duties to which the political culture continued to attach value.

In the first decade or so of the Board's life, its officials acted in Whitehall as the sponsor of local services and capital provision, pressing for powers to facilitate their development. However, increasingly, the Board was forced to become a 'Treasury' for local government, mediating the demands of the local government system on ratepayers, the money markets and the Exchequer. In this role the Board was expected to uphold and work a distinction, based on perceived patterns of consumption and benefit, between the national responsibilities of the imperial government and taxpayers and the private benefits of local consumption. That is, the central authority should be considered an agent of boundary maintenance between local and central government, as much as of central domination of localities. The Local Government Board was obliged to control the national effects of local administrative growth, as well as to stimulate it. And it is this preoccupation with boundary maintenance that prevented the effective development of capital and revenue grants either as a mechanism to secure local compliance with national policy, or to ensure a satisfactory, reasonably uniform, local financial base for the instrumental state.

We have seen in the last chapter that the ambivalence towards the growth of the administrative state reflected by the Local Government Board's management of central-local relations was not unchallenged by those who sought a more uncompromised collectivism and a more positive domination of locality by centre. Particularly, but not exclusively, in the latter part of our period, professional, reformist and ideological lobbies promoted alternative models of central-local relations to the Board's diplomatic-political model. They asserted a technocratic authority, justifying the imposition of defined, universal standards on localities by the central administration, in place of the negotiated, compromised, flexible discretions exercised by the Local Government Board. And, in so far as they succeeded in dissolving the LGB in 1919, they enjoyed an important symbolic success. Yet, these aspirations were limited, and their diagnosis narrow: they asserted in practice a hierarchical chain of command, between centre and locality, based on strengthened legal powers and coercive mechanisms, but they failed to challenge the ideology of possessive pluralism that damaged the resourcing of local government.

Nevertheless, the argument is that their assault on the system of central-local relations symbolised by the Board, and the pressure from the Treasury and the ratepayer lobbies, could not be satisfactorily countered by a lobby of service deliverers. The quasi-judicial culture of the Local Government Board, its paternalistic attitude, its detachment from professional networks, and conflicts over finance with the local authority associations, inhibited the development of an effective, national policy-community representing the interests of the local government system.

A question that arises from this study, then, is whether the ambivalent collectivism symbolised by the Local Government Board is of historical interest only; a prolonged but nevertheless passing phase of our domestic history, representing simply the conflicts and tensions which occurred as the possessive pluralist doctrines of the old Mixed Government model gave way to modern statist or social democratic values. There are three reasons to be cautious about such an easy assumption. The first is that the techniques of central-local relations described here formed the basis of the pattern of controls that has been in use by the centre till the 1980s. This book describes the foundation of our constitutional arrangements between local and central government, not ephemeral administrative history. The second is that the frustrations of central control resonate, as we saw in the first chapter, through the modern political science literature on central-local relations: the corporatist responses of the 1970s and the Thatcherite reforms of the 1980s reflect not the centre's power but the centre's weakness in the late twentieth century system. And the third is the persistent weakness of a technocratic tradition in the central British state. The characteristics of the Local Government Board that have been so roundly censured – the domination of the generalist, the subordination of the specialist, the adherence to precedent and the deference to pressure – are not untypical of the central administration of the UK, then or now. The last lesson of this book is, then, that a history of a government department must be placed in its context – not only the context of the politics and culture of its own time, but the context supplied by an understanding of the political and administrative traditions of the state of which it is part.

Sources

I – Unpublished and official sources

A – *Administrative records in the Public Records Office*

Note: The routine correspondence of the Local Government Board in PRO MH 12, 19 and 25 for the late 1890s and 1900s has been destroyed, and these series peter in the 1890s. It has not been possible, therefore, to use such material for the study of the last twenty years, or so, of the Board's life.

PRO Classes:

MH 12 Local authority files by Union and County

MH 19 (Internal) Departmental Correspondence of the LGB and correspondence with other Departments

MH 25 Miscellaneous correspondence of the LGB (mostly with private individuals and pressure groups)

MH 32 Files of the outdoor staff of the LGB (mostly correspondence with inspectors)

MH 78 Local Government Board establishments and organisation files

MH 107 Personal files of officials and ministers

HLG 29 Policy files, and files of Bills of LGB and Ministry of Health

CAB 26 Papers of War Cabinet, 1916-18

CAB 37 Papers of the Cabinet, 1880-

CAB 41 Letters from Prime Ministers to the Queen, recording main events of Cabinet meetings

RECO 1 Reconstruction papers, 1917-1919

PC 8 Correspondence of the Medical Department of the Privy Council, prior to 1871 (at Chancery Lane)

B – *Personal and private papers*

A. J. Balfour Papers, British Library

Gerald Balfour Papers, Public Records Office, Class PRO 30/60 Burns Papers, British Library

Dilke Papers, British Library

Disraeli Papers, Bodleian Library, Oxford

Campbell-Bannerman Papers, British Library

Harcourt Papers, Bodleian Library, Oxford

E. W. Hamilton Papers, Public Records Office, Class PRO T. 168

Lloyd George Papers, House of Lords Records Office

Long Papers, Wiltshire County Records Office

Monk Bretton (Dodson) Papers, Bodleian Library, Oxford
Ritchie Papers, British Library
Runciman Papers, University of Newcastle Library
Salisbury Papers, Hatfield House, Hertfordshire

C – Other records and series

Reports of the Central Chamber of Agriculture, Ministry of Agriculture
Reports of the Local Taxation Committee, Ministry of Agriculture
Reports of the Poor Law Conferences, Birmingham Public Library
Minutes of the Association of Municipal Corporations, Public Records Office, Class PRO 30/72
Minutes of the County Councils Association, Association of County Councils
Proceedings of the Institute of Municipal Treasurers and Accountants, British Library
Proceedings of the Association of Municipal and Sanitary Engineers and Surveyors, Birmingham Public Library
Transactions of the Sanitary Institute, Birmingham Public Library
Poor Law Officers Journal, including Reports of Poor Law Officers' Union, Bradford Public Library
Miscellaneous papers of the Society of Medical Officers of Health, Association of Poor Law Medical Officers, and various housing and welfare organisations at the British Library

II – Parliamentary papers and returns

Report from His Majesty's Commissioners for Inquiring into the Administration and Practical Operation of the Poor Laws, 1834 (44) XXCLI
Report from the House of Commons Select Committee on the Poor Law Amendment Act, 1837-8 (681) I 36
Report from the Poor Law Commission on the Continuance of the Poor Law Commission and the Amendment of the Poor Law Amendment Act, 1840 (226) 167
Reports from the Committees of Inquiry into Public Offices, 1854 (1715) XXVII 33
Second Report from the Select Committee to Inquire into the Local Government and Local Taxation of the Metropolis, 1866 (452) 317
Return of Local Taxation in Each County and Union in England for 1866, 1867-8 (53) LVIII 707
Return of Estimates of Rental and Rateable Value of the Several Parishes and Townships of England and Wales, and Amounts Levied in Respect of Rates, 1867-8 (497) LIX 679
First Report from the Royal Sanitary Commission, 1869 (C. 4218) XXXII 469
Report from the President of the Local Government Board to the Treasury on

the Incidence of Local Taxation, 1870 (470) LV 177

Report from the Select Committee on the Division of the rates between Owners and Occupiers, 1870 (353) VII 9

Reports from the Poor Law Inspectors on the Boundaries of Unions and Counties, 1870 (122) LVIII 261

Second Report from the Royal Sanitary Commission, 1871 (C. 281) XXXVI

Report from the Select Committee on the Boundaries of Parishes, Unions and Counties, 1873 (308) VIII 1

Report from the Select Committee on the Borough Auditors and Assessors, 1874 (321) VII 1

Reports from the Select Committee on the Continuance of the Turnpike Acts, 1874 (205) XI 565 and XIV 545

Special Report from the Select Committee on the Public Works Acts Amendment Bill and the Local Loans Bill, 1875 (358) XIV 1

Report from the Civil Service Inquiry Commission, 1875 (C. 1113) xxxiii 1

Report from the Select Committee on the Poor Law Guardians, 1878 (297) XVII 263

Return on Visitations by Medical Inspectors of the Local Government Board 1871-1880, 1880 (378) LVI 403

Report of the Select Committee of the House of Lords on the Highway Acts, 1881 (371) X 1

Final Report from the Royal Commission on the Agricultural Depression, 1882 (C. 3309) XIV I

First Report from the Royal Commission on the Housing of the Working Classes, 1884-5 (C. 4402) XXX 1

Report from the Joint Committee of the House of Lords and House of Commons on Private Bill Legislation, 1888 (276) XVI 1

Report from the Select Committee of the House of Lords on Poor Relief, 1888 (363) XV 23

Treasury Minute on the Local Loans Budget, 1887 (166) XLIX 289

Statement of the Proposed Financial Arrangements in Connection with the Local Government Bill, 1888, 1888 (C. 5344) LXXXVI 65

Statements as to the Licence Duties, Probate Grant and Existing Parliamentary Grants Dealt with by the Local Government Bill, 1888, 1888 (C. 5424) LXXXVI 71

Statements as to the Proposed Distribution of the Probate Duty Grant Amongst the Counties of England and Wales under the Local Government Bill, 1888, 1888 (C. 5475) LXXXVI 117

Special Report from the Select Committee on the Government Departments (Transfer of Powers) Bill, 1889 (275) XI 1

Report from the Select Committee on Town Holdings, 1890 (341) XVIII 1

Report from the Select Committee on Town Holdings, 1890-1 (325) XVIII 15

Report from the Select Committee on Town Holdings, 1892 (214-Sess. I) XVIII 613

Report of the Rt. Hon. H. H. Fowler, President of the Local Government Board to the Treasury on Local Taxation, 1893-4 (C. 168) LXXVI 233

Report from the Royal Commission on the Aged Poor, 1895 (C. 7684) XIV 1

Report from the Departmental Committee on Existing Systems for the Maintenance and Education of Children in the Metropolis, 1896 (C. 8027 and C. 8032) XLIII 1

Interim Report from the Royal Commission on Agriculture, 1896 (C.7400) XVII 1

Final Report from the Royal Commission on Agriculture, 1896 (C.7981) XVI 413

First Report from the Departmental Committee Appointed to Inquire into the Sufficiency of the Clerical Staff and Secretariat of the Local Government Board, 1989 ((C. 8731) XI 429

Second Report from the Departmental Committee Appointed to Inquire into the Sufficiency of the Clerical Staff and Secretariat of the Local Government Board, 1898 (C. 8999) XL 447

Report from the Select Committee on the Private Business (Scotland) Bill, 1898 (307) XI 625

Return of the Reproductive Undertakings Carried on by Municipal Boroughs for the Five Years Ending March 1898, 1899 (88) LXXXXIII 1 205

Report from the Select Committee on the Aged Deserving Poor, 1899 (296) VIII 191

Report from the Select Committee on the Cottage Homes Bill, 1899 (261) IX 13

First Report from the Royal Commission on Local Taxation, 1899 (C. 9142) XXXV 795

Final Report from the Royal Commission on Local Taxation, 1901 (Cd. 638) xxiv 413

Report from the Select Committee of the House of Commons on the Repayment of Local Authority Loans, 1902 (239) vii 1

Report from the Select Committee on Private Business, 1902 (378) vii 321

Report from the Joint Select Committee of the House of Lords and House of Commons on Municipal Trading, 1903 (270) vii 1

Report from the Departmental Committee on Workhouse Accounts, 1903 (Cd. 1440) xxvi 567

Report from the Inter-departmental Committee on Physical Deterioration, 1904 (Cd. 2175) xxii 1

Report from the Departmental Committee on the Status of the Board of Trade and Local Government Board, 1904 (Cd. 2121) lxxvii 439

Return . . . of the Counties in England and Wales who have Medical Officers of Health etc, 1906 (316) lxxxii 735

Special Report from the Select Committee on the Housing of the Working Classes Acts Amendment Bill, 1906 (376) iv Pt IV

Return of all Inspectors and Auditors now in the Service of the Local Government Board, 1906 (350) cii 401

Return of Medical Officers of Health and Inspectors of Nuisance Employed by Rural Districts, 1907 (273) lxxii

Report from the Departmental Committee on the Accounts of Local Authorities, 1907 (Cd. 3615) xxxvii 71

Reports from the Royal Commission on the Poor Laws and the Relief of Distress, 1909 (Cd. 4499) XXXVII 1

First Report from the Departmental Committee on Poor Law Orders, 1913 (Cd. 6968) xxxviii 241

Final Report from the Departmental Committee on Local Taxation, 1914 (Cd. 7315) xl 537

Report from the Committee on the Transfer of Functions of Poor Law Authorities in England and Wales, 1917-18 (Cd. 8917) xviii 529

Report on the Machinery of Government, 1918 (Cd. 9230)

III – Published and literary works

A – Books

Unless otherwise indicated, the place of publication is London.

Christopher (Viscount) Addison, *Politics from Within,* Herbert Jenkins, 1924

Christopher (Viscount) Addison, *Four and a Half Years,* Hutchinson, 1934

P. F. Aschrott, *The English Poor Law System,* translated by Herbert Preston Thomas, Knight and Co., 1888

Douglas E. Ashford, *Financing Urban Government in the Welfare State,* Croom Helm, 1980

Douglas E. Ashford, *British Dogmatism and French Pragmatism: Central-Local Policy-making in the Welfare State,* Allen & Unwin, 1982

Douglas E. Ashford, *The Emergence of the Welfare States,* Oxford, Blackwells, 1986

Percy Ashley, *Local and Central Government,* John Murray, 1906

Waldorf Astor, *The Health of the People,* Argus Printing Co., 1917

Lord Avebury, *On Municipal and National Trading,* Macmillan & Co., 1906

D. W. R. Bahlman (ed.), *The Diary of Sir Edward Walter Hamilton, 1880-1885,* 2 Vols. Oxford, Clarendon Press, 1972

W. A. Bailward, *The Charity Organisation Society; a Historical Sketch, 1896-1906,* COS, 1906

J. Bateman, *The Great Landowners of Great Britain and Ireland,* Leicester, Leicester University Press, 1971

R. Dudley Baxter, *The Taxation of the United Kingdom,* Macmillan & Co., 1869

R. Dudley Baxter, *Local Government and Taxation and Mr Goschen's Report,* 1874

R. J. Bennett, *Central Grants to Local Authorities,* Cambridge, Cambridge University Press, 1982

A. S. Bishop, *The Rise of a Central Authority for English Education,* Cambridge, Cambridge University Press, 1971

Sir Courtenay Boyle, *Hints on the Conduct of Business, Public and Private,* Macmillan & Co., 1900

Jeanne L. Brand, *Doctors and the State: the British Medical Profession and Government Action in Public Health, 1870-1912,* Baltimore, Johns Hopkins Press, 1965

C. Fraser Brockington, *A Short History of Public Health,* J. and A. Churchill, 2nd ed., 1966

Kenneth D. Brown, *Labour and Unemployment, 1900-1914,* Newton Abbott, David & Charles, 1971

Kenneth D. Brown, *John Burns,* Royal Historical Society, 1977

J. P. Bulpitt, *Territory and Power in the United Kingdom,* Manchester, Manchester University Press, 1982

Horace Butler, *Confident Morning,* Faber & Faber, 1949

Sidney Buxton and G. S. Barnes, *A Handbook to the Death Duties,* John Murray, 1890

Sidney Buxton, *Finance and Politics: a Historical Study, 1783-1885,* II, John Murray, 1888

David Calladine (ed.), *Patricians, Power and Politics in Nineteenth Century Towns,* Leicester, Leicester University Press, 1982

Edwin Cannan, *A History of Local Rates in England in Relation to the Proper Distribution of the Burden of Taxation*, P. S. King, 1912

Lady Gwendolen Cecil, *Life of Robert, Marquis of Salisbury,* Hodder and Staughton, 1922-31

M. D. Chalmers, *Local Government,* Macmillan & Co., 1883

Richard A. Chapman and J. R. Greenaway, *The Dynamics of Administrative Reform,* Croom Helm, 1980

Winston Spencer Churchill, *Lord Randolph Churchill,* 2 Vols., 1905

J. J. Clarke, *A History of Local Government in the U.K.*, reprinted, Greenwood Press, 1978

P. W. Clayden, *England under Lord Beaconsfield,* 1880, reprinted, Richmond Publishing Co., 1971

Frederick Clifford, *A History of Private Bill Legislation,* I, 1885, reprinted, Frank Cass, 1968

Frederick Clifford, *Local and Private Bills: Some Remarks on Pending Legislation,* Eyre & Spottiswoode, 1904

A. B. Cooke and J. R. Vincent, *Lord Carlingford's Journal,* Oxford, Clarendon Press, 1971

John Dearlove, *The Reorganisation of British Local Government,* Cambridge, Cambridge University Press, 1979

C. Dodd and H. W. W. Wilberforce, *Private Bill Procedure: A Guide to the Procedure upon Private Bills,* Eyre & Spottiswoode & Croom Helm, 1977

A. P. Donajdodzki (ed.), *Social Control in Nineteenth Century Britain,* Croom Helm, 1977

Roy Douglas, *Land, People and Politics: A History of the Land Question in the United Kingdom, 1875-1952,* Allison & Busby, 1976

K. H. F. Dyson, *The State Tradition in Western Europe: A Study of an Idea and an Institution,* Martin Robertson, 1980

H. V. Emy, *Liberals, Radicals and Social Politics, 1892-1912,* Cambridge, Cambridge University Press, 1973

R. C. K. Ensor, *England, 1870-1914,* Oxford, Clarendon Press, 1936

Henry Fawcett, *Pauperism – its Causes and its Remedies,* Macmillan & Co., 1871

Herman Finer, *Municipal Trading: a Study in Public Administration,* Allen & Unwin, 1941

C. D. Foster, R. A. Jackman and M. Perlman, *Local Government Finance in a Unitary State,* Allen & Unwin, 1980

R. F. Foster, *Lord Randolph Churchill: a Political Life,* Oxford, Clarendon Press, 1981

P. Ford, *Social Theory and Social Practice,* Shannon, Irish University Press, 1968

E. H. Fowler, *Life of Henry Hartley Fowler, First Viscount Wolverhampton,* Hutchinson, 1912

Derek Fraser, *The New Poor Law in the Nineteenth Century,* Macmillan, 1976

Derek Fraser, *Urban Politics in Victorian England,* Leicester, Leicester University Press, 1976

Derek Fraser, *Power and Authority in the Victorian City,* Oxford, Blackwells, 1979

W. M. Frazer, *A History of English Public Health, 1834-1939,* Bailliere, Tindall & Cox, 1950

G. K. Fry, *The Growth of Government,* Frank Cass, 1979

R. M. Garnier, *The History of the Landed Interest,* Macmillan & Co., 1893

J. A. Garrard, D. Jary, M. J. Goldsmith and A. Oldfield (eds.), *The Middle Class in Politics,* Saxon House, 1978

John A. Garrard, *Leadership and Power in Victorian Industrial Towns 1830-80,* Manchester, Manchester University Press, 1983

Bentley B. Gilbert, *The Evolution of National Insurance in Great Britain: the Origins of the Welfare State,* Michael Joseph, 1966

Bentley B. Gilbert, *British Social Policy, 1914-1939,* B. T. Batsford, 1970

W. E. Gladstone, *Midlothian Speeches 1879,* Leicester, Leicester University Press, 1971

G. J. Goschen, *Reports and Speeches on Local Taxation,* Macmillan & Co., 1972

J. Watson Grice, *National and Local Finance,* P. S King, 1910

S. Gwynn and G. M. Tuckwell, *The Life of the Rt. Hon. Sir Charles Dilke,* 2 vols, John Murray, 1918

J. L. and Barbara Hammond, *James Stansfeld: a Victorian Champion of Sex Equality,* Longmans, 1932

Jose Harris, *Unemployment and Politics: a Study in English Social Policy, 1886-1914*, Oxford, Clarendon Press, 1972

H. E. Haward, *Imperial Subventions in Aid of Local Taxation: a Review of the Financial Relations between the Imperial Exchequer and Local Authorities of England and Wales, 1889-1910*, IMTA, 1911

J. S. Harris, *British Government Inspectors: the Local Service and the Central Departments*, Stevens & Sons, 1955

J. R. Hay, *The Origins of the Liberal Welfare Reforms, 1906-1914*, Macmillan, 1975

L. M. Helmore, *The District Auditor*, Macdonald & Evans, 1961

Dilys M. Hill, *Democratic Theory and Local Government*, Allen & Unwin, 1974

Frank Honigsbaum, *The Struggle for the Ministry of Health, 1914-1919*, G. Bell & Sons, 1970

Institute of Municipal Treasurers and Accountants, A Short History, 1885-1960, IMTA, 1960

Richard Jay, *Joseph Chamberlain*, Oxford, Clarendon Press, 1981

Sir Ivor Jennings, 'Central control', in H. J. Laski *et al.* (eds.), *A Century of Municipal Progress*, Allen & Unwin, 1935

P. B. Johnson, *Land Fit for Heroes: the Planning of British Reconstruction, 1916-1919*, Chicago, University of Chicago Press, 1968

A. Jones, *The Politics of Reform*, Cambridge, Cambridge University Press, 1972

G. W. Jones (ed.), *New Approaches to the Study of Central-Local Government Relations*, Farnborough, Gower, 1980

R. Jones, *Local Government Audit Law*, HMSO, 1981

M. Katanga, *Radicals, Reformers and Socialists*, Charles Knight & Co., 1973

Royston Lambert, *Sir John Simon, 1816-1904, and English Social Administration*, Macgibbon & Kee, 1963

John Lambert, *Modern Legislation as a Chapter in Our History*, Eyre & Spottiswoode, 1865

Mary Langan and Bill Schwartz, *Crises in the British State, 1890-1930*, Hutchinson, 1965

V. D. Lipman, *Local Government Areas, 1834-1945*, Oxford, Blackwells, 1949

Susan Liveing, *A Nineteenth-Century Teacher: John Henry Bridges*, Kegan Paul, 1926

Marchioness of Londonderry, *Henry Chaplin; a Memoir*, Macmillan, 1926

Walter (Viscount) Long, *Memories*, Hutchinson, 1923

B Keith Lucas, *The English Local Government Franchise: A Short History*, Oxford, Blackwells, 1952

Norman McCord, 'Ratepayers and social policy' in Pat Thane (ed.), *The Origins of British Social Policy*, Croom Helm, 1978

T. Mackay, *A History of the English Poor Law*, III, P. S. King, 1899

J. M. Mackintosh, *Trends of Opinion about the Public Health, 1901-51*, Oxford University Press, 1953

Roy M. MacLeod, *Treasury Control and Social Administration,* G. Bell & Sons, 1968

Bernard Mallet, *British Budgets, 1887-1913,* Macmillan & Co., 1913

M. R. Maltbie, *English Local Government of Today: a Study of the Relation of Central and Local Government,* New York, Columbia College, 1897

Peter Marsh, *The Discipline of Popular Government: Lord Salisbury's Statecraft, 1881-1902,* Hassocks, Harvester Press, 1978

Lucy Masterman, *C. F. C. Masterman: a Biography,* Nicholson & Watson, 1939

A. H. H. Matthews, *History of the Central Chamber of Agriculture, 1865-1915,* P. S. King, 1915

J. S. Mill, *Essay on Representative Government,* Oxford University Press, 1912

W. J. Mommsen (ed.), *The Emergence of the Welfare State in Britain and Germany, 1850-1950,* Croom Helm, 1981

K. O. and Janet Morgan, *Portrait of a Progressive: the Life of Viscount Addison,* Oxford, Clarendon Press, 1980

Bruce K. Murray, *The People's Budget, 1909-10, and Liberal Politics,* Oxford, Clarendon Press, 1980

Sir George Newman, *The Building of a Nation's Health,* Macmillan, 1939

Sir Arthur Newsholme, *The Ministry of Health,* G. P. Putnam, 1925

Sir Arthur Newsholme, *The Last Thirty Years in Public Health: Recollections and Reflections on my Official and Post-Official Life,* Allen & Unwin, 1936

T. J. Nossiter, *Influence, Opinion and Political Idiom in Reformed England: Cases from the North-East, 1832-74,* Hassocks, Harvester Press, 1975

Avner Offer, *Property and Politics, 1870-1914; Landownership, Law, Ideology and Urban Development in England,* Cambridge University Press, 1981

Sir Harry Page, *Local Authority Borrowing: Past, Present and Future,* Allen & Unwin, 1985

Clifford Pearce, *The Machinery of Change in Local Government, 1884-1894: a Study in Central Involvement,* Allen & Unwin, 1980

Albert Pell, *Reminiscences,* John Murray, 1908

Sir Charles Petrie, *Walter Long and his Times,* Hutchinson, 1936

Herbert Preston Thomas, *The Work and Play of a Government Inspector,* Blackwells, 1903

J. W. Probyn (ed.), *Local Government and Taxation,* Cobden Club Essays, 1875

Agatha Ram, *The Political Correspondence of Mr Gladstone and Lord Granville, 1876-1886,* Oxford, Clarendon Press, 1962

William Rathbone, Albert Pell and F. C. Montague, *Local Administration,* Swan Sonnenchien, 1885

J Redlich and F. W. Hirst, *Local Government in England,* Macmillan, 1903

J. F. Rees, *A Short Fiscal and Financial History of England, 1815-1918,* Methuen, 1921

H. A. Rhee, *The Rent of Agricultural Land in England and Wales, 1870-1942,* Memorandum to the Central Landowners Association, 1946

R. A. W. Rhodes, *Control and Power in Central-Local Government Relations*, Farnborough, Gower, 1981

R. A. W. Rhodes, *Power-dependence, Policy Communities and Intergovernmental Networks*, University of Essex Papers in Politics and Government, No. 30, 1985

Gerald Rhodes, *Inspectorates in British Government: Law Enforcement and Standards of Efficiency*, Allen & Unwin for RIPA, 1981

A. Carson Roberts, *Local Administration: Finance and Accounts*, Harrison & Sons, 1931

M. E. Rose, *The English Poor Law, 1780-1930*, Newton Abbott, David & Charles, 1971

Peter Rowland, *The Last Liberal Governments: the Promised Land, 1905-1910*, Barrie & Rockliffe, 1968

Peter Rowland, *The Last Liberal Governments: Unfinished Business, 1911-14*, Barrie & Jenkins, 1971

D. L. Rydz, *The Parliamentary Agents*, Royal Historical Society, 1979

G. R. Searle, *The Quest for National Efficiency*, Oxford, Blackwells, 1971

John Simon, *English Sanitary Institutions*, 1890, reprinted, Johnson Reprint Co., 1970

K. B. Smellie, *A History of Local Government*, Allen & Unwin, 4th ed., 1968

Paul Smith, *Disraelian Conservatism and Social Reform*, Routledge & Kegan Paul, 1967

Gillian Sutherland, *Studies in the Growth of Nineteenth Century Government*, Routledge & Kegan Paul, 1972

Gillian Sutherland, *Policy-making in Elementary Education, 1870-1895*, Oxford University Press, 1973

Robert Taylor, *Lord Salisbury*, Allen & Unwin, 1975

J. A. Thomas, *The House of Commons, 1832-1901, a Study in its Economic and Functional Character*, Cardiff, University of Wales Press Board, 1939

F. M. L. Thompson, *The Rise of Suburbia*, Leicester, Leicester University Press, 1982

Louisa Twining, *Recollections of Workhouse Visiting and Management during Twenty-five Years*, C. Kegan Paul and Co., 1880

P. J. Waller, *Town, City and Nation: England, 1850-1914*, Oxford University Press, 1983

Beatrice Webb, *Our Partnership*, 1948, ed. B Drake and M. Cole, London School of Economics & Cambridge University Press, 1975

Sidney and Beatrice Webb, *English Local Government*, X, 'English Poor Law policy', 1910, republished, Frank Cass, 1963

Sidney and Beatrice Webb, *English Poor Law History*, II 'The Last Hundred Years', Longmans, 1927-9

O. C. Williams, *The Historical Development of Private Bill Procedure and Standing Orders in the House of Commons*, I, HMSO, 1948

R. S. Wright and H. Hobhouse, *An Outline of Local Government and Local Taxation in England and Wales, Together with Some Considerations for Amendment,* Maxwell & Sons, 1884

Ken Young, *Local Politics and the Rise of Party: the London Municipal Society and the Conservative Intervention in Local Elections, 1894-1963,* Leicester, Leicester University Press, 1975

Ken Young and Patricia Garside, *Metropolitan London: Politics and Urban Change, 1837-1981,* Edward Arnold, 1982

B – Articles

C. T. D. Acland, 'County Boards', *Fortnightly Review,* CLXIX, 1881, pp. 93-102

Percy Ashley, 'The financial control of English local authorities', *Economic Journal,* XII, 1902, pp. 182-191

W. H. S. Aubrey, 'Government by chief clerks', *Westminster Review,* CXXXIII, 1890, pp. 105-124

Lord Avebury, 'The growth of municipal and national expenditure', *Journal of the Royal Statistical Society,* LXIV, 1901, pp. 73-86

Lord Avebury, 'Local and imperial burdens', *Journal of the Royal Statistical Society,* LXIV, 1901, pp. 557-572

P. W. J. Bartripp and P. T. Fenn, 'The administration of safety: the enforcement policy of the early factory inspectorate 1844-1864', *Public Administration,* LVIII, 1980, pp. 87-102

C. F. Bastable, 'The taxation of ground rents', *Economic Journal,* III, 1893, pp. 255-263

H. H. L. Bellot, 'The Local Government Act, 1894', *Westminster Review,* CLXI, 1894, pp. 479-489

Neal Blewett, 'The franchise in the United Kingdom, 1885-1918', *Past and Present,* XXXII, pp. 27-56

G. H. Blunden, 'The incidence of urban rates', *Economic Review,* II, 1891, pp. 486-496

G. H. Blunden, 'British local finance I', *Political Science Quarterly,* IX, 1894, pp. 78-118

Jeanne L. Brand, 'The parish doctor: England's Poor Law Medical Officers and Medical Reform, 1870-1900', *Bulletin of the History of Medicine,* XXXV 1961, pp. 97-122

Jeanne L. Brand, 'John Simon and the Local Government Board bureaucrats, 1831-1876', *Bulletin of Medical History,* XXXVII, 1963, pp. 184-194

Edward Bristow, 'The Liberty and Property Defence League and individualism', *The Historical Journal,* XVIII, 1975, pp. 761-789

C. Fraser Brockington, 'Public health at the Privy Council, 1858-1871', *The Medical Officer,* May 1959, pp. 287-290

John Brown, 'Scottish and English land legislation, 1905-1911', *Scottish Historical Research,* XLVII, 1968, pp. 72-85

John Brown, 'The appointment of the 1905 Poor Law Commission', *Bulletin of the Institute of Historical Research,* XLIV, 1969, pp. 239-242

John Brown, 'The Poor Law Commission and the Unemployed Workmen Act', *Bulletin of the Institute of Historical Research,* XLIV, 1971, pp. 318-323

Kenneth D. Brown, 'Conflict in early British welfare policy: the case of the Unemployed Workmen's Bill of 1905', *Journal of Modern History,* XLIII, 1971, pp. 613-629

Kenneth D. Brown, 'The appointment of the 1905 Poor Law Commission – a rejoinder', *Bulletin of the Institute of Historical Research,* XLIV, 1971, pp. 315-318

Kenneth D. Brown, 'London and the historical reputation of John Burns', *London Journal,* II, 1976, pp. 226-237

Kenneth D. Brown, 'John Burns at the Local Government Board', *Journal of Social Policy,* VI, 1977, pp. 157-170, XXXVII, 1959, pp. 367-391

J. M. Caldwell, 'The genesis of the Ministry of Labour', *Public Administration,* XXXVII, 1959, pp. 367-391

Edwin Cannan, 'Ought municipal enterprises to be allowed to yield a profit?', *The Economic Journal,* IX, 1899, pp. 1-9

Edwin Cannan, 'The financial relations of English localities', *The Economic Journal,* XIII, 1903, pp. 6-16

Edwin Cannan, 'The proper relief of buildings from local rates', *The Economic Journal,* XVII, 1907, pp. 34-47

Edwin Chadwick, 'Centralization', *The Edinburgh Journal,* LXIII, 1836, pp. 536-565

Edwin Chadwick, 'On the chief methods of preparation for legislation', *Frasers Magazine,* LXXV, 1867, pp. 673-690

Edwin Chadwick, 'The requisite attributions of a Minister of Health', *The Sanitarian,* 7 Feb. 1879, pp. 59-67

Edwin Chadwick, 'London centralised', *The Contemporary Review,* XLIV, 1884, pp. 794-810

Doreen Collins, 'The introduction of old age pensions in Great Britain', *The Historical Journal,* VIII, 1965, pp. 246-259

P. G. Craigie, 'The cost of local government', *Journal of the Statistical Society,* XL, 1877, pp. 262-288

P. G. Craigie, 'Taxation as affecting the agricultural interest', *Journal of the Royal Society of England,* 2nd series, XIV, 1878, pp. 385-424

P. G. Craigie, 'The English poor rate', *Journal of the Statistical Society,* CI, 1888, pp. 450-93

Valerie Cromwell, 'Interpretations of nineteenth-century administration: an analysis', *Victorian Studies,* IX, 1966, pp. 246-255

Leonard Darwin, 'The taxation of site values', *The Economic Journal,* XVII, 1907, pp. 330-44

D. H. Davies, 'The cost of municipal enterprise', *Journal of the Society of Arts,* XLVII, 1898-99, pp. 224-240 and 265-275

R. Donald, 'John Burns, the workman Minister', *The Nineteenth Century,* LXXXIV, 1906, pp. 191-204

J. P. D. Dunbabin, 'The politics of the establishment of county councils', *The Historical Journal,* VI, 1963, pp. 226-252

J. P. D. Dunbabin, 'Expectations of the new county councils and their realisation', *Historical Journal,* VIII, 1965, pp. 353-379

J. P. D. Dunbabin, 'British local government reform: the nineteenth century and after', *English Historical Review,* XCII, 1977, pp. 777-805

W. Walter Edwards, 'The poor law: a proposal for its abolition', *The Contemporary Review,* XXVI, 1875, pp. 639-644

H. V. Emy, 'The impact of financial policy on English party politics before 1914', *The Historical Journal,* XV, 1972, pp. 103-131

R. C. K. Ensor, 'Some political and economic interactions in later Victorian England, *Transaction of the Royal Historical Society,* XXI, 4th series, 1949, pp. 17-29

T. H. Farrer, 'The imperial finance of the past four years', *The Contemporary Review,* LVIII, 1890, pp. 481-500

T. H. Farrer, 'Local and imperial finance of the past four years', *The Contemporary Review,* LVIII, 1890, pp. 755-784

T. H. Farrer, 'Imperial and local taxation', *The Contemporary Review,* LVIII, 1890, pp. 913-936

J. Moulton Fletcher, 'The taxation of ground rents: a reply', *Contemporary Review,* LVII, 1890, pp. 412-20

M. Foster, 'The growth of the Local Government Board', *The Nineteenth Century,* LIII, 1903, pp. 107-112

H. H. Fowler, 'Municipal finance and municipal enterprise', *Journal of the Statistical Society,* LXIII, 1900, pp. 383-407

John A. Garrard, 'The history of local political power – some suggestions for analysis', *Political Studies,* XXV, 1977, pp. 252-269

P. Lyttelton Gell, 'Reform in the public service', *Nineteenth Century,* XLVIII, 1900, pp. 43-53

R. M. Gutchen, 'Local improvements and centralisation in nineteenth century England', *The Historical Journal,* IV, 1961, pp. 85-96

Edwin Harper, 'Will the rating of land values increase urban congestion?', *Economic Journal,* XVIII, 1908, pp. 28-41

Jenifer Hart, 'Sir Charles Trevelyan at the Treasury', *English Historical Review,* LXXII, 1960, 92-110

Jenifer Hart, 'Nineteenth century social reform: a Tory interpretation of history, *Past and Present,* 1965, XXXI, pp. 36-91

C. Hay, 'Home truths about housing', *The National Review,* XXXIX, 1906, pp. 111-121

C. Hay, 'The Local Government Board', *The Contemporary Review*, XCIV, 1908, pp. 54-63

Roy Hay, 'Employers and social policy in Britain, the evolution of welfare legislation, 1905-1914', *Social History*, IV, 1977, pp. 435-455

R. Heath, 'The rural revolution', *The Contemporary Review*, LXVII, 1895, pp. 182-200

E. P. Hennock, 'Finance and politics in urban local government in England, 1835-1900', *The Historical Journal*, VI, 1963, pp. 212-225

E. P. Hennock, 'Poverty and social theory in England: the experience of the 1880s', *Social History*, I, 1976, pp. 67-91

Gertrude Himmelfarb, 'the writing of social history: recent studies of nineteenth century England', *Journal of British Studies*, II, 1971, pp. 148-169

Royston J. Lambert, 'Central-local relations in mid-Victorian England: the Local Government Act Office, 1858-71', *Victorian Studies*, VI, 1962-63, pp. 121-150

Royston J. Lambert, 'A Victorian National Health Service: state vaccination 1855-71', *The Historical Journal*, V, 1962, pp. 1-18

H. J. Laski, 'The personnel of the English Cabinet', *American Political Science Review*, XXII, 1928, pp. 12-31

B. Keith-Lucas, 'Municipal business and ultra vires', *Public Administration*, XXVII, 1949, pp. 87-90

Baron Lyttelton, 'The Poor Laws', *The Contemporary Review*, XXVI, 1875, pp. 169-192

Norman McCord, 'The implementation of the 1834 Poor Law Amendment Act on Tyneside', *International Review of Social History*, XIV, 1969, pp. 90-108

Oliver Macdonagh, 'The nineteenth century revolution in government: a reappraisal' *Historical Journal*, I, 1958, pp. 52-67

Roy M. MacLeod, 'The Alkali Acts administration 1863-1884: the emergence of the civil scientist', *Victorian Studies*, XI, 1865, pp. 85-112

Roy M. MacLeod, 'Social policy and the floating population: the administration of the Canal Boats Act, 1876-1899', *Past and Present*, XXXV, 1966, pp. 101-133

Roy M. MacLeod, 'The frustration of state medicine, 1880-1899', *Medical History*, XI, 1967, pp. 15-40

Roy M. MacLeod. 'Statesmen undisguised', *American Historical Review*, LXXVIII, 1973, pp. 1386-1405

A. S. MacNalty, 'The history of state medicine in England, Lecture III: the Medical Department of the Local Government Board', *Journal of the Royal Institute of Public Health and Hygiene*, II, 1948, pp. 9-46

M. R. Maltbie, 'The English Local Government Board', *Political Science Quarterly*, XIII, 1898, pp. 232-258

Clive Martlew, 'The state and local goverment finance', *Public Administration*, LXI, 1983, pp. 127-147

J. S. Mill, 'Centralisation', *The Edinburgh Review,* CXV, 1862, pp. 323-358

G. H. Murray, 'Notes on the growth and incidence of local taxation', *The Economic Journal,* III, pp. 698-704

James E. O'Neill, 'Finding a policy for the sick poor', *Victorian Studies,* VII, 1964, pp. 265-284

The Earl of Onslow, 'The rise and development of local legislation by private bill', *Journal of the Royal Statistical Society,* LXIX, 1906, pp. 1-31

Albert Pell, 'The making of the land in England', *Journal of the Royal Agricultural Society of England,* XXIII, second series, 1887, pp. 355-374

E. Leigh Pemberton, 'Private Bill legislation', *The Fortnightly Review,* XLIV, 1885, pp. 228-239

Harold Perkin, 'Individualism versus collectivism: a false antithesis', *Journal of British Studies,* XVII, pp. 105-118

J. Roland Phillips, 'Local debts and government loans', *The Edinburgh Review,* CLIII, 1881, pp. 548-581

R. J. Phillips, 'E. C. Tufnell; Inspector of Poor Law Schools, 1847-74', *History of Education,* V, 1976, pp. 227-240

Mary Ransome, 'Some recent studies of the composition of the House of Commons', *University of Birmingham Historical Journal,* VI, 1958, pp. 1132-1148

William Rathbone, 'Local Government in England and Wales', *The Nineteenth Century,* XIII, 1883, pp. 297-313 and 509-528

R. A. W. Rhodes, 'Some myths in central-local relations', *Town Planning Review,* LI, 1980, pp. 270-285

David Roberts, 'Jeremy Bentham and the Victorian administrative state', *Victorian Studies,* II, 1959, 193-210

J. E. Thorold Rogers, 'British finance: its present and future', *The Contemporary Review,* XXXIV, 1979, pp. 281-303

W. A. Ross, 'The Local Government Board and after', *Public Administration,* XXXIV, 1956, pp. 17-25

C. H. Sargant, 'The taxation of ground values', *The Contemporary Review,* lvii, 1890, pp. 282-289

Nassau Senior, 'Poor Law reform', *The Edinburgh Review,* LXXIV, 1841, pp. 1-44

W. E. Snell, 'Administrative reform', *The Westminster Review,* CLIV, 1900, pp. 504-509

Gillian Sutherland, 'Recent trends in the study of nineteenth century administration', *Victorian Studies,* XIII, 1970, pp. 408-411

Tom Taylor, 'Local and central action', *Transactions of the National Association for the Promotion of Social Science,* 1851, pp. 478-480

D. A. Thomas, 'Anomalies of the civil service', *The Fortnightly Review,* LXXI, 1903, pp. 874-886

R. J. Thompson, 'Local expenditure and local indebtedness in England and

Wales', *Journal of the Royal Statistical Society,* LXVII, 1904, pp. 337-367

R. S. Thompson, 'An inquiry into the rental of agricultural land in England and Wales during the nineteenth century', *Journal of the Royal Statistical Society,* LXX, 1907, pp. 587-616

Charles Trevelyan, 'Land value taxation and the use of land', *The Economic Journal,* XVII, 1907, pp. 30-35

W. S. Weston, 'History of the Society of Medical Officers of Health, 1856-1956', *Public Health,* 1956, pp. 160-226

Paul Wilding, 'The administrative aspects of the 1919 Housing Scheme', *Public Administration,* LI, 1973, pp. 307-326

IV – Unpublished theses

K. Isaac-Henry, *The Association of Municipal Corporations and the County Councils Association: a Study of Influences and Pressures on the Reorganisation of Local Government 1945-72,* University of London PhD thesis, 1980

Steven Stacey, *The Ministry of Health, 1919-29: Ideas and Practice in a Government Department,* University of Oxford DPhil thesis, 1984

Dorothy E. Watkins, *The English Revolution in Social Medicine, 1889-1911,* University of London PhD thesis, 1984

Index

accounts, local authority, 169-70; Departmental Committee on 1907, 171, 180, 187

Adderley, Charles, 120

Addison, Christopher (Viscount), 250, 251, 252, 253, 254-8

Adrian, (Sir) Alfred, LGB official, 133, 248-9

advisory committees, 235-6, 257

agricultural depression and rating issue, 38, 48, 49

agricultural interest, grievances on rates, 28, 31; attitudes to 1870 local government bills, 33; impact on central-local relations, 12, 24; influence in Conservative Party, 48-9

agricultural rates, proposals partially to derate, 43, 49

Agricultural Rates Act, 1896, 49-50; renewal of, 55-60

Asquith, H. H., and housing, 95, 96; and local finance, 57, 100, 98; and poor law reform, 251; appoints Macnamara to LGB, 58

assigned revenues, abolition of, 57; arrangements of 1888 for, 44-7; problems of, 48, 52-5; proposals for, 33, 38-9, 43, 45; proposals to extend, 53-4

Association of Municipal Corporations, and Borough Funds Act, 200-2; and 1909 Budget, 58; and default powers, 217; and devolution of government powers, 243-5; and education loans, 100; and housing, 95; and municipal audit, 86, 181-7;

and Police and Sanitary Regulations Committee, 204, 205; and private bills, 315; establishment of, 200; relations with government, 60-6; relations with LGB, 235-6

Astor, Viscount, 252

Audit Commission, proposals for, 186

Audits, Inspector of, 170, 171

audit, see District Audit

Austin, John, on central-local relations, 5, 7

Avebury, Lord, 185

Balfour, A.J.; as Leader of House of Commons, 56, 184-5; as President of LGB, 43, 49; on 1909 Budget, 57-8

Balfour, Gerald, President of LGB, 56, 96

Balfour, Lord, 51-4

Baxter, R. Dudley, 30

Beach, Michael Hicks, 27, 43-4

Bedwelty Union, 178, 191-2n

Bentham, Jeremy, 5

Benthamism, 5, 6, 7

Bircham, Thomas, General Inspector, 150, 154

Bolton Local Board, 218

Booth, George Sclater, President of LGB, 27, 35-6, 126, 183, 241

Borough Auditors and Assessors, Select Committee on, 182-3

Borough Funds Act, 1872, 63, 64, 196, 199, 200-2, 212

boroughs, see municipal corporations, Association of Municipal Corporations;